THE ARCHAEOLOGY OF
RELIGIOUS
HATRED
IN THE ROMAN AND EARLY MEDIEVAL WORLD

THE ARCHAEOLOGY OF RELIGIOUS HATRED

IN THE ROMAN AND EARLY MEDIEVAL WORLD

EBERHARD SAUER

First published in 2003 by Tempus Publishing

Reprinted in 2009 by
The History Press
The Mill, Brimscombe Port
Stroud, Gloucestershire GL5 2QG
www.thehistorypress.co.uk

© Eberhard Sauer, 2003, 2009

The right of Eberhard Sauer to be identified as the Author of this work has been asserted by him in accordance with the Copyrights, Designs and Patents Act 1988.

All rights reserved. No part of this book may be reprinted or reproduced or utilised in any form or by any electronic, mechanical or other means, now known or hereafter invented, including photocopying and recording, or in any information storage or retrieval system, without the permission in writing from the Publishers.

British Library Cataloguing in Publication Data.
A catalogue record for this book is available from the British Library.

ISBN 978 0 7524 2530 6

Typesetting and origination by Tempus Publishing.
Printed and bound in Great Britain.

CONTENTS

Acknowledgements		6
Preface		8
1	The tip of the iceberg	23
2	Pagan 'vandalism' and iconoclasm in peacetime	45
3	Destruction in war and peace	53
4	Image destruction seen through Christian eyes	64
5	Hilltop sanctuaries	70
6	Large Mithraic cult images	79
7	Destruction at Dendara: a colossal task	89
8	Destruction and re-use in Egypt and Palestine	102
9	The speed of Christianisation in Egypt	106
10	A world waiting for Christianity?	114
11	Afterlife and oriental cults: serious competition for Christianity?	131
12	Money and Mithraism	143
13	Christianisation and bloodshed	157
14	A past phenomenon or future threat?	160
15	Conclusions	165
Bibliography		174
Picture credits		187
Index		188

ACKNOWLEDGEMENTS

I am very grateful to Dr Martin Henig for reading the entire book and his very valuable comments and improvements. I would like to thank in particular Deborah Miles-Williams for all the time and talent invested in producing the two splendid drawings specifically for this book (**colour plates 3** & **14**); they are invaluable in giving some visual idea of the process of image destruction in Antiquity and the early Middle Ages, a phenomenon which is virtually unrecorded in contemporary art. I am grateful to Ian R. Cartwright for his skills and efforts in reproducing photographic images, to Dr Colin Adams for kindly reading and commenting on the section on Dendara, to the always helpful staff of the Sackler library in Oxford where much of this book was written, and especially to Tim Clarke and Peter Kemmis Betty for all their efforts and improvements in seeing the book through publication and in designing the cover. This book was written during the first half of my tenure of a British Academy Postdoctoral Fellowship, and I am indebted to the British Academy, as well as to Keble College and the Institute of Archaeology of Oxford University and the School of Archaeology & Ancient History of Leicester University, for their kind support. The book has also significantly benefited from the advice offered by all those who read and commented on an earlier monograph on a related subject (Sauer 1996) and who are acknowledged there.

I am very grateful to all individuals and institutions who kindly consented to the reproduction of images and often even provided new prints, slides or scanned images or helped in some other way with the illustrations. (Places of original publication are listed in the picture credits.) In particular I would like to thank Professor John Baines (University of Oxford), Professor Manuel Bendala Galán (University of Madrid), Mrs Bettina Braun (Stiftsbibliothek St Gallen), Dr Hélène Chew (Musée des Antiquités nationales, Saint-Germain-en-Laye), Dr Helen Cockle (Roman Society, London), Mrs Theres Flury (Stiftsbibliothek St Gallen), Mrs Joyce Fongers (Brill Academic Publishers, Leiden), Dr Henri Gaillard de Sémainville (Revue Archéologique de l'Est, Dijon), Mrs Sabine Hengster, M.A. (Museenverwaltung Hanau), Professor Michał Gawlikowski (University of Warsaw and Cairo), Dr Chiara Guarnieri (Museo Archeologico Nazionale di Sarsina), Dr Jean-Olivier Guilhot (Service régional de l'archéologie de Bourgogne, Dijon), Dr Jenny Hall (Museum of London), Dr Berndmark Heukemes (Lobdengau Museum, Ladenburg), Professor Günther Hölbl (University of Vienna), Dr Peter Horne (English Heritage, York), Dr Ralph Jackson (British Museum, London), Dr John A. Larson (University of Chicago); Professor Ramsay MacMullen (Yale University), Dr Jacques Meissonnier (Service régional de l'archéologie de Bourgogne, Dijon), Dr Francesco Menotti (University of Oxford), Mrs Maria Porzenheim M.A. (Kreis- und Stadtmuseum Dieburg); Mr Fabio Remondino (Swiss Federal Institute of Technology, Zürich), Dr Elizabeth J. Shepherd (Soprintendenza per i Beni Archeologici di Ostia), Mrs Elke Schwichtenberg (Bildarchiv Preußischer Kulturbesitz, Berlin), Mrs Christine Speroni (Musée Archéologique de Strasbourg), Professor Margareta Steinby (University of Oxford), Dr Volker Thewalt (Wiesenbach, Germany), Dr Christian Vernou (Musée Archéologique de Dijon), Professor Gerd Weisgerber (University of Freiburg), Dr Engelbert Winter (University of Münster), Dr Ann Woodward (Birmingham University Field Archaeology Unit), Dr Marta Zuchowska (University of Warsaw) and Mrs Karin Zuleger M.A. (Kreis- und Stadtmuseum Dieburg). Needless to say that it should not necessarily be assumed that the theories advanced here correspond to the opinions of those who provided help in various ways.

PREFACE

Imagine the scene: followers of religion X force their way into your local parish church. They attack the crucifix, century-old images carved in stone, paintings and beautiful stained-glass windows with iron bars, sledgehammers and bricks. Then they pour petrol over the wooden seating and set the ancient building alight. All over the country such events are taking place. Affected are not just churches, but places of worship of all other religions except for those of religion X. Elsewhere parishioners are hiding the contents of their local churches fearing similar attacks. Charismatic spiritual leaders of religion X mastermind the assault on the religious competition in a spontaneous and uncoordinated manner. Their targets cluster around their domiciles and travel routes. Some towns and villages, like your own, are only left with burnt-out ruins where their churches had once been, while many others have, as yet, largely escaped. You walk past the smouldering shell of your parish church to buy a newspaper. The roof of the old building and parts of the church steeple have collapsed. The ruined walls are blackened with soot, and they display gaping holes where a few hours before doors and windows had been. Smoke is still rising from the debris, and the smell of burnt wood hangs in the air. Opening the newspaper, you read that the government has declared visits to existing churches and religious buildings as well as most forms of worship illegal, except for religion X. Depending on the nature of the offence, penalties range from expropriation and drastic fines (or unspecified punishment for those who cannot pay) to the death penalty. Whether or not you are religious, how would you feel towards those responsible?

Had you lived in the Roman Empire in the AD 390s (already divided for most of the decade into a western and an eastern half) the above scenario might have unfolded itself before your eyes. There are just a few small differences: there are no newspapers, but the imperial edicts of AD 391 and 392 are passed on to you by word of mouth. The building affected is not your local parish church, but an old temple close to your home, quite possibly as ancient then as your parish church is now. It does not contain a crucifix or stained-glass windows, but awesome old stone images which your ancestors had worshipped since time immemorial. Of course, the assailants are not using petrol, but your local temple probably has a lower and thus more easily combustible roof than your parish church, therefore being an easy target for arson.

Our journey into the archaeology and history of image destruction and religious hatred, however, commences somewhat later, in the year AD 610, some 220 years after the edicts and more than 270 years since the policy in the Roman Empire had turned from anti-Christian to anti-pagan. Even in AD 610 there are still some pagan images that survive above ground. This is due to the unsystematic nature of the attacks, spearheaded by individuals, and due to the sheer numerical scale and wide geographic spread of Western Europe's once abundant pagan monuments. Despite all missionary efforts, some have even been recently erected. After over 200 years of destructive raids, Christian anti-pagan passion continues unabated as we will see whilst accompanying two monks and missionaries on their journey through what is nowadays part of Switzerland and Austria.

Yet before following as silent observers in the footsteps of the two holy men through small settlements in which paganism was rampant and yet about to be crushed, let us guard our distance for a moment. What was the world like some 1,400 years ago, the time of our missionary journey? North-western Europe and the Mediterranean had changed significantly in the preceding centuries, and similarly momentous events had begun to unfold in south-west Asia without anybody yet anticipating that these events would entirely change the course of world history. At the beginning of the fourth century the majority of the Roman Empire's population still venerated a multitude of deities, and Christianity was a persecuted minority religion. The Empire was vast: it stretched then, and still for another century, from Britain, Gaul and the Iberian peninsula in the West to Anatolia (modern Turkey), Syria, westernmost Iraq and Egypt in the East. Much of the eastern half of this large Empire and the islands and some coastal possessions in the western Mediterranean were still part of the surviving eastern Roman (or Byzantine) Empire in AD 610 whose Christian rulers resided at Constantinople (or Byzantium). Now, however, the Empire was involved in the most devastating war it had ever fought against the invading Persians. It was also around AD 610 that, unnoticed by the Persians and Byzantines, the prophet Mohammed (AD 570-632) started to preach on the Arabian peninsula. Nobody could foresee at the time that by the middle of the century all of weakened Persian and half of the Byzantine Empire would have fallen to the forces of the new religion, Islam, changing the religious landscape of the world forever. Our book, however, will mainly look at the changes which had taken place prior to the expansion of Islam.

The Western Roman Empire had ceased to exist in the fifth century, and its territories were now under the control of Germanic kings, most of which, however, had converted to Christianity. We tend to think of them as 'Christian' states, but what does this mean? Are we dealing with a population united by an unshakable belief in the same God – or rather with a mixture of ardent followers of Christ, superficial Christians and surviving pockets of pagan population? How had Christianity achieved its dominance while, at the same time, it was still a minority religion in the Persian Empire where it did not enjoy state support?

The written sources speak a very clear language. By following the two monks, Columbanus and Gallus (**colour plates 1 & 2**), for some of their way in AD 610, we shall have the opportunity to look at one episode in more detail before turning our attention to the archaeological evidence. The events are reported by Wetti and Walahfridus, biographers of St Gallus, who were monks themselves. While living in the ninth century, they drew on an earlier common eighth-century source. Both Columbanus and Gallus were of Irish origin, but the strength of their faith had made them migrants and missionaries. It is reported that Columbanus's mother begged him not to leave her and blocked the door with her body, but he stepped over her wishing her well, saying that he would never see her again in this life. Whether or not the details are true, the episode would certainly be typical for his restless mind, which led him to travel for over 25 years through the Frankish kingdoms and into Lombard Italy. It also led him to found monasteries, some of them in deliberately remote locations without settlement at the time. The monastery at Luxeuil at the foothills of the densely forested low mountain range of the Vosges, for example, was at the site of an old spa. This ancient Roman health resort is reported to have been long abandoned and returned to a state of complete wilderness. Even many pagan images survived here, probably overgrown by forest vegetation and up to then unnoticed by Christian image-haters when Columbanus arrived there in AD 590. Much later, in AD 610, just five years before his death – in yet another newly founded monastery at Bóbbio in a valley in the north Italian Apennine mountains – Columbanus, in company of his disciple Gallus, came to the region south of the upper Rhine (nowadays northern Switzerland and westernmost Austria). This area had gone through a turbulent history. Until the fifth century it had been part of the Western Roman Empire. Its history after the final collapse of the Empire in AD 476 is still partially shrouded in mystery. The, at least superficially, Christianised Romanic population stayed on, but in the sixth century the Germanic Alamanni began to infiltrate the area. The Alamanni at the time were under the overlordship of the Franks who had recently converted to Christianity. Paganism was still strong amongst the Alamanni, even though Christianity had made inroads in the sixth century and became the dominant religion in the course of the seventh. In the early seventh century there were pagans and Christians amongst both the Germanic and Romanic elements of the population. It is not clear to what extent the struggle against paganism which ensued was directed against natives who had given up the genuine or superficial Christian faith of their ancestors or against recent immigrants from pagan communities in the North.

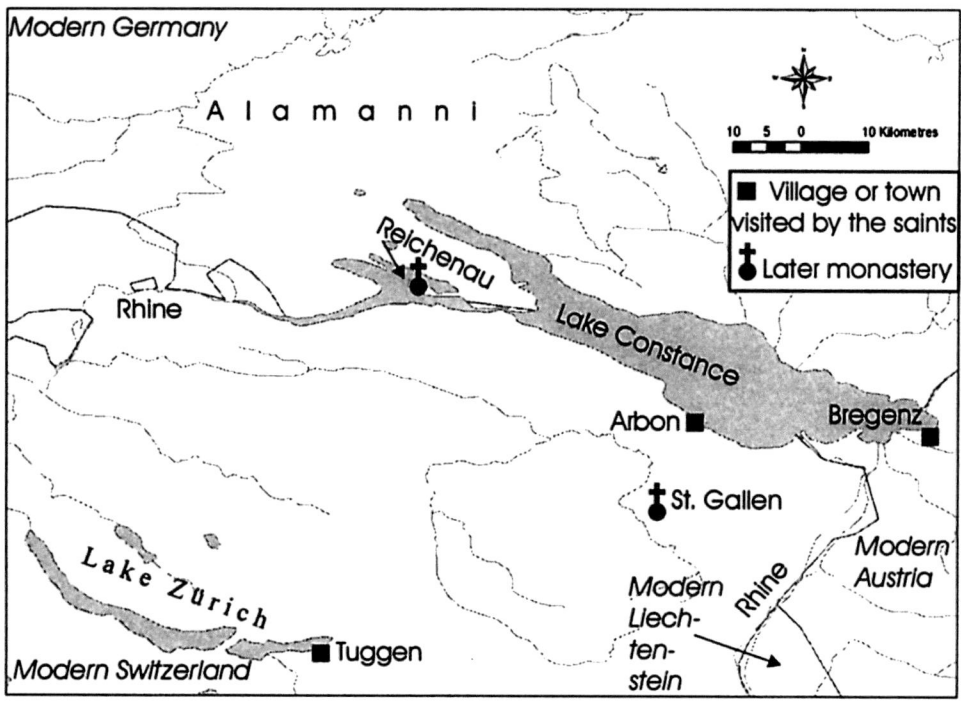

1 *Sites visited by St Columbanus and St Gallus on their missionary journey in the area of Lake Constance*

The first encounter of the saints with paganism in the area, at Tuggen village at Lake Zürich, was dramatic (**1**). Gallus's biographer, Walahfridus, reports that the people who lived there, much to the dislike of the two missionaries, did not believe in God, worshipped images and venerated 'idols'; they made sacrifices, were involved in soothsaying and divination, and pursued many other 'superstitious' activities. The holy men started to live amongst them. 'You should believe in the Father and the Son and the Holy Spirit,' they preached, yet to no avail. What could be done to force the obstinate minds, deaf to the monks' words, onto the path of righteousness? Fire and deposition in deep water seemed the only right responses to deal with the material manifestations of evil, which stood in the way of conversion. 'The blessed Gallus,' we are told, 'the disciple of the holy man, armed with the zeal of piety, set fire to the temples, in which they made sacrifices to the demons and whatever votive objects he found he sank in the lake.'

The villagers had apparently not minded the strangers settling amongst them, and they had even tolerated their uncompromising admonitions. Yet, seeing their heritage and what was holy to them falling prey to arson and going up in flames was more than they could bear. It comes as no surprise that they were enraged and pursued the men. After public consultation, they intended to kill the perpetrator, Gallus, and to whip and humiliate his master,

Columbanus, and to expel him from their land. Only speed saved the clerics from bodily harm and lynch-law, and not without having asked God to bring down his divine revenge upon the villagers and their children, they moved on in search for worthier subjects of their missionary efforts.

Yet this was not the last encounter with deep-rooted paganism they made in the area. After having spent seven days with a like-minded priest who lived within the massive walls of the over 300-year-old late Roman fort at Arbon at Lake Constance, it was time to go again to a place where their intervention was needed. A boat brought them over the lake to the old Roman town of Bregenz, now largely in ruins, yet still with people living amongst the dilapidated structures. One building left standing was an oratory once dedicated to the Christian saint Aurelia; the holy men were to discover that not only had the stone buildings deteriorated as a result of neglect (a fact of little concern to them), but that Christianity itself had suffered a setback. The oratory had been transformed into a pagan temple with three gilded bronze images fixed to the wall. The people venerated and made sacrifices to them having abandoned the altar of the sacred Christian religion. 'These are the old gods and the ancient protectors of this place,' they told the saints, 'their appeasement has protected us and our belongings to the present day.'

As at Tuggen, public exhortations formed the prelude of the missionaries' struggle against idolatry. Unlike the Abbot Columbanus, Gallus had acquired considerable proficiency in the local tongue, and it was he who spoke to a big crowd when it assembled on the occasion of festivities at the above-mentioned temple (and former church). Men and women of all age groups had gathered, not only because of the repute of the festivities, but also to see the foreigners whose arrival they had heard about. When they assembled, Gallus, on the order of the abbot, began to speak and to show the people the way of the truth; he urged them to become converts to the Lord, to give up the falsehood, to worship God, the father, the creator of all things and his only son, in whom is salvation, life and the resurrection of the dead; Jesus Christ, the son of God, had unlocked the gates of the heavenly kingdom to human kind which had grown cold in the filth of their sins. And in view of all, he seized the images, smashed them to pieces with stones and threw them into the lake.

The passionate speech, culminating in such dramatic and irreversible destruction of what had been central in the religious lives of the audience, split the stunned crowd. Some were converted and, we are told, 'confessing their sins, they praised the Lord for their illumination.' Others were angry, furious and enraged about the smashing of the images, yet in their shock they did not lift a hand to the perpetrator, but went home feeling devastated by this irreplaceable loss. 'But saint Columbanus,' we read, 'asked for water to be brought and, after he had blessed it, he besprinkled the temple with it and while they walked around the temple, singing psalms, he re-consecrated it as a church.'

This is just one amongst many passages in early Christian literature reporting the destruction of pagan temples and images. Some may question whether we can take such reports at face value, considering that the above is based on sources written after the last eyewitnesses had died. Yet the earliest common source whose relevant passages were lost was written merely a century after the events, and the oral tradition must have been vivid considering that St Gallus had the famous monastery of St Gallen, not far from Lake Constance, named after him. Both Walahfridus and Wetti were based at the nearby monastery on the Reichenau, an island in Lake Constance. A second possible objection against the reliability of such hagiographical sources, written by clergymen, is the stereotypical nature of virtually all works of this genre. The saints are portrayed as being virtuous and brave, and destroying pagan monuments in the face of opposition was a deed which distinguished them as fearless and charismatic men of God, untainted by and in power superior to the forces of evil. Might the incidents of image destruction therefore have been invented to make them fit the stereotype? This seems exceedingly unlikely; the very fact that image destruction features so prominently in these and in many other biographies of saints proves undoubtedly that it was something to be aspired to. Furthermore, as we shall see, both pagan sources, at least in the late Roman period, and the sad remains of mutilated sculptures all over the ancient world confirm that image destruction was a significant phenomenon. Many sources, not just Wetti and Walahfridus, confirm that a substantial number of Christian saints, like St Gallus and St Columbanus, did not normally shy away from discomfort and danger. While the devout biographers, unsurprisingly, portray all deeds of the saints in shining colours and all actions of unconvertible pagans in a negative light, there is nothing to suggest that any part of the above-mentioned story has no basis in true events, albeit seen and interpreted from a Christian viewpoint. It would have been easy, for example, to make the saints appear even more fearless by inventing that they stayed in Tuggen after the image destruction, braving the threatened lethal revenge by the villagers to be rescued by a divine miracle at the last minute. Yet, while Wetti finds a passage in the Bible, 'leave room to the wrath' (*Romans* 12,19), to justify why St Gallus, in company with St Columbanus, fled for his life, no attempt is made in either biography to disguise this rather humiliating episode.

There were several reasons why the elimination of all material remnants of paganism was seen to be both justified and necessary. The conversion of non-believers was considered a religious duty to the adherents of a religion with a monopoly on the truth. The destruction of temples and images made a continuation of traditional forms of worship impossible, especially if something irreplaceable was destroyed, such as the gilded bronze images at Bregenz. These must have been Roman bronze statues, 300-500 years old at the time of their destruction, and in the seventh century the technological knowledge of how to produce bronze sculpture no longer existed in the area. The very fact that it was beyond human ability at the time to produce anything of the kind will have given them sanctity in the eyes of the worshippers. Furthermore, their antiquity and local tradition about their worship since time immemorial made these images venerable to the local population. Once smashed to pieces there was no going back. The destruction marked a cultural revolution which broke the link of the people with their past.

Furthermore, not only pagan worshippers, but also Christian iconoclasts thought that there was more to pagan images than mere empty shells. Christians at the time did not consider pagan deities to be non-existent; contrary to modern enlightened views, pagan deities were considered to be dangerous demons. These demons inhabited images and pagan sanctuaries. Acts of worship, in particular sacrifices, gave them strength. Even though they were far inferior in power to God and his saints, they could bring peril to human souls.

The views of non-Christians did not matter, and the question of tolerance did not arise for Christian missionaries. With an unshakeable conviction in knowing the absolute truth, the idea that there could be anything valuable in pagan cults was as alien to them as the idea that there is any merit in false equations to the mathematician. Had God not ordered that pagan altars be destroyed, the sacred groves cut down, the stone images broken (*Exodus* 34,13) and the carved wooden images of the pagan gods burnt with fire (*Deuteronomy* 7,25)? In complete contrast to the later Renaissance, there was amongst many late Roman and medieval clerics, no concept of pagan art worth preserving. Its destruction was a necessary step in the process of 'freeing' the world from paganism. But the destruction of pagan images cannot be viewed on an entirely rational level. In early Christian literature one can often sense a hatred of anything non-Christian. The Christian writer Tertullian (*On the Games*, 30) rejoices around AD 200 at the prospect of seeing not only the persecutors of the Christians burning in hell (perhaps understandable at a time of persecution), but also a wide range of representatives of other professions whose only fault was to be part of pagan culture, like philosophers, actors etc. Later attitudes became more discriminating and a love-hate relationship to classical culture evolved in Late Antiquity and the Middle Ages. Mythological scenes in art were sometimes tolerated for their art-historical merits and sometimes still produced in Mediterranean cities in the fourth and fifth century. Some ancient sculpture was also Christianised by incision of a cross. Yet much more often pagan images had to make way for the new religion. Representatives of the same institution, the Church, assiduously copied and thus preserved the literary wisdom of the ancient world, including texts on paganism, while breaking the visual remnants of the abolished religion to pieces.

It is not the intention of this book to deny that Christianity had much to offer or to imply that its success can be ascribed merely to destruction and suppression of dissent. The identification of Jesus with the poor, the social nature and mutual care in many early Christian communities, the loving father, the clear moral orientation, the promise of eternal life in paradise to the faithful etc. made it a very attractive religion. In fact, Christianity had been so attractive that many had been prepared to die for this religion during persecutions, notably in the Roman Empire between the first and early fourth centuries AD; it had been so attractive that this 'Hydra' in the eyes of the pagan state continually grew no matter how many heads were cut off. No doubt, Christianity would have continued to spread and would have gained the devotion of large numbers of human minds over wide areas even if it had not turned from persecuted into persecutor after it had gained imperial support in the fourth century. Yet, would it ever have become the dominant, let alone the sole religion in the West without force?

By focusing upon destruction, this book is not about belittling all the other factors which contributed to make Christianity the – in numerical terms – most successful of all religions today. Yet these have been discussed much more extensively before, so there is no need to re-examine them here. As far as destruction is concerned, the written sources have been studied on several occasions. Still, many remarkable episodes like the one chosen as an introduction for this book are little known. Even less well known is the archaeological evidence. In fact, except on a regional basis, it has rarely been endeavoured to study the phenomenon comprehensively. One would have thought that such acts of image smashing so frequently reported in biographies of saints should have left clear material traces, and wonders why they do not feature more prominently in archaeological literature. One might even ask whether we are dealing merely with a few isolated incidents, despite the observations above, blown out of all proportion by early Christian literature in order to cultivate the stereotype of the brave saint combating idolatry. The investigation of material traces of destruction may thus form a yardstick to assess how prevalent or otherwise the phenomenon was in antiquity and to what extent it can be blamed on Christians as opposed to pagan invaders or other potential suspects.

There has been an astonishingly low level of interest in the material traces of image destruction in archaeological literature. The reasons for this lack of interest have to be sought in scholarly tradition and fashion. Currently scholars who have been strongly influenced by the pacifist movement in the 1960s and 70s have reached the peaks of their academic careers, resulting in a phenomenon recognised and currently studied by Simon James at Leicester University who coined the term 'pacification of the past'. In sharp contrast to the obsession with anything military in the nineteenth and first half of the twentieth century, evidence for warfare, violence and destruction is now ignored as far as possible and any interest in such aspects in the culture of past societies is frowned upon as old-fashioned. Profound cultural changes in prehistory are now hardly ever interpreted as being the result of invasion, but almost always of acculturation (despite good historical analogies for the former

2 *Found beheaded: Mithras and the bull, the central cult image in a crypt, serving as a temple, underneath a bath-house in Ostia*

as well as the latter), Iron Age hillforts are no longer of any defensive, but of purely ritual or symbolic significance etc. While there are undoubtedly some merits in these new approaches, it is clear that the pendulum of interpretation has swung from one extreme to the other, and that the new one-sided interpretations are often just as far removed from the truth as the ones they replaced. People smashing sculpture and setting alight religious buildings is not an image that fits easily into the new vision of the peaceful past we are meant to have, irrespective of whether the perpetrators were invaders or religious zealots. It is much more fashionable to elaborate on the complex social changes which were behind the transformation of the religious landscape in Late Antiquity. Undoubtedly there were complex social changes, yet what is the justification for the implicit assumption that within the framework of the complex interlinked historical, religious, cultural and social developments, violence was not an important factor? We shall come back to this question later, citing concrete examples. Suffice it to say, in order to demonstrate that this is a real phenomenon, the contemporary researcher Richard Gordon (1999, 688) is convinced that it would be 'misguided to believe that direct violent intervention by Christians was the dominant or even critical factor in the wider process of the decline of paganism', and is quick to accuse those

3 Perfectly restored – concealing all traces of the violent attack to the modern spectator

who think otherwise of research which 'has a 19th-c. whiff about it', without feeling a need to justify why such 'old-fashioned' views have to be wrong by definition, because they found support in the nineteenth century.

Yet, is the lack of interest in destruction of monuments only, or even mainly, due to current fashion? The answer is negative; traditional, classical archaeology has, for quite different reasons, failed to show much of an interest in the phenomenon either. Archaeology and history suffer from an increasing level of over-specialisation. There are numerous classical art historians who lack all interest in the post-classical periods or non-artistic aspects in the study of sculpture. The damage to a mutilated statue is of interest only in so far as it poses the challenge of restoring the image to its original splendour. Parts of the work hacked off by an image-hater long ago have often been restored with such perfectionist skill that the visitor to the modern museum will not notice that it had been damaged at all, let alone be able to differentiate between deliberate and accidental damage. The statue of Mithras from Ostia is symptomatic (**2** & **3**): it has been reproduced in numerous articles and books, yet virtually always after its restoration. The same mind-set, namely the ideology that only the art and architecture of Greece and Rome in their 'glorious golden ages' are worth studying for the classically educated person, have led to the unrecorded removal of any evidence for the decline or destruction of temples in uncountable instances. Numerous past excavations, especially in the Mediterranean, some of them even decades after excavation techniques had been revolutionised by some British and German scholars in the later nineteenth and early twentieth century, basically consisted of vigorous clearance operations. The workmen merely stopped for inscriptions or major works of art. In the case of old excavations in the Mediterranean one often searches in vain for any records about other datable material, such as coins or pieces of pottery recovered from a building, let alone any descriptions of occupation or destruction layers or lists of material embedded in them. With luck an inscription, tile stamp or architectural element may allow us to establish when a temple was constructed, yet there is normally no way of telling when it was abandoned or destroyed, with the exception of the rare cases when small objects found in temple interiors were kept and their findspots recorded. Where intentionally destroyed sculpture was found in such sanctuaries it will be unknown forever when it fell prey to iconoclastic attack; and short of having any indications for the date, it will often remain guesswork as to what precise historical developments led to the outburst of violence. Neither will we get a very clear idea of the mode of destruction, unless there are plans showing where fragments of the smashed sculpture fell or were deposited.

Ostia, the town next to the harbour of imperial Rome, forms a prime example. Even by imperial standards the religious life in the bustling cosmopolitan town was unusually diverse, and we know of no other settlement in the Empire apart from the capital itself, which contained, for example, a larger number of temples where devotees of the oriental god Mithras assembled. In a temple located in an underground room of a bath-house (the Mitreo delle Terme del Mitra) the above-mentioned life-sized statue of the god kneeling over and sacrificing the bull, a scene central in the Mithras mysteries, was subject to a savage and brutal attack (**2 & 3**). Not only the heads of Mithras and the bull, but also both arms of the god were chopped off and thrown into a sewer. An ear of the bull, fragments of his horns, tail and a knee made of a different marble shared the same fate and attest that the sculpture had already been damaged and repaired prior to the brutal execution and slaughter of Mithras and the bull. In this case there is little doubt who it was the god had to make way for or when it happened. Two marble supports of a screen, decorated with Christian *chi-rho* symbols of mid- to late fourth-century type, found on the ground floor of the same building attest that parts of the building were then adapted for Christian worship (**4**). In other mithraea at Ostia the case is less clear-cut. One would have liked to know how long the sanctuaries continued to be visited despite the economic decline of the town in Late Antiquity. Where deliberate damage was observed, one would have liked to know when it was inflicted (namely in the case of a smashed marble altar from a different temple, the Mitreo delle Pareti Dipinte, with depiction of the sun god, and the

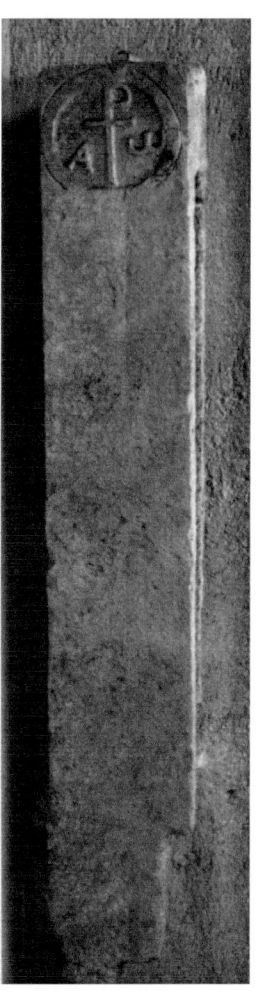

*4 Two marble supports of wooden or metal railing with Christian symbols: parts of the same bath-house in Ostia, where the Mithras statue (**2** & **3**) was found, were re-used for Christian worship*

torchbearers, central figures in the Mithras mysteries). Yet, no information on pottery and virtually none on coins from the Mithras temples is published and, presumably, was not kept, neither for excavations in the late nineteenth to early twentieth century nor for the excavations from 1938 to 1942. In these years much of the architecture of the town was unearthed in a mammoth operation, erasing any traces of later life. This is not a cheap plea for perfectionism in difficult circumstances with the benefit of hindsight, but even crude excavation methods combined with a very selective sampling strategy for small finds and a few sections could have told us a great deal without necessarily multiplying the resources or time required to excavate. Ostia forms an unfortunately not atypical example of a quarrying operation for the recovery of architecture, works of art and inscriptions without any signs that the early excavators had any notion that evidence other than stone monuments and works of art was worth looking for. Such excavation and recording standards make any in-depth study of late Roman paganism at Ostia and many other sites impossible.

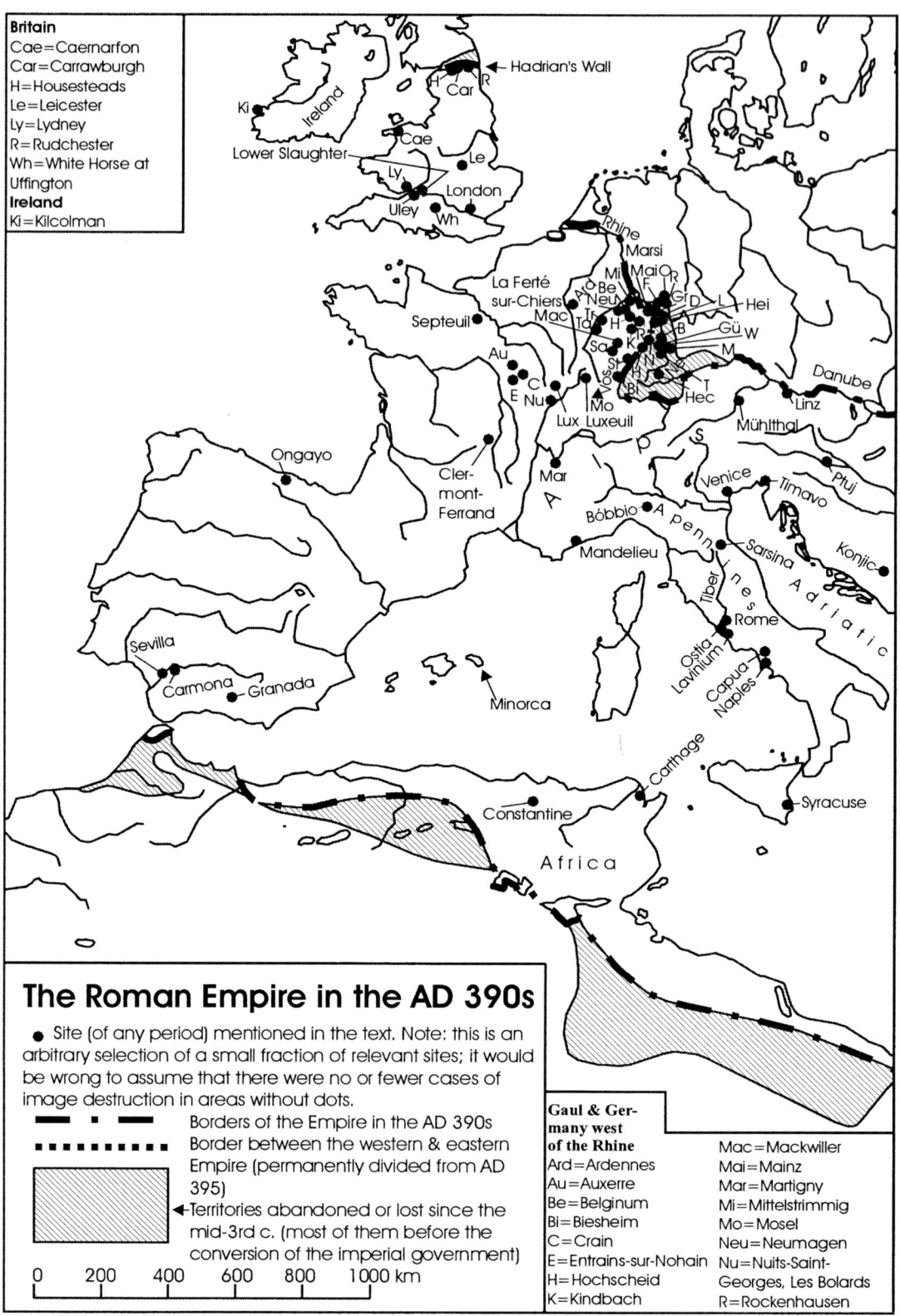

5 *Map of sites mentioned in the text*

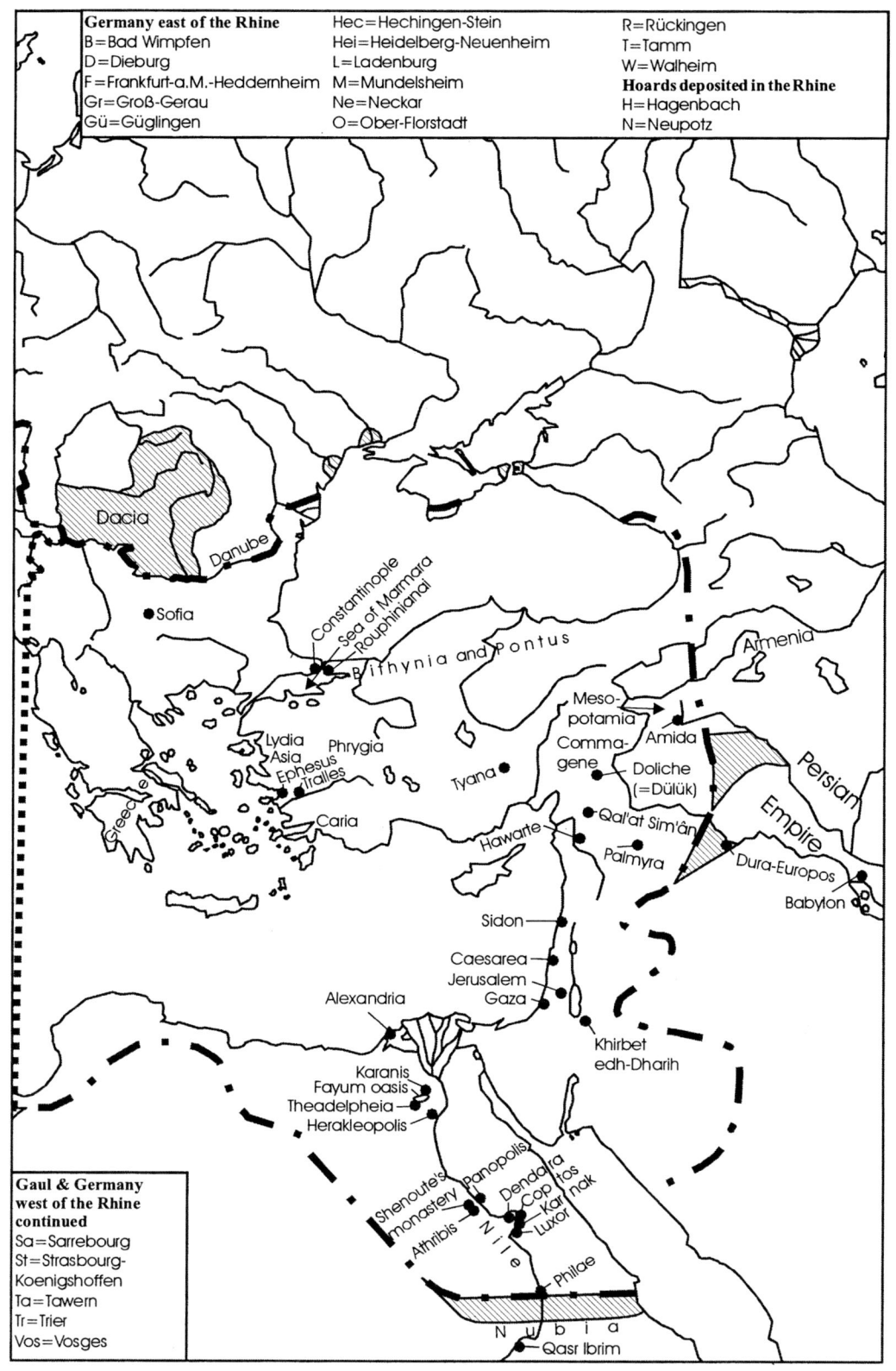

If there is a bias in this book towards examples from north-western Europe, then this is mainly due to the fact that there is a larger number of well excavated temples north of the Alps (**5**). As today most excavations within the territories of the former Roman Empire are carried out and published to high standards; this is likely to change. It also ought to be pointed out that evidence for the destruction of images and cult objects has never been systematically compiled over a large geographic area. There is a boundless number of publications which would merit being scrutinised for evidence of this phenomenon, and there will be many instances I am not aware of, and others which there is no space to mention in the present study. Yet, if by picking out the odd example here and there, the book will demonstrate just how much the mute traces of destructive mania can tell us about past and even about present developments, it will have served its purpose.

1
THE TIP OF THE ICEBERG

The holy rage of men, like St Gallus, undoubtedly left permanent traces. Some modes of destruction are, however, easier to detect than others. Cases of arson (such as at Tuggen), unless preceded by image smashing, cannot easily be differentiated from accidental fires. Thus they are not studied in this book. The deposition of votive objects in deep water (as practised by St Gallus at both Lake Zürich and Lake Constance) can, of course, be detected, but often leaves room for more than one interpretation, such as accidental loss or ritual deposition of cherished items or, indeed, permanent concealment of utterly detested objects. When St Gallus smashed the bronze images prior to throwing them into Lake Constance, he may have created a material manifestation of religiously motivated destruction that archaeologists could recognise, should the remains ever be found (although we would still not know whether the bronze fragments were discarded deliberately or were intended for the melting pot and fell off a boat). The shattered remains of an image made from stone, by contrast, can form a permanent testimony of the iconoclast's hatred as clear and lasting as any surviving traits of anatomy or dress of the artistic creator's devotion. However, while emotions, both love and hatred, can be engraved in stone, there may be more than one ideology and more than one set of circumstances which can trigger outbursts of rage. Is there any way to differentiate between the material traces of the proverbial 'barbarian' destructive mania and anti-pagan hate on the part of Christians? In this chapter we shall explore two difficult examples to sharpen our awareness of the dangers of jumping to conclusions one way or another. Both are crystal-clear manifestations of outbursts of hatred, yet, by whom?

Whose hands, for example, are holding the chisel and driving it with a hammer deep into the skilful work of art shown on **colour plate 3**? It is a revolving cult image, decorated on both sides (**6** & **7**). The image is positioned in a stone frame, and it can be rotated around two central pivots. Yet, at the very moment captured by the artist the pressure of the chisel is tearing deep fractures into the relief, radiating from the point of impact. Seconds later the fragments of the work of art will lie shattered on the ground.

THE ARCHAEOLOGY OF RELIGIOUS HATRED

6 *Obverse of the main cult relief from the Dieburg. (See **colour plate 3** on the possible method of destruction)*

Contrary to the widespread assumption that the dedication of elaborate art was the domain of an elite, people practicing ordinary professions, living in the provincial small town of Dieburg, Upper Germany, had once dedicated it, presumably in the second half of the second or early third century: Silvestrius Silvinus, a stonemason, his brother Silvestrius Perpetus, a shoemaker and the latter's grandson, Aurelius. They were all devotees of the Mithras mysteries. Their work of art shows that they were remarkably well versed in Mithraic theology and classical mythology, even if the deeper meanings of some of the scenes are now lost to us. Centrally on the obverse we see the god Mithras himself as a hunter. Left (second panel from the bottom) we witness how he is born out of a rock. Soon he is to hunt down the sacred bull (top and upper two scenes right), the prelude to the holy sacrifice of the divine animal, not depicted here. In the bottom right corner we see how Mithras and the sun god

7 *Reverse of the Dieburg cult relief*

take the sacred meal to commemorate this sacrifice and act of salvation. Then Mithras and the sun god ascend to heaven in the sun god's horse-drawn chariot, a destiny Silvinus, Perpetus and Aurelius presumably hoped to share. At some point during the ceremonies in the fire-lit windowless temple the revolving cult image was turned around and the assembled votaries could see a scene from the Phaeton myth on the reverse. Phaeton asks his father, the sun god, for permission to drive the sun chariot over the sky resulting, as the votaries knew well, in the inferno of the blazing earth and sky. The scene is unique in Mithraism, and thus we cannot tell whether the votaries believed that such was the fate awaiting the world, whether Phaeton symbolised the votary's wish to ascend to heaven as well or whether the mythological scene had some other hidden meaning. Surely the brothers had been proud to furnish their local temple (**8**) with such an erudite work of art to be enjoyed by present and future generations.

Peace and prosperity in Upper Germany, however, were not to last for reasons other than universal conflagration (whether or not there was such a belief). The newly formed Germanic tribal group of the Alamanni invaded the region in AD 233 and, though Roman rule was re-established, the safety and economic prosperity of earlier years had gone for good. Finally, in AD 260 or soon after, the Empire, while being engaged in a series of wars against internal and external enemies, abandoned all territories in Germany beyond the Rhine and the Danube, including Dieburg. Precisely when within the third century the last Mithraic ceremonies were celebrated at Dieburg is unknown, yet there are no signs that worship continued in any temple in those territories after Rome's withdrawal. Pagan Germans settled and now controlled the area east of the Rhine, and it was not for another 300–400 years that Christianity gained a foothold here. Only in 1926 did archaeologists uncover the remains of the temple and traces of the wave of devastation which had once swept through it. The marks of damage speak a language as clear as words: a deep wedge-shaped mark where once the head of the central figure, the hunting Mithras, had been, must have been inflicted with an iron blade with sharp cutting edge. (A similar mark may be discernible to its right along the same fracture line.) The tool appears to have been positioned at a right angle to the surface, the long side of the blade being at a horizontal level, if the monument was upright. It was not a massive tool, and its blade was little more than two inches wide. The combination of precision-targeting

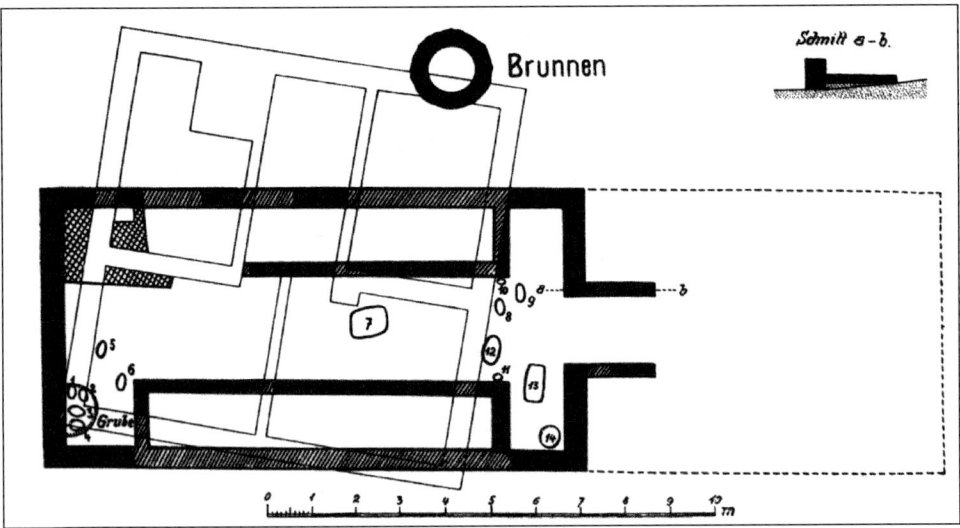

8 *The Mithras temple at Dieburg. The Roman walls are indicated in black, modern walls in white.* 'Brunnen': well with a fragment of the big Mercury and two fragments each of Mithras carrying the bull and Juno; 3: pit with the rock-birth, Mithras as a bowman and the two Genii; 5: two fragments of Hercules; 6: un-inscribed pedestal; 7: findspot of the main cult relief; 8: very small mother goddess (escaped destruction); 9: small altar; 12: basis with the feet of the big Mercury; 13: un-inscribed altar; 14: thigh of big Mercury

and forceful impact at a right angle to the surface is best explained by the use of a broad chisel (or by using a similar tool, like a pane hammer, as a chisel). It was certainly a deliberate and calculated act by which the work of art, once dedicated by a shoemaker and a stonemason, perished, and it was not the only such act to affect the cult inventory of the temple. The sculpture of Mithras born out of the rock was beheaded (**9**), and so was the image of Mithras as a bowman (**10**). Another relief showing Mithras carrying the bull was smashed to pieces (**11**). Two fragments comprising the torso and legs of the god had been thrown into the temple well outside the building; the part with the head has never been found. Other divinities on display in the temple of the saviour god fared no better. A Hercules relief was broken into two parts and the head was removed (**12**). Two Genii, protective supernatural beings, equally appear to have fallen prey to the decapitation frenzy (**13**), though one of the heads escaped obliteration and could be fitted back onto its trunk in the 1920s. Together with what remained of Mithras as a bowman and the rock-birth, they were hidden from view in a pit within the temple.

The worst treatment of all was reserved for Mercury (**14**). He was hacked into 23 pieces, not counting the missing parts, which, once again, included the head. The survival of the chin may suggest pulverisation within the temple rather than deposition at a yet to be discovered spot outside the building. The fragments were scattered all over the interior of the temple, and one part, the left hand with the caduceus, an attribute of Mercury and once a symbol of peace, was carried out of the temple and thrown into the well. Never should anybody be able to reassemble the shattered remains of the deity. One wonders why Mercury in particular attracted the rage of the intruders. Was it because, without sense of shame and decency, the god had displayed his private parts, wearing no more than a cloak? Such improper posture he shared amongst the surviving images only with Hercules and some figures on the reverse of the cult image. The small Hercules relief, as we have seen, was punished by beheading. The main cult relief does not appear to have been touched again, once it lay broken on the ground, apart from being removed from its likely place of destruction at the end of the sanctuary and, disrespectfully, placed on the floor of the nave. It would go too far to scrutinise here the fate of each recovered fragment of sculpture. Suffice it to say that further deities perished in the onslaught, including Minerva and Juno (**15**). The latter's head survived, but was again hidden from view in the well together with some of the torso in high relief. There is nothing to suggest that those who reduced the temple inventory to rubble had any deeper knowledge of individual pagan cults, and they need not even have known who Mithras was (or, if so, they hated him no more or less than his divine companions). There was perhaps some particular bias against 'immodest' images, but otherwise the attack was quite indiscriminately directed against all pagan deities or elaborate art. A large altar not inscribed but merely decorated with some abstract sacrificial tools (which may not have been recognised as such) was spared.

9 (Opposite, top left) *Beheaded: rock-birth of Mithras from Dieburg*

10 (Opposite, top right) *Decapitated: Mithras as bowman from Dieburg*

11 (Opposite, below left) *Surviving parts of Mithras carrying the bull from Dieburg*

12 (Opposite, below right) *Mutilated Hercules relief from Dieburg*

13 (Above left) *Equally beheaded: one of the two Genii from Dieburg*

14 (Above right) *Remaining parts of the large Mercury statue from Dieburg, smashed into 23 preserved fragments*

15 (Right) *Thrown into the well next to the Dieburg temple: the remains of the goddess Juno*

Who was responsible? The excavator, Friedrich Behn (1928, 45-7) believed the Christians to have destroyed the temple inventory at the time when Rome lost control over the territory east of the Rhine in the mid-third century. Ernst Künzl (1989, 203) seems undecided whether to attribute the blame to Christians (even though there is no way to decide whether or not there were Christians in the area prior to AD 260) or to the Alamanni; he appears to share Behn's assumption about the date of the destruction. Egon Schallmayer (1989, 253) believes in destruction by the Alamanni. Ingeborg Huld-Zetsche (1986, 46) equally argues for a mid-third-century destruction of Roman monuments in the area and, for this reason, excludes the possibility of Christian involvement. Richard Gordon (1999, 686) goes as far as to postulate that plotting temples with damaged sculpture on a map allows us to trace the invasion route of the Germans. That there is one perfectly well preserved mithraeum in one settlement on the invasion route (the first mithraeum in Heddernheim) is explained with the assumption that it might have been abandoned in the AD 230s, while he is unaware of the extensive destructions in the Mundelsheim mithraeum in the Neckar valley, an area thought by him to be beyond this invasion route. Franz Fischer (1991) by contrast (not specifically referring to Dieburg) thought that most such cases of thorough destruction were not perpetrated around AD 260 as the above-mentioned scholars argue, but in the early Middle Ages and, indeed, by Christians. Hans-Peter Kuhnen (1992, 42-3) postulates that both Christians and Alamanni were involved in image destruction.

Does the archaeological and historical evidence allow us to decide between this bewildering array of interpretations? Firstly, while it is a fair assumption that Christians could have lived in the area in the mid-third century, there is no convincing evidence for Christian image destruction that early anywhere in the Roman Empire. Apologetic Christian writers excel themselves in portraying Christians as law-abiding in anything other than matters of personal belief. A Christian council held at Granada in southern Spain two generations later, some time between AD 295 and 314, ruled that if anybody had smashed idols and fallen prey to lynch-law as a result, he should not be counted amongst the martyrs. It was stressed that there was no example for iconoclasm in the Gospels or under the Apostles. At the time of the council, held just before, during or after the last great persecutions in the Roman Empire, Christians were still discouraged from such acts. The phenomenon of Christian iconoclasm, quite apparently, originated before the persecutions had come to an end, but the virtual silence of Christian and pagan authors suggests that we are dealing with a few isolated instances. Image destruction exploded only when Christianity enjoyed imperial backing. To judge by the written evidence, the frequency of such acts of destruction by individual clergymen mirror the increasingly anti-pagan attitude of the imperial government, now Christian itself. The phenomenon seems to have increased in frequency between the

AD 320s and AD 361 (the time of Constantine and his sons), but had not yet reached the momentum to put the survival of the religious landscape of the ancient world at threat. The reigns of the last pagan Emperor Julian (AD 360/361-63), the Christian but tolerant Emperor Valentinianus I (AD 364-75) and his imperial brother Valens (AD 364-78) provided a breathing space before the onslaught on the Empire's pagan heritage eventually spiralled out of control in the last quarter of the fourth century. Christian image destruction in Dieburg around AD 260 thus seems exceedingly unlikely. The alternatives are thus destruction by Germans during the third-century invasions or the subsequent period of settlement, or by Christian missionaries no earlier than the sixth or seventh century when the area was converted to Christianity.

It could be argued that exceptionally laborious modes of destruction for no obvious purpose other than complete annihilation of the monuments concerned, points to a high level of determination and thus, probably, to religious fanaticism. There is no doubt that the damage at Dieburg was extensive, yet in terms of efforts it cannot be compared with the destruction of massive temples in Egypt or even the large Mithraic cult images of Sarrebourg or Koenigshoffen to be discussed below. One doubts that it would have taken a single, physically fit man equipped, as we have seen, with iron tools more than an hour – at a very rough estimate – if the missing parts were removed or a few hours if they were pulverised. The stone fragments from the well were of a size that a strong person would have been able to carry on his own. The group or individual responsible undoubtedly felt hatred against the artwork or those whose culture or religion it symbolised. The culprit(s) lacked any intention of re-using the stones or the well. All of these motives could be ascribed to pagan Germans and early medieval Christians alike. The former might even have had the intention to destroy the well, if it was during a raid; the latter would have found it long abandoned and as such a convenient depository.

Yet, does the particularly thorough destruction of the almost naked Mercury reveal it as an act of prudish Christians? Would 'barbarians' – if involved in image destruction on any scale at all – not, by contrast, have been motivated by hatred towards the provincial population and their culture, by superfluous destructive energy or by a desire to transform the area into a cultural and religious wasteland, less attractive to re-settle for the fled population? Would they thus not have spread their energy more evenly or selected the most elaborate monuments for special treatment? Yet, Mercury was not only almost naked, he was also the biggest surviving statue. Might he have been singled out for this reason by people who aimed to cause the maximum damage, quite irrespective of what they thought about male nudity in art? A further stone monument, the base of a statue, may help to decide between these two options: no more than parts of a pair of bare human or human-like feet survive next to a hoofed animal foot (**16**). There can be no doubt that these are the feet of a second Mercury statue next to a ram, the god's typical

THE ARCHAEOLOGY OF RELIGIOUS HATRED

16 *All that survived the onslaught: the feet of the second statue of Mercury (with a ram) from the Dieburg temple*

companion. To judge by the surviving part, this statue was only about half the size of the big Mercury and thus no larger than several other less thoroughly destroyed images. All except the feet of the statue was removed or crushed to stone powder; the small Mercury appears to have fared no better than his larger counterpart. We have to be cautious in our interpretation, considering that also much of the statue of the fully dressed goddess Minerva perished. Nevertheless, it is still hard to think of an explanation for the exceptionally thorough destruction of the two Mercury statues other than outrage about the god's nudity.

Mercury's treatment could be seen as an indication for Christian responsibility. Yet, are the indications strong enough? Is there another way to swing the camera around to see whether the arms on **colour plate 3** belong to a pagan Germanic invader or settler or to an early medieval Christian? (I exclude the rather less likely possibility that it was the act of a psychopath which, in any case, can hardly explain the universality of iconoclasm during the late Roman/early medieval transition, even if it should account for the odd example.) In modern cases of vandalism it is the exception rather than the rule that the perpetrators are caught, even if the targets and method of destruction may well allow one to form an opinion as to the motive and potential circle of suspects. 'Vandals' would not normally leave items behind which revealed their identity. If it is difficult today to expose the culprits on the basis of the material traces of their activities, how much harder is it if the destruction took place before living memory: no witness accounts are available, not even on the situation before and after; additionally any organic traces or even footprints have long since vanished.

First, we have to ask whether there is a way of knowing when the Dieburg temple was attacked. It is common practice in archaeology to assume that items (like fragments of sculpture) were deposited shortly after the time when the latest datable artefact in the assemblage was manufactured. On such a premise it would seem absurd to even contemplate the possibility that deposition of the shattered remnants of pagan statuary could have taken place during the Christianisation of the area, some 400 years after the last dated object from the temple we know of was produced. Yet, while occupation of a site or industrial activity tends to produce extensive debris, the destruction of artwork during a short visit to a building will in the vast majority of cases not involve the loss of datable artefacts or objects which provide clues to the origin or religion of the perpetrators. Notwithstanding the fact that our contemporaries produce a vastly higher number of low-value objects made of non-perishable materials than either Germanic tribesmen or early medieval Christians, in the majority of modern vandalism cases no datable artefacts, let alone objects which reveal the ideology of the perpetrators, are lost. The Dieburg temple will indeed have been abandoned in the third century, yet the solid stone structure and the images in its interior could easily have lasted for centuries if simply left to natural decay. Careful modern excavations might well have established whether or not an abandonment layer built up over the last occupation layer and prior to the deposition of the remains of sculpture, but the 1920s excavation report does not allow us to tell. The mithraeum collapsed eventually whether as a result of progressive dilapidation or deliberate action, burying all the smashed debris. The absence of heads, wide scattering of sculpture fragments and chisel marks leave not the slightest doubt, however, that the extensive damage to the works of art had been inflicted deliberately and could not have been caused by elements of the collapsing roof and walls falling onto fragile sculpture. The wooden entrance hall, by contrast, burnt down. We cannot be sure whether this was the result of an accident or of arson, and neither do we know when it happened and whether it preceded or post-dated the image destruction. We shall see that the roof truss of parts of the Strasbourg-Koenigshoffen mithraeum stayed intact for centuries. It is possible that the entrance hall at Dieburg was set alight following the image destruction, but it could equally have perished in a fire, whether caused accidentally or deliberately, at a much earlier date; the recently excavated temple of Mithras at Güglingen, equally in south-west Germany, burnt down twice and was refurbished after the first conflagration. There are no compelling reasons to exclude the possibility that the stone-built main temple could have been left to natural decay whether or not the timber entrance hall was still standing. We know that the new masters of the land, used to timber houses, neither re-occupied such buildings nor had any use for the stone and thus no incentive to demolish them. There is nothing to compel us to think that they were obsessed by a persistent and collective destructive mania, even if some monuments perished during the invasions. It is perfectly conceivable that they kept their distance from temples, whether out of disinterest or caution, not knowing what powers foreign deities carved out of stone might be able to exercise if provoked.

We may get further not by asking the question whether we can acquit with certainty pagan invaders or settlers from potential responsibility in individual cases of iconoclasm, such as at Dieburg (which, indeed, we cannot), but by asking what we should expect to find, had there, indeed, been persistent destructive mania. Even if we assumed, purely theoretically, that pagan

THE ARCHAEOLOGY OF RELIGIOUS HATRED

17 *Spared despite its sizeable dimensions (1.80 x 1.75m): there are no signs that this (or indeed any other monument) in the first mithraeum at Frankfurt am Main-Heddernheim has ever been deliberately attacked until it eventually fell over whereby the reverse suffered some accidental damage: a counter-argument against systematic image raids by the invading Germans?*

Germans had been responsible for all acts of image destruction in southern Germany, it is still astonishing how many such monuments survived unscathed without having been buried prior to Roman withdrawal. The above-mentioned extensive collection of stone monuments recovered from the first of five mithraea in Frankfurt am Main-Heddernheim shows no signs of deliberate damage at all. Like Dieburg, it contained a revolving cult image (**17** & **18**), but of larger dimensions than that of Dieburg. It had fallen onto an altar resulting in some accidental breakage. Nearby Rückingen has yielded the third of the revolving cult images (**19** & **20**), a peculiarity only known from this part of Roman Germany. Like the Dieburg specimen, it was violently broken

18 *The reverse of the same image: Mithras and the sun god take the holy meal and, like in Christian Communion, consume wine (the sun god is holding grapes) and bread rolls. Note that the nineteenth-century restoration gives the false impression of a monolithic block. In reality the central part of the relief could be rotated in the stone frame which therefore has only one display side (see **17**)*

off its anchorage and mutilated, which involved the hacking off of the heads of all eight pagan main figures on both sides of the relief. Three images do not allow statistical evaluation, but is it at least possible that the two smaller images at Rückingen and Dieburg rested in their frames for centuries, perhaps until the Christianisation of the region, whereas the specimen from Heddernheim collapsed as a result of its greater weight at an earlier date.

Heddernheim is not an isolated case. In another Mithras temple at Groß-Gerau, just 25km from Dieburg, a lion sculpture and a stone image of the god Mercury survived unharmed in the nave between the benches of the mithraeum buried eventually beneath the collapsed roof. Might the

19 *The faces of all three main figures attacked: the obverse of a third revolving cult relief, from Rückingen*

monuments at Heddernheim and Groß-Gerau have escaped iconoclasm because they were already buried at the time? It does not seem likely that they would have been buried beneath debris as early as the end of Roman dominion around AD 260 and since it seems scarcely conceivable that such buildings would have been overlooked for decades or even centuries, we may conclude that at the very least a high proportion of the new Germanic settlers were content for Roman images to survive undamaged. To stay with the example of the Mithras cult for a moment, the very fact that those territories in southern Germany abandoned by Rome over half a century before the conversions of the imperial government to Christianity have yielded some of the best preserved of the large cult reliefs anywhere in the Empire speaks for itself; besides the relief from Heddernheim we may add magnificent undamaged reliefs from Ladenburg and Heidelberg-Neuenheim. Such works of art could have been shattered with a single blow and yet were

20 *Mutilated faces: the reverse of the same image*

not even touched by the new German masters until they were eventually covered under debris. This is hard to reconcile with the assumption that pagan enemies more than Christians are responsible for widespread destruction of religious art.

Biographies of saints leave no doubt that much pagan artwork was still extant in Christian as well as pagan regions in north-west Europe as late as the sixth and seventh centuries and only then met its fate. The story of St Gallus and St Columbanus is by no means an isolated case. Turning the camera, we cannot discern with absolute certainty who is smashing the Dieburg images through the nebulous clouds of historical distance, even though we can see clearly how it was done. Yet, while many individual cases remain unresolved, the balance of probability is shifting towards Christians; they certainly were not responsible for all unresolved cases, but the above observations suggest that they were probably responsible for the majority of them. The reasonably certain cases of Christian iconoclasm are no more than the tip of the iceberg; many other cases leave room for more than one interpretation and in even more instances evidence has partially or entirely vanished as a result of the re-use of temple stone and smashed images in lime kilns or elsewhere.

I propose that the occurrence of any one of the following indications render religiously motivated iconoclasm likely, as shall be further explored in the course of this book:

1. exceptionally laborious and thorough modes of destruction without any obvious practical purpose like re-use of stone,
2. cases where pagan images appear to have targeted, but other artwork spared,
3. cases where naked deities were more thoroughly destroyed than their modestly dressed counterparts,
4. temples in which items of value, notably coins or other metal items, were deliberately left behind, and, of course,
5. iconoclasm in temples which soon thereafter were consecrated as churches or built over by churches.

Criterion 3 can be observed at Dieburg; whether criteria 1 and 2 apply as well is debatable.

Needless to say that these are only strong indications and not necessarily ultimate proof in each individual case. In the majority of instances even such criteria cannot be applied. The first criterion can only be used reliably if the temple inventory contained artwork on a truly massive scale. There is no way in which to establish whether a single statue in a temple *cella* was destroyed by iconoclasts who had the same level of determination as those responsible for image destruction at the Egyptian temple of Dendara (to be explored below). Neither can criteria 2 or 3 in such an instance be applied. If no valuable items were left behind, we cannot know whether they had been robbed, whether they had never been there in the first place or were concealed by the votaries themselves. Only a minority of temples were re-dedicated as churches (**colour plate 4**). This depended on whether the building was suitable and in an appropriate location, whether there was a need for additional places of worship at the time of destruction, and whether the necessary workforce was available to carry out the required alterations. Occasionally, churches seem to have been built on the sites of natural sanctuaries as this was the only way to re-focus traditional religiosity. That only a small proportion of sanctuaries was re-dedicated as churches renders it impossible to draw any conclusions from the fact that it was decided not to adapt a temple for Christian worship. Both literature and archaeology provide plenty of cases of temples which were destroyed by Christians without ever being re-used as churches. Where temples were re-dedicated as churches, pagan art had mostly been removed from the premises prior to re-dedication. While it is a safe bet that the sculpture of temples re-dedicated as churches was not treated respectfully and disposed of elsewhere, firm evidence to link the phenomena of image destruction and re-dedication of temples as ecclesiastical buildings is in the majority of cases lacking.

While the criteria above allow us to conclude that Christian responsibility is in many cases a more likely explanation for the destruction than enemy action, in numerous others there is no certain way to tell one way or the other. As a rule of thumb the proportion of modern scholars who explain an incident of image destruction as the work of 'barbarians' increases with the vicinity of the site to the borders of the Empire. We have already seen that in the case of image destruction in southern Germany roughly the same proportion of scholars argue with equal conviction for Christian or Germanic responsibility. Virtually identical observations can lead to diametrically opposed interpretations, as may become obvious by comparing just two modern views on how to explain the strong fragmentation of images recovered from two sites in southern Germany. Stefan Schmidt-Lawrenz (1999, 40-1 in translation) interprets the discovery of fragmented images from a variety of small shrines in a sacred enclosure next to the villa of Hechingen-Stein as follows:

> The fact that, in case of the statues and reliefs, heads and arms were found separated from the bodies points towards a deliberate and targeted destruction. We are probably dealing with early Christian missionaries who destroyed the last visible remnants of the pagan religions.

By contrast, Dieter Planck (1991, 48 in translation) comes to very different conclusions when discussing numerous pieces of sculpture recovered from three wells in the Roman village of Walheim:

> The images of deities were mostly very fragmented, probably also a violent consequence of the third-century incursions of the Alamanni.

The further we get from the northern frontiers of the Empire, the less frequently the blame is attributed to invading enemies. The so-called 'Tomb of the Elephant' in the necropolis of Carmona near Sevilla in southern Spain was undoubtedly the site of an iconoclastic attack as well and provides a useful analogy to Dieburg. This complex had been cut almost 5m deep into the natural rock and comprised no less than three cultic dining rooms and various side chambers, suggesting that it served for religious assemblies (**21**). Before dealing with the destruction of the pagan images in this unusual monument, it is necessary to explore what its original function had been. The cult inventory

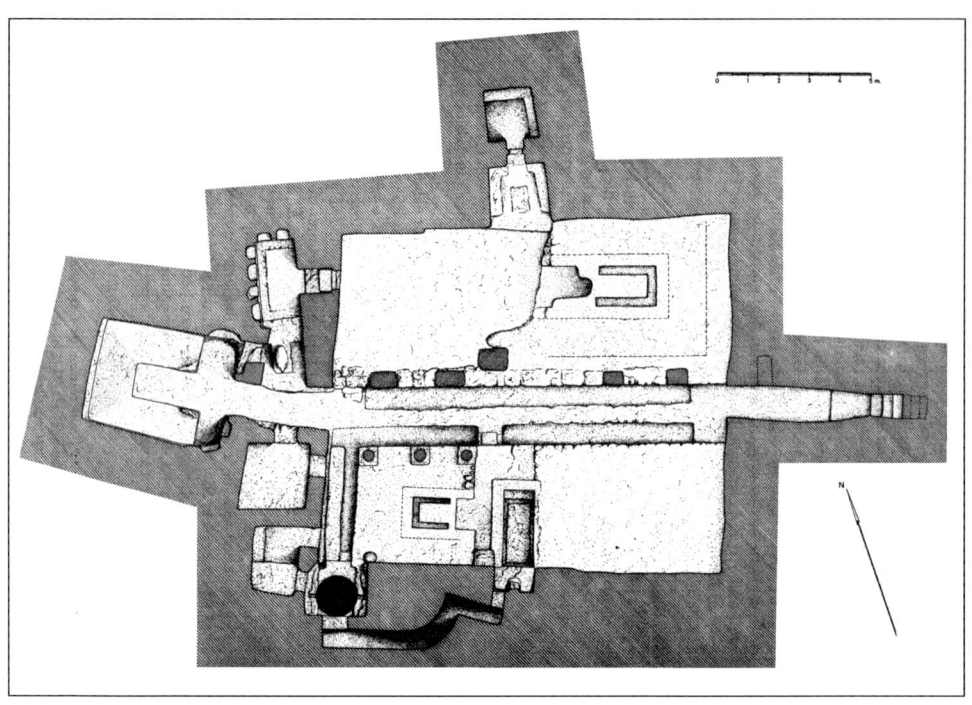

21 *The so-called 'Tomb of the Elephant' at Carmona: the well in the south-west of the rock-cut installation is depicted as a black circle*

22 *Badly damaged: the statue of the god Attis from the 'Tomb of the Elephant'*

gives essential clues. It included a statue of the god Attis (**22**), mutilated to such an extent that it is just barely recognisable as such on the basis of the characteristic way the god crosses his legs. Such a posture is otherwise only adopted by torchbearers in the Mithras mysteries, but the discovery within a non-Mithraic installation and in a cemetery renders such an interpretation exceedingly unlikely. A 63cm-high ovoid stone monument presumably represented a *betyl*. Such a holy stone had been specifically brought from Anatolia to Rome in 204 BC to form a central cult object in the capital's main temple of Cybele, the divine partner of Attis and mother goddess of Anatolian origin. While *betyls*, holy stones, are otherwise hardly ever depicted in the context of the Cybele and Attis cult, it is indeed likely that the stone from Carmona is meant to represent the conical and possibly meteoritic stone at Rome suggesting that those who used the complex worshipped the divine pair who had defeated death: Attis, according to the legend, had to die, but, at the initiative of Cybele, his body had never been allowed to decompose, and he was even partially revived. Thus he became an icon of pagan hopes that death was not the end. There are six burial niches in one underground side chamber. The extensive banqueting facilities and pagan works of art suggest it was intended to be a place for pagan assemblies whether merely for commemorative funerary meals for a select few or for wider gatherings of adherents of the Cybele and Attis cult.

Iconoclasts may not have cared whether it was more a temple or a funerary monument, and there was enough art on display to attract their attention. Only the lower parts of Attis' body survived the onslaught. Once again heads were the main targets. A rock-cut relief of a badly damaged figure, tentatively identified as a priest, displays a gaping hole above the truncated neck (**23**). A large rock-cut niche had largely protected it from accidental damage, suggesting that some of the damage affecting the lower body parts was due to hammering rather than natural erosion. Incidentally, two further statues of Attis were found in Carmona's necropolis. One had lost half of his head, the other head and shoulders. Returning to the 'Tomb of the Elephant' we can observe a second parallel between the procedure here and that adopted at Dieburg. The iconoclasts again did not content themselves with removing heads, they equally found some secondary use for the temple well. A statue of an elephant (**24**) was thrown down in the over 20m deep shaft and, while the records of the excavations do not appear to give certainty, it appears that the *betyl* was recovered from the same once watery depository. The inscriptions from the 'Tomb of the Elephant' had been hacked into such small pieces that we are no longer able to make any sense of them. At least one inscribed marble fragment derives from the temple well. It is worth stressing that the Dieburg temple well had less than a tenth of the depth of its equivalent in the 'Tomb of the Elephant'. Those who decided to fill up the bottom of the latter with heavy stone monuments destroyed not only a piece of infrastructure, which was particularly useful in the hot Mediterranean climate, but was also difficult to replace. Who were they?

THE ARCHAEOLOGY OF RELIGIOUS HATRED

23 *This figure, cut into the rock in the 'Tomb of the Elephant', is thought to represent a pagan priest who had his head chopped off*

Again we have no precise chronological fixed-points. We know of merely three coins, all from the temple well, ranging from the first to the fourth century, but we do not know whether or not all of them were found below the dumped stone monuments. Thus we cannot even be absolutely certain that the deposition of the fourth-century coin pre-dates the violent attack. At least, however, we know that the damage was done no later than the late Roman or the migration period. The 'Tomb of the Elephant' was filled up with soil or debris, intentionally one would have thought, and burials of the Visigothic period (fifth to eighth century) were found as much as 2m above the ancient surface. Muslims who conquered this area and much of the rest of the Iberian peninsula in the eighth century thus cannot have been responsible for any of the damage. Considering that southern Spain had been much more sheltered from invasions than the hinterland of the northern frontiers of the Empire, one would agree with Manuel Bendala Galán (1976, 64-5 and 1986, 390) that it is highly probable that Christians were responsible. One feels reminded of a letter written by North-African estate owner Publicola to St Augustine (letter 46) expressing fear that drinking water from a temple well might be perilous for a Christian. Those who threw stone monuments into the well may not have seen this as the destruction of a useful piece of infrastructure, but as a dangerous source of ritual pollution. Admittedly, we cannot exclude alternatives with absolute certainty. Southern Spain had been subject to extensive Moorish incursions in the AD 170s, and the Vandals temporarily conquered it in the early fifth century. The term 'vandalism' is, incidentally, a modern creation, and the Vandals were to no greater (or lesser) extent involved in acts of devastation than several other contemporary Germanic tribes. It thus seems very unlikely that the Vandals (having only just converted to Christianity themselves) were responsible for the destruction at Carmona during their short period of presence in the area.

The incidents of iconoclasm at Carmona and at Dieburg are comparable in labour investment, method and indiscriminate ferocity. If anything, the destruction of the Dieburg required more time. Can we be sure that the Dieburg incidence was committed by invaders and the destructions at Carmona by Christians solely on the basis of geography? Admittedly, the targeting of heads and the deposition of parts of the cult inventory in the temple well does not require particular ingenuity, and it would be dangerous to read too much into the parallels. Indeed, it is perfectly plausible to assume that invaders caused significantly more damage in the immediate hinterland of the frontier than in the interior of the Empire. Yet, if the forms of image destruction are similar, we should probably at least consider both options rather than attributing responsibility categorically to the 'barbarians'. The treatment of the nude Mercury representations at Dieburg suggests that here as well, the images had to perish because they were pagan, not because they

24 *Thrown into the well: this statue of an elephant gave the monument its modern name*

embodied the culture of a hostile power. Had there been no representations of Mercury then it would be difficult to tell one way or the other, and so it is in uncountable cases, not to mention images re-used as spoils or burnt to lime at a later date. The instances where we can point the finger clearly to either Christians or invaders are only the tip of the iceberg. The number of cases of image destruction must have exceeded many-fold those whose traces we have discovered and can understand.

2

PAGAN 'VANDALISM' AND ICONOCLASM IN PEACETIME

'Tolerance' in Pagan Rome

The adjective 'tolerant' is nowadays generously applied to the mainstream interpretations of all of the world's principal religions. Notwithstanding that, it could be argued that there was a greater degree of religious freedom in the Roman Empire of the first three centuries AD than there is in large parts of the world today (even if Christianity and Manichaeism formed an exception to the rule as we shall see). Polytheism, the belief in the existence of a variety of supernatural powers, was a system open to change and expansion. Unlike in Christianity, Judaism or Islam, the exploratory mind, who chose to add new divine powers to the personal pantheon to seek divine protection in a specific field, to fulfil spiritual or social needs or out of sheer curiosity, did not need to abandon traditional deities instead. The Emperor Severus Alexander (AD 222-35) is reported to have kept in his shrine of house gods (*lararium*) besides images of the *lares* themselves and those of his personal and imperial ancestors representations of Apollonius of Tyana also, who enjoyed wide religious veneration as a wise man and miracle worker of the first century, Christ, Abraham and Orpheus (a mythical musician and legendary founder father of a complex religious movement). The source, the *Historia Augusta* (Severus Alexander 29,2), is not always reliable. However, whether Christ indeed attracted the emperor's admiration as the charismatic founder of a remarkably successful, even if outlawed religion or whether this detail was invented by the late Roman author to demonstrate pagan open-mindedness, he could be sure that his readers would find such an unrestricted combination of religious key figures from the most different traditions, based purely on personal preferences, by no means implausible. Indeed, the transformation of the Roman state from an entity centred on Italy and dominated by conservative values to a vast and cosmopolitan Empire went hand in hand with a spread, exchange and diversification of religious cults and rituals on an unparalleled scale. No other state has ever controlled the majority of Europe's population, not to mention the Near East and northern

Africa for a period anywhere near as long as the Roman Empire, namely over 500 years. One of the reasons was the superiority of the army to those of Rome's enemies at least until the third century. Yet, equally important was the remarkable ability of the Empire to integrate its new subjects.

By contrast, it would probably be true to say that a member of a conservative Christian, Jewish or Muslim society today intending to change his or her religion or to pick and choose deities or key elements from a variety of religions is likely to face a significant degree of resistance and social stigma. Codified monotheistic religions claim by definition that there is only one God and one way to the truth and are thus inherently resistant to change. Cosmopolitan Western societies are presumably the first in Europe and the West since the time of the Roman Empire where there is similar or greater freedom in religious choice – or indeed the freedom to adopt an atheistic or agnostic worldview.

Imperial iconoclasm

In view of this large degree of religious freedom, would it be fair to lay the blame for each and every archaeologically traceable case of image destruction at the door of Christians? The biographies of saints leave no doubt that Christian iconoclasm was a widespread phenomenon, yet was it an exclusively Christian phenomenon? It is interesting to note that earlier iconoclastic excesses are equally linked with the spread of monotheistic religions, religions which proclaimed the existence of only one God at the exclusion of all other deities. Pharaoh Akhenaten (1372-1355 BC) is the earliest example. He promoted his solar god Aten and had names and representations of other deities erased from monuments, only to cause a violent backlash after his death. The Old Testament not only legitimised, but demanded the destruction of pagan images, and it is well known that, for example under King Herod, some Jews sacrificed their lives to remove the king's golden cagle from the temple at Jerusalem. Later Islam, the third of the monotheistic world religions, adopted iconoclasm as well. The politically motivated destruction of images and names of deceased Roman emperors or political figures who fell victim to official damnation need not concern us here. It is almost always possible to differentiate between such political and religiously motivated acts since there is little overlap in the types of images affected. In case of votive inscriptions with reference to a name of a condemned emperor, damnation would normally result in a neat erasure of the imperial name only while Christian iconoclasm would involve the destruction of the whole object.

Yet, while political damnation was largely confined to images depicting and inscriptions naming emperors despised by their successors, there was also state-sponsored destruction of religious images within the Roman state long before the victory of Christianity. Indeed, in the first century BC and at the beginning of the first century AD the policy towards some of the foreign Eastern religions, especially the cult of Isis, was changeable, but often conservative and hostile. Temples of Isis at Rome were repeatedly destroyed. Yet, interestingly, in one instance in 50 BC none of the workmen dared to lift an arm against the sanctuary until the consul, Lucius Aemilius Lepidus Paullus, himself attacked the temple doors with an axe. Ordinary men refused to obey the highest representatives of the state out of religious fear and respect. What could be more striking evidence that violent action against religious buildings and images, even if sacred to an exotic deity, broke a deep-rooted taboo? Isis and tolerance were soon to win the battle against the last conservative die-hards. The latest temple destruction is recorded for the year AD 19 sparked by a scandal when the trust of an Isis devotee married into a leading senatorial family had been abused. An admirer had persuaded her to have sexual intercourse with him in the temple by successfully pretending that he was no less than the jackal-headed Egyptian god Anubis himself. The Emperor Tiberius (AD 14-37), disgusted by the crime, had the Isis priests crucified for their complicity, the temple of the goddess razed to the ground and her cult statue thrown into the River Tiber. These cases of pagan iconoclasm, however, remained isolated incidents, largely confined to the old capital Rome.

Yet, the heart of the most cosmopolitan and culturally diverse Empire the West had ever seen could not survive as a bastion of religious conservatism. Religious freedom facilitated successful political integration, and the elite itself increasingly appreciated and took advantage of the unrestricted religious choice on offer to them. Image destruction and religious persecution no longer occurred after the death of Tiberius, not even at Rome itself. Only the Christians who condemned the Empire's 'worship whomsoever and whatever you like' system and who placed themselves outside the umbrella it provided, could not count on any protection or tolerance. Christianity was not a traditional religion and had strong missionary tendencies which made it dangerous and suspect in the eyes of the pagan majority. Judaism as the other exclusive one-God-religion faced some discrimination as well. Yet on the whole it was tolerated, as were virtually all other traditional religions and religious practices for the sake of promoting the cohesion of the state. The only other exceptions to the rule were institutions or rituals perceived to be politically dangerous or ethically unacceptable, namely Druidism and human sacrifices in general. Much later Manichaeism, another new religion emanating from the hostile Persian Empire in the third century, was outlawed, as it was erroneously associated with the Persian state.

There is no attempt here to justify or to belittle the cruel treatment many followers of Christ and of the prophet Mani had to suffer, yet it does not alter the fact that the majority which was content to stay within the pagan system enjoyed virtually unlimited freedom of choice. With Christianity being virtually the only and initially largely image-less religion subjected to persecutions, religiously motivated image destruction was a non-phenomenon within the Empire. There is no evidence to suggest that there was mindless 'vandalism' against images as in the Western world today; belief in the potency of deities to take revenge besides social and legal sanctions prevented people from conceiving such ideas, let alone carry them out. If ever people dared to violate the divine in peacetime, then it was done for financial profit. A few cash-stricken emperors melted down metal votives, a sacrilege which did not fail to attract strong condemnation by historiographers.

The second and early third century marked also the peak in the creation of pagan stone monuments, a peak which was followed by a sharp decline between the AD 230s and the AD 280s when the Roman world was affected by a string of civil wars, large-scale invasions and a severe economic downturn. Not only were far fewer works of art produced during the crisis, but priorities shifted, and elaborate stone monuments began to be re-employed as mere building material, especially in hastily erected defences. The phenomenon of using works of art as spoils escalated in the second half of the third century, but reached its peak only in the fourth century. Stone images, ornamental stonework and inscriptions, often broken into suitably shaped blocks, were re-used in such constructions. These spoils derived from pagan shrines as well as from funerary and secular structures. Some will have been taken from already dilapidated buildings, others were specifically demolished for the purpose. Sections of the riverside-wall of London (**25**), hastily erected during a time of an increasing threat of sea-raids in the third quarter of the third century (though it is disputed whether the re-use of spoils dates to this period or to a fourth-century phase), form one example for the re-use of earlier stone monuments. The use of spoils in Roman Britain was comparatively scarce in contrast to the Continent, which was to a far greater extent affected by invasions. Famous are the elaborate funerary monuments re-used in the foundations of the early fourth-century fortification at Neumagen in the Mosel valley, and many hundreds of stone monuments have been found in the third- and fourth-century walls of Mainz in Germany. Securely dated to the third century is a building inscription of AD 270 or 271 for a military stronghold on the reverse of a dedication to three indigenous deities from Mittelstrimmig in Germany. The indiscriminate re-use of whatever suitable building material was available demonstrates that we are in most instances not dealing with targeted anti-pagan iconoclasm (even though there are examples for the latter as we shall see in the case of Gaza in Palestine). The pragmatic nature of the re-use is confirmed by the distinct preference for squared stones, such as altars, bas-reliefs or torsos of statues. In the case of the stones from the riverside wall at London, unnecessary damage was avoided and facial features normally spared. The phenomenon of large-scale use of works of art as building material certainly attests to a dramatic change in the religious landscape, but is no reliable indicator for specifically anti-pagan measures.

PAGAN 'VANDALISM' AND ICONOCLASM IN PEACETIME

25 *The construction of a section of the riverside Wall in London, re-using fragments of religious stone monuments, as envisaged by Peter Warner*

It is noticeable that few examples can be found for cases of image destruction which carry distinctive signs of religious hatred firmly datable to the period before the conversion of the imperial government while they abound in the late fourth century and thereafter. The temple of the war goddess Allat at Palmyra in Syria forms a revealing example for the differences in the treatment of images in the late third century at the hand of pagans, and over 100 years later, presumably at the hands of Christians. The rich trading centre of Palmyra in a Syrian desert oasis became, in the early AD 270s, the nucleus of an independent Empire that stretched from Egypt into the area of modern Turkey. Emperor Aurelian (AD 270-275) crushed the rebellion and brought the East back under central control. Palmyra had to be subdued twice. The sources allege that deliberate destruction followed the second capture of the city, yet archaeology has found little evidence of it on the ground. A possible exception, however, was formed by the temple of the warrior goddess Allat, whose sacred enclosure seems to have suffered some damage prior to its restoration around AD 300. Funerary monuments as well as pagan sculptures were re-used in wall foundations of this period (**26**). They include the parts of a monumental 3.5m-high lion (**colour plate 5**) who carefully guarded an antelope between his paws to remind visitors that the goddess did not allow blood to be spilled in her sanctuary, a message reiterated in an inscription.

49

THE ARCHAEOLOGY OF RELIGIOUS HATRED

26 *The retaining wall of c.AD 300 around the sacred precinct of the temple of Allat in Palmyra with funerary sculpture (bottom) and the trunk of a statue of a local god wearing a cuirass (top)*

We have no certainty whether or not it were indeed Aurelian's troops who deprived the goddess of this powerful protector who must once have guarded her sacred enclosure or under what other circumstances the sculpture was demolished. A series of figures wearing civilian dress and one equipped with a cuirass and a sword fared less well than the lion and were reduced to torsos prior to being re-used as building material in the foundations of the new temple. The draped men could be funerary sculptures, while the cuirassed figure resembles first-century representations of Palmyrene gods. Whether coincidence or not, it is worth noting that the published torsos all seem to belong to male humans plus the one probable god in military dress. A funerary image with a Greek inscription referring to Zeus, depicting a woman together with her son remained undamaged and so did a statue of the goddess Allat in the guise of Athena. Might this reflect that the rage of Aurelian's soldiers was directed in the first instance against male adults, even though the rebellion had effectively been led by a woman, Zenobia? The funerary sculpture of mother and son was found inserted in the late foundations as well, while the goddess Allat was even allowed to stay in her temple.

PAGAN 'VANDALISM' AND ICONOCLASM IN PEACETIME

Even if a small number of pagan images besides funerary sculpture should have perished when Aurelian took the city for the second time, not a single temple in this centre of rebellion can be shown to have suffered complete or permanent destruction. Neither the temple of the god Baalshamen nor the vast sacred complex of Bel appear to have been significantly damaged, and both continued to function as cult centres until their central sanctuaries were transformed into churches much later. The temple of Allat equally was not destroyed and the damage confined to the sacred enclosure. The complex was not only restored around AD 300, but continued to flourish in the fourth century as is attested by almost 200 oil lamps of this period from within the temple. It was not before AD 383 at the very earliest, to judge by coin evidence, that the temple met its fate. This time the intruders showed no respect to the divine mistress of the temple (**27**). A heavy blow with a metal tool from behind (**28**) struck off the head of the 2.14m-tall white marble

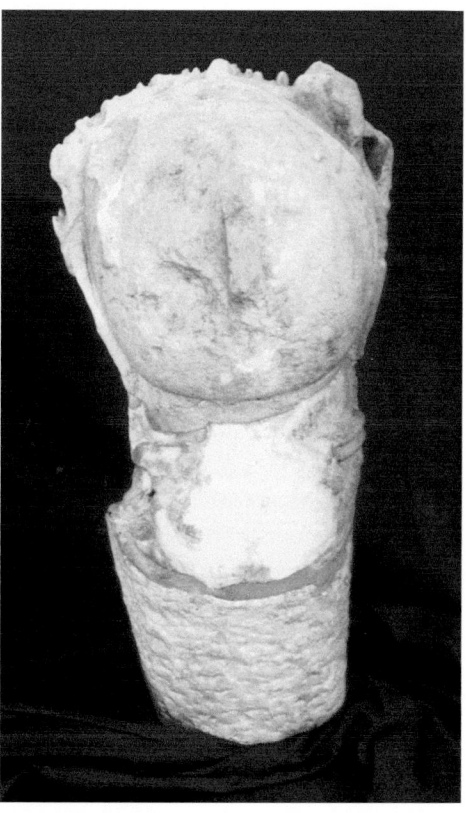

27 (Left) *The over life-sized marble statue of the goddess Allat*

28 (Above) *The marks of the tool which struck her from behind, knocking her head off the torso*

29 (Above) *The mutilated head of the goddess was found broken into eight fragments*

30 (Right) *The shoulder of Allat was chopped off*

statue in fine classical style. Further fragmentation followed until the goddess's head was broken into eight pieces (**29**). Not only the left arm, but the whole shoulder was cleanly chopped off (**30**). The decently dressed torso required no further mutilation and was left lying in the ruins of her sanctuary. The decapitation of a second smaller statue of the goddess and the horizontal dissection of the altar completed the destruction of the interior; the building followed later. The contrast between the at most half-hearted pagan iconoclasm even in a city responsible for repeated rebellion and what was to follow over a century later is striking. One cannot help thinking that Aurelian and his troops felt more fear or respect for the pantheon of the defeated city than hatred for their enemies. They did not erase a single temple and probably could not even have imagined the catastrophe, which was to descend on the rich visual world of Roman paganism about five generations later.

3

DESTRUCTION IN WAR AND PEACE

We have already seen when discussing the fate of the Dieburg relief that there was no concerted action against surviving Roman art after the Germanic Alamanni had taken control over south-west Germany around AD 260. Indeed, several major works of art survived unscathed, such as the whole inventory of the first temple of Mithras at Frankfurt am Main-Heddernheim. The cult relief itself eventually fell over causing some accidental damage, but did not suffer any deliberate mistreatment. It seems highly unlikely that all monuments would already have been covered by sediments or debris as early as AD 260. It is true that also in several temples of Mithras in the Mediterranean well-preserved works of art have come to light despite the fact that these territories, unlike southern Germany, had not been abandoned prior to the Christianisation of the Roman state. But do these really prove that Christians did not mind the continued display of pagan art? For the most part, the excavations did not conform to modern standards, and we often have no way of telling whether these buildings had been sealed off at the time when Christian image-raids reached their apogee or whether they were still accessible. Occasionally the reports provide clues as to why images in Mediterranean temples escaped destruction. In ancient Capua the colourful paintings on the wall of an underground temple of Mithras (**colour plate 6**) have never been touched. Some time after AD 330/35, the date of the latest of three identified coins from the occupation levels of the temple, earth mixed with debris of tiles, mortar and stone were dumped through the air holes into the interior of the subterranean place of worship. We do not know who has been responsible for this, whether votaries who considered filling up the temple with debris the only way to stop image destruction or non-fanatical Christians who saw no point in defacing images condemned to be buried under heaps of debris. Either way, the heaps of building waste ensured that the paintings were safe from both, being the object of illegal pagan worship and legal Christian image destruction. There is nothing to suggest that any temple in south-west

Germany was intentionally filled up with debris, especially considering that the Alamanni had no tradition in this kind of earth-moving operation. The survival of unprotected images on open display in pagan south-west Germany may well prove that there was no general hatred against the visual remnants of the Roman past amongst the new masters of this region.

Yet, it is not my intention to imply that Germans and Romans showed great mutual respect for each other's culture and religion during periods of warfare, even if literary evidence for temple destruction in the course of military conflicts is sparse. The nature of destruction was, from what we can gather from ancient authors, however, not specifically targeted against religious monuments. In AD 9 the Germans had annihilated three of Rome's legions, with auxiliary troops and support staff probably well in excess of 25,000 men. The Empire took revenge. A surprise raid against the German tribe of the Marsi in AD 14 formed the prelude to three years of sustained campaigning. Tacitus (*Annals* 1,51) reports the deeds of Germanicus, the nephew of Emperor Tiberius, and his army:

> He devastated an area fifty miles across with fire and sword. There was no mercy for either sex or for any age. Profane and sacred places were indifferently razed to the ground, also the most famous temple amongst these people, which they called the temple of Tanfana. The soldiers who had slaughtered people half-asleep, unarmed or dispersed, escaped without a wound.

Tacitus paints a picture of totally indiscriminate carnage and destruction. Religious sites were neither spared nor treated worse than profane sites. The famous sanctuary, which must have consisted of wood, will have been an easy target whose destruction involved minimum effort and had maximum effect.

Is there evidence for the Germans acting likewise? Gregory of Tours (*History of the Franks* 1,32) reports on events some two and a half centuries after the raid of Germanicus. Then, apparently, the Alamannic king, Chrocus, overran all of Gaul and destroyed all ancient buildings to their foundations. There is no doubt that the Germanic incursions affected much of Gaul at the time. Nevertheless, the claim that all old buildings were destroyed in such a thorough manner is incompatible with the evidence on the ground and certainly at least an exaggeration of the facts. The pagan king's deeds included, according to Gregory, the burning and destruction of a monumental temple with lavish interior and lead roof at Clermont-Ferrand in Gaul. A massive temple with debris of its lead roof, molten in fire, have actually been found at Clermont. While archaeology has been unable to establish the date of the inferno, it is thought that Gregory saw the massive ruins some 300 years after the alleged date of the destruction. Other than undated traces of fire, archaeology has as yet been unable to find direct evidence for the legendary devastations of King Chrocus anywhere in the town, although the town apparently suffered a decline in population in the third century. Tradition knows of another Germanic King Chrocus who committed very similar deeds in the fifth century. This raises the question whether two historical figures might have been confused. Nevertheless, Gregory's architectural description fits so well to the excavated temple (especially as a lead roof was very unusual) that one is tempted to think that he reported a by and large correct local tradition. If so, the remains of the temple suggest that fire was used as a quick and easy form of destruction. There is no positive evidence for destruction of stone images or walls. Some fragments of sculpture have been found in the immediate vicinity of the remains of the temple, but they bear no signs of targeted iconoclasm. Even the head of Mercury on the preserved part of a stone relief has not been touched.

Was image destruction entirely alien to Rome's military adversaries? A monument from Ladenburg, a Roman town near Heidelberg in Germany, provides one of the few incidences of destruction, which can be dated. It was a Jupiter giant column (**colour plate 7**). This type of monument was particular popular in the German frontier zone. Details of the composition of this type of monument need not concern us here, but it was invariably a large column crowned by an image of the father of gods, Jupiter, normally on horseback, brandishing a thunderbolt and riding over a defeated giant. Classical mythology explains the image: the giants were legendary beings of a ferocious nature and of fearsome appearance with huge muscular bodies, a wild hair-style and legs in the shape of snakes. They tried to gain world domination, but suffered a bloody defeat at the hands of Jupiter, his fellow deities and semi-gods. However, Jupiter is not normally depicted as a horseman in classical art, and this particular monument is a peculiarity of the north-west of the Roman Empire. Some of these monuments were deliberately destroyed, including the monument in question (one of no less than thirteen such giant columns from Ladenburg alone). At the bottom of a well in Ladenburg one such rider group was found (**31**), buried beneath building debris; it was visibly damaged as a result of having fallen off a column. Pottery sherds from underneath the sculpture attest that the deposition occurred some time after the early third century. After an interlude when snail shells accumulated on top of the building debris, the remains of an entire column were dumped in the same well, now filled up almost to the rim. Parts of the monument were fire-reddened, further proof for the turbulent events which affected the town when Roman rule collapsed. The dedicatory inscription of the monument stating specifically that the monument had been restored was carved into the stone on top of an earlier inscription. An associated altar equally carries two superimposed inscriptions. This suggests it had been the same column which had been demolished twice. It is scarcely conceivable that early medieval missionaries would have disposed of the remains of pagan monuments in the

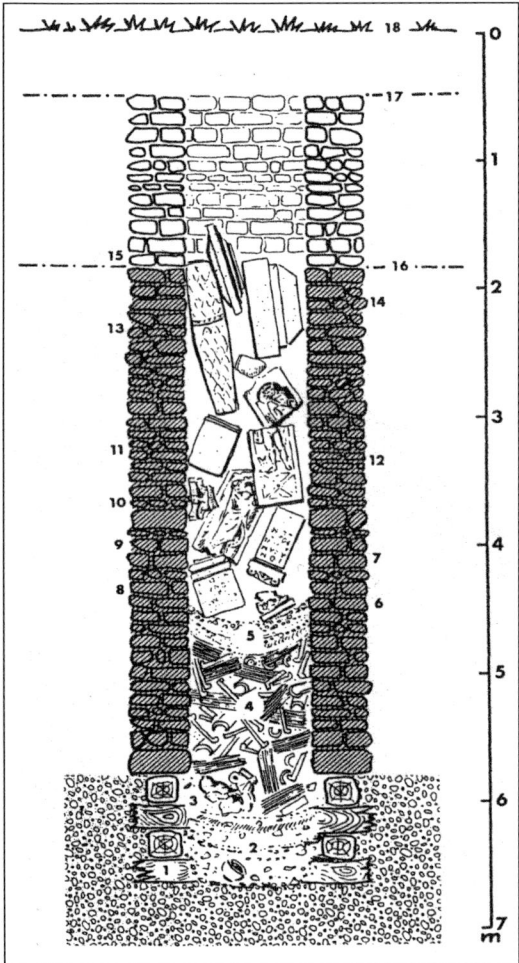

*31 A well in Ladenburg with fragments of a Jupiter giant column (**colour plate 7**): evidence for an image raid by pagan Germans*

same well in two separate episodes, several years apart. And if the restoration inscription indeed refers to the same monument whose crowning sculpture was deposited in the well, as seems likely, then we have firm evidence that at least the first incident of destruction (and almost certainly both) occurred in the third century. The invasion by the tribe of the Alamanni in AD 233 and the final takeover of power around AD 260 might conceivably have been the dates of destruction. Is this really evidence of indiscriminate Germanic destructive mania or did the invaders feel particularly provoked by this specific type of monument? If one had to select just one single visual symbol of Rome's claim to superiority, surely the Jupiter giant columns would have been it. The image of the Roman father of the gods riding over a wild and seemingly uncivilised creature, proudly on display on a column, sent out a message blatantly obvious to friend and foe alike: Rome was superior to its 'barbarian' enemies. It is most significant in our context that this clear example of pagan German iconoclasm does not bear the hallmarks of the 'overkill' mentality, concerning central parts of the divine anatomy, we have witnessed at so many other sites. Jupiter has lost his upper body, but this need not have been the result of deliberate action, but merely of the fall from 4m height. A single blow each would have sufficed to permanently disfigure the faces of the four deities at a lower level and yet the pagan Germans refrained from doing so – a striking contrast to Dieburg and so many other cases.

It is difficult to assess whether it was such symbolism which sparked Germanic image destruction or whether it was a more widespread phenomenon. It is noticeable that in the Germanic frontier zone wells served exceptionally often as convenient dumping grounds for smashed sculpture not just at Ladenburg and Dieburg, but elsewhere. In Bad Wimpfen a statue of the goddess Minerva was found smashed into six pieces which bear traces of fire from the conflagration of the building, while the base of the same statue was thrown into a well, 50m from the other debris; the goddess's head has never been found. Numerous other shattered fragments of stone images nearby attest to the systematic and indiscriminate nature of the attack. At Walheim, like Bad Wimpfen and Ladenburg on the River Neckar, three wells were filled with numerous debris of deliberately smashed votive sculpture and inscriptions. The distances of the three wells from each other range from $c.100$m to over 140m and it appears that in a fairly systematic clearance operation all the pagan monuments in reach were specifically targeted, smashed, carried to the nearest well and disposed of. In contrast to the Ladenburg example, the jury is still out as to whether these cases were perpetrated by Germanic invaders or, much later, by Christian missionaries. A well in an abandoned settlement could have stayed open for centuries, and those responsible for smashing stone monuments and carrying the remains to the deep shafts were unlikely to lose datable artefacts while doing so. We have seen in the introductory chapter that lakes certainly formed an appropriate depository for pagan votive objects as recovery was difficult or impossible. Wells could have fulfilled a similar function, and we ought to keep an open mind as to who was responsible. At Entrains-sur-Nohain six Mithraic bull-slaying reliefs and the heads of several deities were found close together on the bed of the local river. Many of them were distinctively mutilated, such as the corner of a relief with beheaded Mithras next to the sun god. The latter's forehead and face are disfigured by a deep scar inflicted with a metal tool with a long cutting edge (**32**). The river could have fulfilled a similar function to the wells. Surely the settlement in Gaul was well within the range of Germanic invaders, but the quite systematic nature of the mutilation and removal of the pagan heritage raises major doubts as to whether pagan 'vandalism' is a more likely interpretation than Christian image destruction.

The Germanic invasions in the third century involved, at least occasionally, episodes of destruction of a quite indiscriminate nature but with a preference for easy modes of destruction, such as arson. The cases where Germanic responsibility for the more arduous smashing of stone images can be proved

32 *A deep scar in the sun god's head: proof that this relief from Entrains in Gaul fell prey to deliberate attack. It was found together with several other pagan monuments on the bed of a small river*

beyond doubt are very few. Even though Christian responsibility in those cases outside the borders of the late Roman Empire is similarly difficult to prove, the question remains as to why some images at least do not appear to have been touched after the Germanic takeover of those territories. Biographies of saints leave no doubt that at least to the west and south of the Rhine Christian missionaries were still busy smashing images which must have been 300-500 years old at that time in the sixth and seventh century. We cannot exclude the possibility that they could have acted in a similar manner in the same period east of the river in territories previously under pagan rule. Indeed, the systematic and arduous procedure of the iconoclasts at Walheim makes me think that Christian intervention in the early Middle Ages is the more plausible explanation. However, the excavations at Walheim have not yet been fully published, and we will have to await the final report to see whether there is further evidence to decide one way or the other.

It would be interesting to carry out an Empire-wide study concerning what proportion of religious monuments in different provinces ended up in wells. While this cannot be offered here, it seems clear that there are signifi-

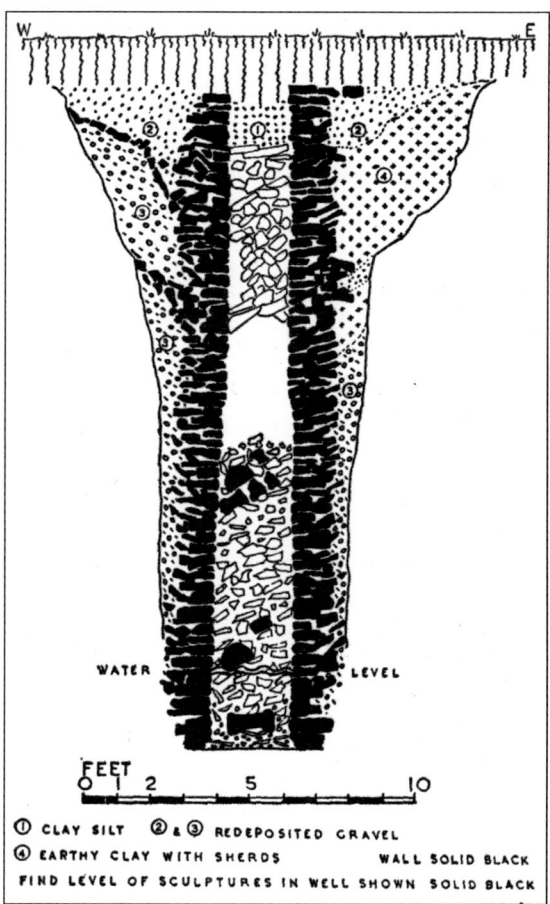

33 *A fourth-century well at Lower Slaughter in Gloucestershire contained pagan stone monuments (in black), some of which had been mutilated*

cant differences, between southern Germany and Britain, for example. A well at Lower Slaughter in Gloucestershire (**33**) has yielded a collection of altars without inscriptions, votive slabs and small sculptures of two seated deities, both deliberately beheaded prior to deposition (**34** & **35**), most probably deriving from a small rural shrine. Yet, in comparison with the numerous examples of deposition of pagan stone monuments in the German frontier zone such evidence pales into insignificance. No matter whether responsibility is attributed to invaders or Christians or both groups, much iconoclasm has to pre-date the time when in Germany or south-east Britain stone became once again an important building material in the second millennium. While there was never a gap in the Mediterranean, in many of the former provinces of the Roman Empire in central or north-western Europe the technique of constructing buildings in stone was discontinued for several centuries after the end of the western Empire. Then, for several centuries more it was applied only in case of a small number of key buildings, notably churches. Thus we cannot reasonably explain the lower proportion of stone monuments thrown into wells in Britain with the greater scarcity of natural stone suitable as

34 (Left) *Statuette of a headless deity from the well at Lower Slaughter*

35 (Right) *Statuette of a second headless deity (a goddess) from the well at Lower Slaughter*

building material in much of southern Britain; it has to have its reason in a real difference in the extent or the modes of iconoclasm between southern Germany and Britain. Whether this was due to Britain being less affected by invasion or to a greater degree of respect towards pagan deities will be further explored below. As far as Lower Slaughter is concerned, the well was only constructed in the fourth century, thus pointing with a high degree of probability to a Christian image raid in this particular instance.

Britain seems to form a special case. Apart from Mithraic art there is astonishingly little evidence for iconoclasm in Britain. The beheaded sculpture from Lower Slaughter forms an exception to the rule. While there is no scarcity in Britain as elsewhere of statues without heads and isolated heads, the example of distinctively mutilated images (with tool marks, for example) which cannot be explained as a result of an accident are far fewer than in Gaul or Germany as a survey of the images now in their majority conveniently compiled in the *Corpus Signorum Imperii Romani* (volumes I,1-8) will confirm. The transition from paganism to Christianity in Britain was less of a cultural revolution. Even where statues were broken, we do not normally witness the same degree of destructive violence as in many other former parts of the Empire. In Uley, for example, the head of Mercury (**colour plate 12**), formerly the lord of a major rural shrine was buried with great care in a votive pit once his time had passed and a new building, quite possibly a church, erected at the site in the early Middle Ages. A single blow with a metal tool or even stone would have sufficed to permanently disfigure his youthful face. Yet, apart from some minor, presumably accidental, damage to the nose, he suffered no mistreatment. There was no hatred, perhaps even a degree of respect or superstitious fear on the part of those who laid him to rest. Perhaps we can even trace a survival of the cult of the human head, well attested in Roman Britain. Other fragments of sculpture were re-used in the new constructions whether for purposes of desecration, pragmatic re-use or belief in continuing magic power.

Rural cults flourished in late fourth-century Britain, and coin series in many temples run to the end of the fourth century, the time when coin supply to Britain and other northern territories of the Empire ceased. New mosaics with pagan subjects were laid in private villas and as late as the last third of the fourth century in a temple at Lydney. There was astonishing ritual continuity in the case of many sanctuaries in Britain, a part of the Empire which appears to have seen comparatively little immigration, from the pre-Roman period to the very end of Roman rule in the early fifth century and beyond, attesting to the strength of local cults. The most striking example may be the White Horse at Uffington, a figure cut into the chalk visible from kilometres away. Recent scientific dating has established that it is about 3,000 years old. Yet adjacent monuments attest that it continued to be a centre of worship throughout the Iron Age and Roman periods. It had to be cleared of vegetation at regular intervals, and we know that this continued to be done right to the nineteenth century, attesting to three millennia of religious continuity. Paradoxically, it may have been the same deep-rooted religious traditionalism of Britain which never allowed the alien cult of Mithras to gain a foothold in the countryside, consented to its early eradication and which did not allow another foreign religion, Christianity, to use excessive force against what were perceived to be native cults.

Interestingly, not only the Germans, but also Rome's Persian enemies seem to have been content to leave the pagan art of their opponents undamaged. Dura-Europos was probably captured by the Persians in c.AD 252, then taken for a second time by storm and transformed into a ghost town in AD 256. Yet despite its dramatic end, Dura has yielded many exceptionally well preserved works of art. Dura's image-rich places of worship dedicated to a range of different deities and religions have yielded a fair number of damaged sculptures (besides many undamaged images). Yet, at least some of the damage has been plausibly explained by the excavators (Rostovtzeff et al. 1939, 243-4) as a result of wall and roof collapse and later stone robbing. The loss of heads or the discovery of isolated heads which can be observed at Dura, as at many other sites across the Empire, often poses problems of interpretation. Unless, as at

Dieburg, there is a clear pattern with virtually all images being found without their heads, one cannot be sure whether this was not simply the result of accidents: when a statue collapsed or was hit by falling debris the thin neck was intrinsically likely to break (though identifiable remains of the shattered head should normally survive the impact of falling debris). One searches in vain at Dura for unmistakable traces of iconoclasm, such as paintings with gouged out faces or sculpture which carries deep incisions inflicted with sharp tools. The most likely candidate for iconoclasm I could find amongst the numerous images from Dura is formed by a small relief dedicated to Nemesis, the goddess of revenge, found at one of the city's gates. The heads of all four figures on the relief, Nemesis herself, a priest, a griffon and the sun god, have been destroyed. Yet, even in this case an explanation that it was an accident is possible: a deep fracture, conceivably the result of falling debris, split the bust of the sun god in two, and the fracture line is close enough to the head of the griffon to explain its splintering off. The cracking off of the faces of Nemesis and the priest might equally be due to falling debris or the collapse of the image, as might the loss of Nemesis' lower arms. The observation that the fracture was mended in antiquity adds further doubts as to whether this is really an example of Persian iconoclasm. Yet, even if it could be shown that the odd image was destroyed in AD 256 (and it cannot), the large number of images without any trace of intentional destruction renders it doubtful that Persian anger over the fierce Roman resistance released itself in systematic image destruction, despite the fact that it had not been an easy siege; the highly dangerous operations which must have inflamed mutual hatred involved the Persians undermining the walls while a counter-mine was dug by the defenders of the city. Dura became a ghost town (**colour plate 8**) and never again had a Roman garrison. It demonstrates quite strikingly the fundamental difference in the fate of pagan images within and outside the sphere of influence of Christian iconoclasts.

Intentional damage, by contrast, is frequent in temples whose territories remained under Roman control. Six mithraea, for example, are known in the Syrian provinces (an area stretching from south-east Turkey to Israel and Palestine). Two of them are not relevant in our context: the Dura-Europos mithraeum has yielded a rich collection of art and no signs of iconoclasm whatsoever. However, being positioned close to the city walls, its extant remains were covered in the wake of a last desperate attempt to strengthen the fortifications by an embankment. Much of the description of the possible Sidon mithraeum is probably invented and thus there are uncertainties about its interpretation; yet, there are indications that the rich collection of undamaged marble statues had been intentionally hidden towards the end of the fourth or in the fifth century whether or not as a result of a real threat of Christian iconoclasm. Amongst the remaining four temples, one, the mithraeum at Caesarea, appears to have been abandoned at an unknown date after the late third century. There were no large stone monuments left in the building and no signs of intentional destruction, but whether this was the result of a concealment of stone monuments outside the temple in the light of a Christian threat or whether the votaries abandoned the temple without outside pressure has to remain a matter of speculation.

The remaining three temples were intentionally destroyed and all of them demonstrably by Christians. At Hawarte, a mithraeum which was still furnished with new paintings in the AD 360s, and, on the basis of coin evidence, used until at least AD 383, but probably beyond, had as much as 1.5m of rubble heaped into it, before its natural rock ceiling was deliberately destroyed and a church built on top of it at the turn of the century.

Two mithraea in natural caves adjacent to each other at Dülük (ancient Doliche), only discovered in the 1990s during an archaeological survey by Anke Schütte-Maischatz and Engelbert Winter, appear to have been visited up to the mid-third century when the town was destroyed by the Persian king Shapur I. Yet, the rock-cut images were apparently not touched by the Persian invaders. Later, they were not only attacked, but the perpetrators even left their signature in form of Christian crosses. Most dramatically, the over 2m high main cult relief in the first mithraeum was systematically destroyed by deep chisel blows, so that no more than a negative impression survived where once Mithras and the bull had been (**colour plate 9**). Yet, these negative impressions of body shapes alone were sufficient to identify the picture. A Christian cross, cut into the rock precisely where once the head of the god had been, forms a powerful visual symbol of victory over paganism and leaves no doubt who carries responsibility for this act of image destruction. Such signatures were, however, exceedingly scarce and normally confined to pagan sanctuaries re-dedicated as churches or chapels. Why was it that Christians hated images so much?

4

IMAGE DESTRUCTION SEEN THROUGH CHRISTIAN EYES

> Then God spoke all these words. He said, 'I am Yahweh your God who brought you out of the land of Egypt, out of the house of slavery. You shall have no gods except me. You shall not make yourself a carved image or any likeness of anything in heaven or on earth beneath or in the waters under the earth; you shall not bow down to them or serve them. For I, Yahweh your God, am a jealous God and I punish the father's fault in the sons, the grandsons, and the great-grandsons of those who hate me . . .'
>
> (*Exodus* 20,1-4)

A glance at any extensive concordance of the Bible under the word 'image' or its plural, 'images,' demonstrates just how numerous examples of religiously motivated image destruction are in the Old Testament. Yet God's commandment allowed an even wider interpretation: nothing at all should ever be depicted, no matter for what purpose. The opposition of early Christians to creating images accounts partially for the fact that there is no material evidence for the existence of Christians prior to the late second century. (Another reason was, of course, that creating Christian imagery, symbols or monuments would have been extremely dangerous for the members of an outlawed religion.) Yet, Christians in the Roman Empire lived in a culture dominated by magnificent works of art, and over the centuries the hostile attitude to the visual culture eroded. From the late Roman period to the present, Christianity has had on the whole a much more liberal attitude to images than Judaism or Islam. They even played an increasingly dominant role in the religion itself, and Jesus, scenes from the Bible and saints were increasingly often depicted in the late Roman period and early Middle Ages, despite occasional backlashes, notably the famous phases of iconoclasm directed against Christian icons in the eighth- and ninth-century Byzantine Empire. We have already seen that this liberal attitude did not in any way

IMAGE DESTRUCTION SEEN THROUGH CHRISTIAN EYES

encompass pagan images even though there were borderline cases, notably divine or symbolic personifications of cities (like Rome itself) or general virtues. Victoria, the goddess of victory, for example, still features prominently on many imperial coins of the late Roman period as a victory symbol long after most of her fellow deities had been condemned to obliteration.

Normally, however, the depiction of pagan deities was unacceptable. This even applied to depicting a pagan image during the process of its destruction. Repeatedly we read in early Christian literature about evil demons thought to inhabit images. Such works of art were used by them to attract worship and sacrifice, which they depended upon to maintain their malignant power. An image of a pagan deity, presumably even in the context of its destruction, was thought to have the potential to attract evil forces, pollution and peril to human souls. The contrast between the recurring theme of the early Christian saint reducing pagan images and monuments to rubble and the scarcity of representations in art showing saints doing so is indeed striking. It was through the passage of time that attitudes softened here and even naturalistic images of pagan deities occasionally found their place in churches in such contexts. It had been many centuries since people in the area had worshipped images of Mars, the sun god and the moon goddess when they were depicted, strikingly similar to ancient originals, around AD 1200 or a few years later on colourful gold-ground mosaics on the walls and a vault of the church of San Marco at Venice. With the distance of time they were no longer considered to be serious competitors for the church; their powers were now beyond resuscitation, though it was still considered to be an edifying lesson for church-goers to depict their destruction. To what extent such visual allusions to Christian martyrs struggling against paganism may have been considered meaningful in the light of the contemporary Crusades is open to debate. The tradition that dark demonic powers were hiding in the guise of innocent-looking images had not yet been forgotten. We see St Simon and St Jude forcing down the chariots of the sun god, Sol, and of the moon goddess, Luna, drawn, as often in antiquity, by horses and oxen respectively, from the high columns on which they had been venerated (**colour plate 10**). Yet, dark green demons with horns, large ugly teeth and an evil expression on their faces, one with wings and one without, appear on top of the columns trying desperately to hold back the descending chariots and to prevent their own dethronement. In a manner we would now consider to be racist the artist chose to depict the demons who are naked, except for their loincloths, in dark colour to form a visible contrast to all the other fair-skinned figures in the scenes. While only depicted around 1200 in art, this scene probably closely reflects the visual idea a late Roman Christian had of demons. The fourth-century text the work of art is based upon (which has little to recommend itself in terms of historicity, but all the more in reflecting contemporary Christian beliefs) describes how St Simon and St Jude instructed the 'most evil' demons to come out of the statues of the

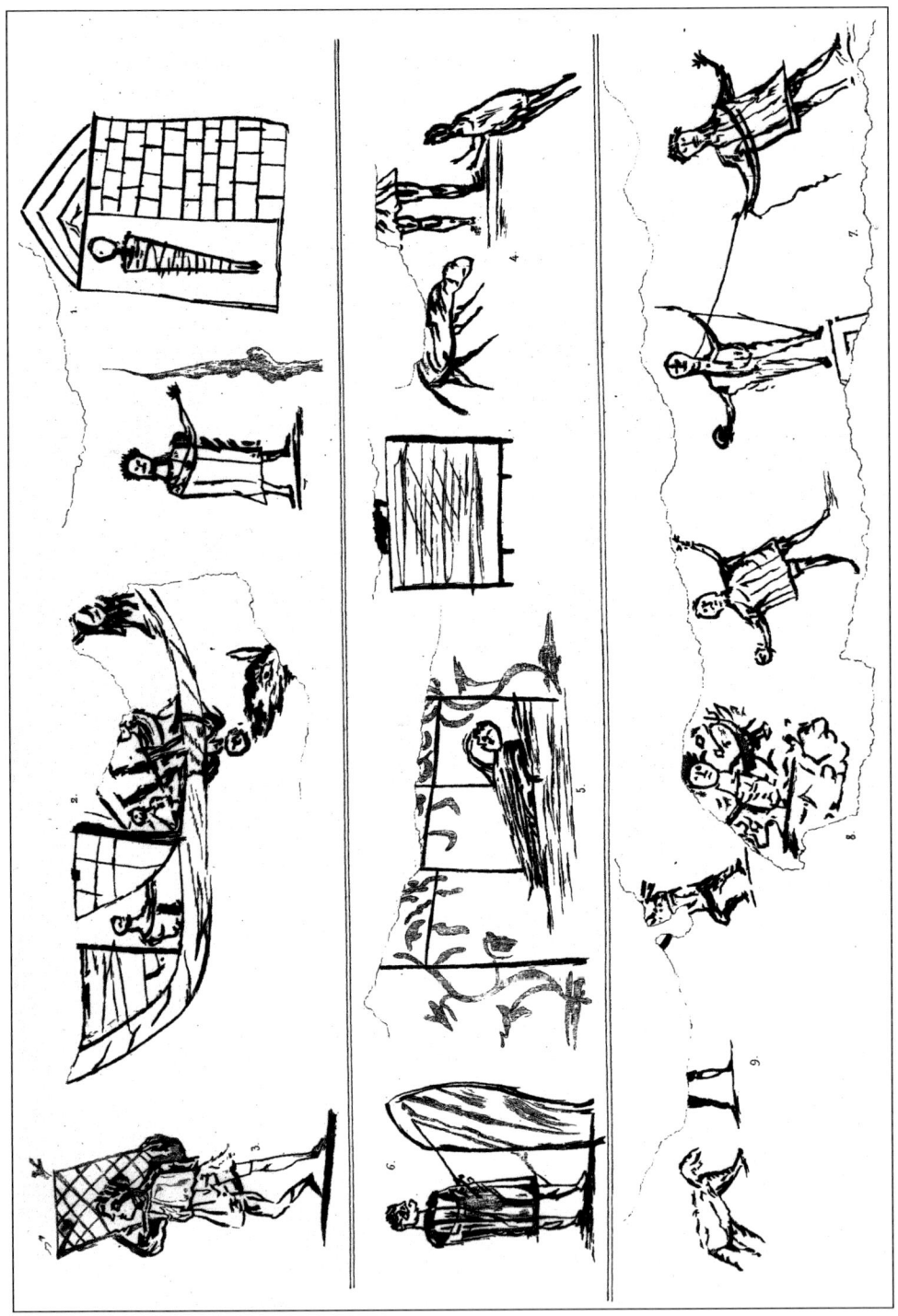

36 *A Christian painting from the catacombs at Rome depicting the destruction of a pagan statue (scene 7)*

sun god and of the moon goddess and to crush them to pieces together with the sun god's chariot. Indeed, according to this legend, the assembled pagan crowd, which was soon to murder the apostles, saw how the demons, namely two 'Ethiopians' departed, 'black, naked, of horrible appearance, yelling and emitting dreadful sounds'. When, on St Philip's instigation, a statue of Mars is pulled down with a rope, equally from a high column, a winged dragon appears (**colour plate 11**). While far removed in time from the main period of image destruction in the Mediterranean and in Western Europe in the late Roman period and the early Middle Ages, these pictures may give us the closest visual idea we can get of what was going on in the minds of pious men who felt the destruction of works of art, possessed by the forces of evil, was their religious right and duty.

Yet, as a representation of image destruction by Christians per se, such high medieval works of art are not entirely the first in their genre. It was in the Roman catacombs where the first and, to my knowledge, only ancient depiction of image destruction through the agency of Christians was discovered. The catacombs were subterranean cemeteries outside the walls of Rome consisting of an extensive network of underground passageways and chambers with large numbers of graves inserted into the walls. They were a response to the increasing scarcity of land in Rome whose population is thought to have numbered roughly one million inhabitants and in a few other big cities in the ancient Mediterranean. While not an exclusive Christian phenomenon, this form of underground cemetery was particularly popular with members of this new religion from the late second century until the early fifth. It was Giovanni Battista de Rossi, the founder father of the sub-discipline of Christian archaeology, who discovered in the Roman catacombs this unique ancient depiction of Christian image destruction. De Rossi embarked on one of his discovery tours of the remains of the catacombs just to the north of the city of Rome in January 1865. Some of the underground passageways and rooms he explored had been visited before. He saw the bones from plundered burials attesting to the activities of grave robbers, and he rediscovered frescos seen 82 years earlier by the art historian Seroux d'Agincourt.

Yet, finally he found something extraordinary, nobody had seen or paid attention to previously, and few only have seen after him: black line drawings decorated three of the white walls of one of the underground chambers. The drawings did not impress him from an artistic point of view (in fact he found them clumsy, infantile and unrefined, more caricatures than works of art), but because of the subject matter of one of the scenes (**36**). The unusual style and, as we shall see, motive may suggest that we are dealing with a lay artist who was not fully familiar with techniques, fashionable styles and normal repertoire. The subject matter of the majority of scenes, it ought to be stressed, is perfectly normal in early Christian art and leaves no doubt that the artist and his client were of Christian faith. Unsurprisingly in a cemetery, interventions by God and Jesus resulting in the physical salvation of those who trust in God are the dominant themes; such allegorical representations reinforced the Christian belief in God's power and will to ensure salvation and resurrection of the faithful: Jesus raising Lazarus from the dead (scene 1), Jonah thrown overboard into the sea and about to be swallowed up by the great fish (and to be rescued later) (scene 2), a man healed by Jesus and now fit enough to carry his bed on his shoulders (scenes 3 & 5?), probably Abraham, spared by God from offering his first-born and then only son, Isaac, as a human sacrifice (scenes 4 & 9) and Moses with God's help creating an abundant spring for the thirsty Israelites in the desert by touching a rock with a rod (scene 6). Another scene (8) refers, according to De Rossi, to the men allegedly thrown in a 'burning fiery furnace' by the Babylonian king Nebuchadnezzar (605-562 BC) for refusing to worship an image made of gold. As is well known, the three men, according to the Bible (*Daniel* 3), survived the ordeal unharmed and thus convinced the king of the power of the God of the Jews. If so, it would be yet another scene referring to divine rescue in an otherwise hopeless situation. Only one person is shown burnt at the stake and raising his hands in prayer whereas in early Christian art, in accordance with the Bible, normally three are depicted. However, since the left part of the scene is not preserved (and the relative position of the different scenes does not appear to be shown to scale on **36**), three could have been depicted originally. If meant to show the men in the burning fiery furnace, one of the most popular themes in early Christian art, and not a martyr, one still wonders whether the image might not also have reminded observers of the Christian martyrs burnt alive during the more recent persecutions.

Most unusual and interesting in our context, however, is the remaining scene (7): it depicts a male pagan deity on a pedestal holding a long sceptre and a roundish object, probably a globe or possibly a *patera* (a sacrificial bowl to pour out wine as an offering) surrounded by two figures, one in the process of pulling him down from his pedestal with a rope, attached to the god's neck, the other hurling a stone at the strangulated deity soon to fall. Is this the image that the men in the fiery furnace refused to worship? De Rossi rightly dismisses this idea since the Bible does not mention any image destruction, attempted or successful, in this context, and it seems somewhat doubtful anyway that the adjacent scene depicts one of the men in the fiery furnace. Was it meant to depict another Biblical event which involved image destruction? The iconography, it ought to be pointed out, is typically Roman: the pedestal is right-angled and appears to bear a rectangular field, presumably for an inscription; the attributes of the male deity, the long sceptre and the globe, are characteristic of Jupiter. This in itself need not rule out that the artist might have had a Biblical scene in his mind, since it is unlikely that he would have been familiar with the iconography of pagan deities in the Near East in the times of the Old Testament (and even though he could have included an oriental symbol, such as the Phrygian cap, a type of headgear worn by many male oriental deities in the Roman period). However, in the absence of parallels and iconographic clues it would have been equally impossible for the ancient Christian observer as it is for us to link the scene with any particular passage in the Bible. There can be no doubt that Christians would in the first instance have thought of contemporary image destruction when seeing this picture. In parallel with other catacomb art our drawing dates probably to the fourth or, at the latest, early fifth century; an earlier date is unlikely since written evidence suggests that Christian image destruction did not normally occur before the fourth century. The juxtaposition of the pious man burning alive, whether one of the men in the fiery furnace or a Christian during the persecutions and the imminent downfall of Jupiter, the most powerful pagan deity, captures in the most dramatic manner how times had changed. There can be little doubt that the artist had seen himself how images were pulled down and destroyed. It must have strongly engaged him emotionally, so that he depicted himself in art that he wanted to be erased from the artistic record. Others saw the contradiction between destroying the images of pagan deities and creating such images themselves, whatever the context and no matter how abstract. The virtual absence of scenes of image destruction in early Christian art has to be explained by fear of and contempt for pagan 'idols' and demons, not by unfamiliarity with the phenomenon.

5
HILLTOP SANCTUARIES

While there can be no serious doubt that Christians had powerful motives for their sustained onslaught on pagan art, the question remains how we can differentiate between Christian and pagan image destruction. We have seen that in the majority of cases we neither have a signature in form of a cross, nor an immediate re-use of the building as a church, nor a selective attack on immodest images. In the following three chapters I shall suggest that the sheer effort involved in destruction may form one decisive criterion.

Hilltop sanctuaries

No sacrifice was too great for the most ardent supporters of the new, Christian religion. While during the time of persecutions significant numbers had been prepared to suffer torture and to sacrifice their lives for their faith, after (and already before) the conversion of the Empire into a Christian state more and more adherents of this religion adopted an ascetic lifestyle and denied themselves all worldly pleasures. Christian asceticism sometimes took extreme forms: not only could it involve fasting, the rejection of all non-vital possessions, frequently, as far as possible, the avoidance of human company, the deliberate exposure of the body to the elements in extreme climatic conditions (whether in hot deserts or cold mountain ranges) and sometimes even self-imprisonment. Some Christian ascetics went even further than that; we know of a Syrian hermit who chose to live in complete darkness, another who lived in a wooden box so small that he had to bend his body permanently and there are numerous other examples of the most extreme forms of self-chastisement. Particularly famous was St Symeon who spent over 40 years of his life on the top of columns (**37**), each new one higher than the one before, at what was to become the important pilgrimage site of Qal'at Sim'Çn in northern Syria. By freeing themselves from dependence on anything pleasurable in the world, Christian ascetics could focus their minds entirely on God. While the most extreme cases of such asceticism cluster in the Levant and adjacent territories, imitators can also be found in the West. It comes as no surprise that religious

37 *Christian asceticism could take extreme forms: St Symeon is reported to have lived over forty years on top of columns. The site became a major pilgrimage centre. This fifth- or sixth-century Syrian relief is further proof of the saint's fame*

conviction strong enough for many to subject themselves to the most excruciating forms of self-chastisement for decades of their lives only to be ended by death equally knew no limits in the time and effort devoted to eradicating anything which stood in the way of complete Christian victory.

When the historian Gregory, Bishop of Tours (*History of the Franks* 8,15), travelled through the low mountain range of the Ardennes in AD 585, he met the deacon Vulfilaicus, a prime example of a Christian who, according to his own testimony and report to the bishop, thought no suffering or effort too great in his pursuit of getting closer to Christ and eliminating paganism. Apparently inspired by St Symeon, Vulfilaicus built himself a column on which he stood for long periods barefoot even in winter, icicles forming in his beard. The sermons of the determined servant of Christ did not fail to impress the local population, and he gained converts from idol worship to Christianity. The dominant hill on which his column stood at La Ferté sur-Chiers was the site of an old pagan sanctuary and had presumably been chosen for this particular reason. Stone images, which must have been 300-400 years old at the time had, up to then, still attracted devoted pilgrims. The saint broke all the more easily destructible ones personally to pieces. Only one proved beyond his physical strength: a statue of the goddess Diana of gigantic size. It required the joint efforts of a large number of converts, repeated attempts and a tearful prayer to the Lord until they finally succeeded to pull it down with ropes. Afterwards it was smashed with iron hammers until no more than powdered stone remained.

Even allowing for rhetorical exaggeration, this passage (which is not without parallels) serves to demonstrate the extraordinary efforts devout Christians were prepared to undertake in their endeavour to eradicate the visible remnants of paganism. Even more remarkable than the community effort to pull down the image is the laborious transformation of its remnants into powdered stone. Why was this necessary? Once tumbled to the ground and broken apart, the goddess will no longer have been awe-inspiring and, by means of contemporary technology, she could not have been restored to her former splendour. There will have been a strong element of religious zeal to ensure that no part of the image could ever be re-used for any non-Christian act of worship. It might also have been seen as part of a heroic struggle; the evil powers embodied by pagan imagery are often reported to try to fight back though they are always defeated by the might of God and his saints. Indeed, allegedly all of Vulfilaicus's body was soon covered in ugly pustules after Diana's image had been destroyed, ascribed to the intervention of the devil himself, though cured later, we are told, with oil from the church of St Martin.

Yet, despite such recurring topoi, it is still worth stressing that I am not aware of any clear literary or archaeological evidence for similarly arduous and systematic destructions out of non-religious motives (e.g. hate or delight in destruction during a hostile incursion). A study of the comparative scale of effort involved in different modes of destruction or removal of images of different sizes may thus be worthwhile. It is certainly fair to argue that the more time-consuming a particular act of destruction was, the more likely it was the work of a person of strong motivation and conviction.

Giant images, as described by Gregory of Tours, were comparatively scarce and most life-sized or smaller representations of pagan deities in stone or any other material could indeed have been destroyed by any reasonably fit person equipped with a suitable iron tool within seconds or, at most, minutes. Even when sophisticated tools were not available, a stone statue could hardly have sustained an attack with a more primitive instrument, such as a thick plank of timber or a large stone. There is no way of knowing whether some damage to a single statue was the work of an invader or an ardent Christian believer. Often we cannot even be sure whether we are dealing with deliberate action or an accident. A single monument can suffer damage when it falls over or is hit by elements of a collapsing building's roof. The resulting breakage can easily resemble that caused by deliberate destruction with a blunt tool. Only if a series of images with similar damage (e.g. with head or face splintered away) are found at the same spot or if sharp metal tools have left distinctive marks (e.g. **32** & **68**) can we be sure that this is the result of deliberate action rather than an accident. The most laborious forms of iconoclasm, however, cannot possibly be confused with an accident, provided the preserved remains of the mutilated image come from a well recorded excavation, so that we can be sure that the absence of any part of the image is real (and any single tool mark is ancient rather than the result of an accidental strike with the excavator's mattock or pickaxe). Indeed, while falling debris or the collapse of the image itself can easily result in a head becoming detached from a statue, the dislocation of the severed head as a result of such natural processes would follow the law of gravity; neither could they account for the complete removal of a head or its deposition in a well outside the building in which the statue stood, nor could they ever lead to the complete pulverisation of the head.

Is there archaeological evidence for religious sites on the summits of hills that perished in similar attacks? While Gregory of Tours does not specifically refer to a temple, it is likely that the assortment of pagan images that fell prey to the religious zeal of Vulfilaicus at La Ferté sur-Chiers had been on display in an old Roman hilltop sanctuary, one of many in eastern Gaul. It might have looked similar to the reconstructed temple complex at Tawern on the slope of a hill some 13km south-west of Trier (**colour plate 13**). Not only the nature of the sacred sites, but also the end they met may have been similar. While the imposing image of a giant Diana had presided over Vulfilaicus's site, a slightly over life-size statue of the god Mercury guarded the latter. Like its counterpart, Mercury was not pardoned from the death sentence on pagan culture. His head was struck off and, instead of pulverising it, it seemed safe enough to put it beyond the reach of humans by depositing it in the over 14m-deep temple well. This fate he shared with two altars, the fragments of a large inscription and two reliefs all thrown into the same well. One of the reliefs from the well depicts the Egyptian deities Isis and Serapis, and the sacred enclosure has even yielded a broken statuette of the goddess Artemis from Ephesus, the very same deity whose followers had opposed the missionary activities of St Paul in their city in the first century. It was indeed a colourful and diverse pantheon that perished in the fanatical onslaught by image-haters in this single provincial temple precinct.

Some hint for the date of the attack is furnished by a coin minted in the closing years of the fourth century or the very beginning of the next. It was found very near the bottom of the well and underneath the desecrated cult images. Several contemporary issues from the sacred site indicate that pilgrims continued to make their way up the hill to pay their respect to the divine powers who resided at this lonely spot at the very least until the late fourth century. How long thereafter the religious visits continued is impossible to establish. Base metal coinage virtually ceased to be used north of the Alps after the late fourth century and so do most other closely datable categories of artefact. Our ability to trace human activities in the fifth, sixth and seventh centuries is therefore severely limited. The contrast between the abundance of evidence for events of the fourth century all over north-west Europe and the extreme scarcity of traces of activity (except burials) for subsequent centuries is striking. It can be observed at secular habitations as well as on religious sites. There is no way the population could have shrunk to such a minute fraction of what it had been before to account for the virtual absence of artefacts. People simply reverted to using

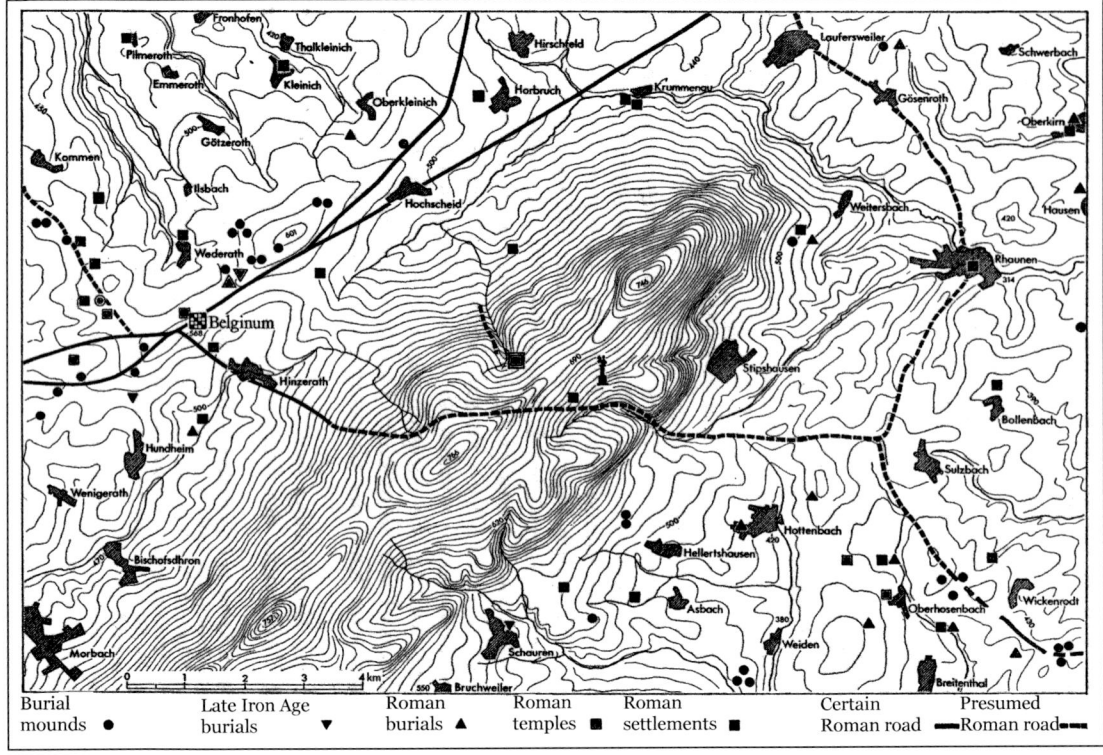

38 *Devastated despite its remoteness: the temple complex at Hochscheid (concentric square symbol at the centre of the map) was located, several kilometres from the next settlement, in mountainous terrain*

almost exclusively organic materials for most items of everyday use; and these have perished at most sites leaving barely a trace. Human occupation during these centuries is difficult to prove, visits of peasant pilgrims to a site almost impossible. Textual sources, like the above-quoted episode on Vulfilaicus, leave no doubt that visits to pagan sanctuaries came by no means to a grinding and lasting halt once they had been declared illegal in the fourth century. Whether the deities at Tawern met their fate at the end of the fourth century or only in the fifth, sixth or seventh century or still later, is impossible to establish. Neither is any evidence known (though the site is not yet fully published) which would allow us to tell whether the natural sanctuary in its solitude continued to attract devotees right down until its brutal end or whether the visits had ceased beforehand. Date and manner of the hilltop sanctuary's end at Tawern suggest strongly, in my view, Christian responsibility. Yet, it might be objected that a functioning temple might have seemed a worthwhile target for invading plunderers as well as for religious zealots. It would be more difficult to find a motive for invaders to search for and devastate abandoned ruins in a remote location and mountainous terrain. The following archaeological example thus will allow more definite conclusions.

HILLTOP SANCTUARIES

Not only vibrant and functioning sites drew iconoclasts upon themselves, yet, as in the case of the Taliban in the recent past, it was even felt necessary to annihilate the visible remnants of pagan religion at sites, which had long ceased to be places of worship. The spring sanctuary of Hochscheid was in mountainous and presumably densely forested terrain, at 645m above the sea-level, over 5km from the next village (named Belginum) (**38**). When this settlement went into serious decline, presumably as a direct or indirect result of the devastating Germanic incursions in the second half of the AD 270s, the spring sanctuary appears to have been abandoned as well. At some stage, however, the statue of the naked spring god Apollo (**39**) was violently destroyed; indeed, his head and torso have never been found, and all that remained are parts of his limbs and his lyre as well as the beheaded griffon adjoining him. Much more survived of his modestly dressed female partner Sirona (**40**); only the lower legs were missing while the remainder was found broken into three pieces. Surprisingly, a second statue of Apollo, equally naked, was found remarkably well preserved (**41**). The damage it suffered could easily have been caused by falling debris, but it bears no marks of deliberate destruction. The torso was

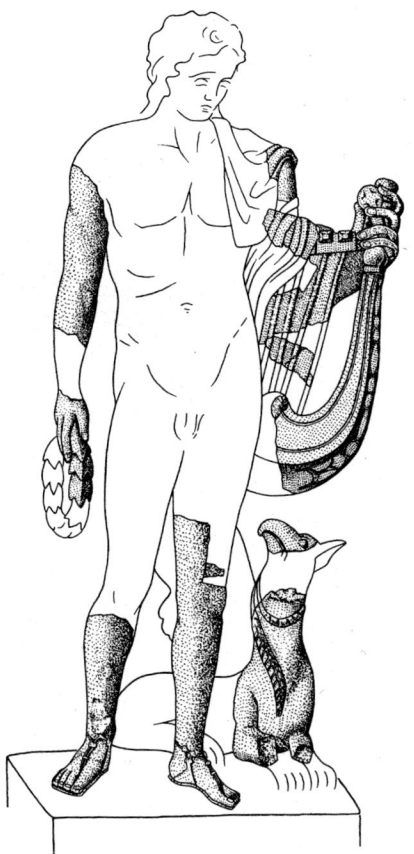

39 *Only fragments survived of the big statue of the naked god Apollo at Hochscheid*

40 *Apollo's divine partner Sirona*

41 *The small Apollo from Hochscheid*

lying next to the wall of the *cella*, and the other fragments of this sculpture were found in the temple *cella* as well, but no information is available allowing to assess whether their distribution may be the result of the image being hit by elements of the roof and eventually tumbling over or whether they were deliberately scattered. Whether the iconoclasts contented themselves with pushing over the small Apollo and Sirona (even her head was found undamaged hurled into the catchment installation for the spring in the centre of the *cella*) or whether some of the monuments were already engulfed by a boggy layer which formed itself in the area of the *cella* around the spring thus escaping destruction is impossible to establish on the basis of the published information. The position of the torso of the small Apollo is best recorded; there is no doubt that mortar had crumbled out of the wall, some elements of the roof had fallen down and earth washed into the temple, before he came to lie at his final resting place. Professor Gerd Weisgerber (1975) who published the excavations is thus certainly right in postulating that there must have been a considerable gap between abandonment of the temple and the destruction, which he attributes to the Christians. This must be true no matter whether the small Apollo and Sirona had already been hit and partially covered by building debris at the time, only the big Apollo being subject to systematic destruction or whether the two other figures had equally been pushed over on this occasion.

It was undoubtedly an effort to pulverise or remove parts of the big Apollo image at Hochscheid, and one wonders whether this type of action would really have been considered worthwhile for a pagan invader out of hate or in pursuit of mindless delight in destruction. There may be a degree of risk in imposing our own rationale on Germanic invaders or in assuming that they would necessarily have acted in a manner comparable to modern 'vandals' who take delight in hearing and seeing the glass splinter when smashing street lamps, yet would not normally painstakingly disassemble the metal and plastic parts, even if there was no risk of detection. Yet, the question must be allowed what would have motivated a pagan invader, even if hate or destructive mania drove him to smash images, to go beyond what modern 'vandals' would do. Surely, in case of most life-sized and under-life-sized statues, no more than a few blows (and presumably often no more than a single blow) with a weighty and hard instrument was needed to fragment the image. Once the parts were lying on the ground and the image beyond repair, what additional satisfaction could be gained from selecting significant parts of the sculpture, such as the head, and to obliterate any human or divine features in a much more arduous and time-consuming manner (and without anything like the original 'bang')? There is no evidence for a superstitious Germanic belief which demanded complete destruction of the head to neutralise the divine power. Even if there had been any such belief, we would have difficulties to explain why (as we have seen) the Germanic invaders spared so many images. An explanation of the destructions at Hochscheid with a similar sort of Christian zeal as attested for Vulfilaicus is much neater.

There are thus three indications which indeed point towards Christian responsibility in the case of the Hochscheid temple: 1. the considerable gap in time between the abandonment of the temple (not before the late third century) and the final deposition of the remaining fragments of sculpture, 2. the remote location of the site which renders it unlikely that any later invaders passing through the area would have found their way to it by accident or would have had a motive to search for abandoned ruins in the forest, and 3. the efforts involved in the complete removal or pulverisation of head and torso of the large Apollo statue (whether his nakedness had provoked particular rage or whether he was the only statue left standing at the time of the attack).

6
LARGE MITHRAIC CULT IMAGES

While the thorough fragmentation of the life-sized large Apollo at Hochscheid and the assault on the slightly over life-sized Mercury at Tawern had involved some arduous efforts, greater challenges posed themselves to image-haters in the northern provinces of the Empire. Some of the main cult images on display in temples of the god Mithras were amongst the biggest and heaviest works of art ever produced in those territories. The sheer size of the largest specimens of this type of monument rendered their destruction one of the most physically demanding tasks awaiting the determined iconoclast in the northern frontier provinces of the Roman Empire. The cult relief at Sarrebourg (**42**) with the crowning bust of the sun god was 3.27m high (and without it 2.6m), 2.2m wide and 0.58-0.68m thick and consisted of huge stone blocks of up to 1.75m by 0.85m by 0.58m size fixed to each other and to the back-wall with iron clamps; that at Strasbourg-Koenigshoffen together with its base was once even about 4-4.15m high, 2.46m wide and up to 0.36m thick. It was not only a major effort to destroy such images, but might even have been a dangerous or impossible task for an iconoclast acting on his own. An individual trying to break such heavy and tall stone monuments while still upright would have been at serious risk from falling debris. Since the main panel at Koenigshoffen appears to have been as thin as 0.05m between the protruding images in high relief of presumably up to *c*.0.3-0.36m in thickness, it seems doubtful that it would have been easy to hack off the protruding parts without taking the risk of the whole monument splintering and collapsing onto the iconoclast. It thus seems likely that these images were pulled down first in a manner similar to the one described by Vulfilaicus, presumably with the joint efforts of a group. Afterwards further fragmentation would have been safe, even if time-consuming; and fragmented they were indeed with remarkable thoroughness: over 360 pieces of the Koenigshoffen main relief could be identified and over 300 of its equivalent at Sarrebourg.

Yet, even these astonishing figures under-represent the true scale of destruction, for those parts crushed to unrecognisable chips or powder must vastly

42 *Smashed into over 300 recognisable pieces: the Sarrebourg relief*

LARGE MITHRAIC CULT IMAGES

43 *Mostly pulverised or removed: the 360 recovered fragments constitute only a smaller part of the Strasbourg-Koenigshoffen relief*

outnumber the identified pieces; they probably even exceed them in volume in case of the Koenigshoffen relief as a glance at the monument (**43**) suggests. It is worth pointing out that not all of the sanctuary has been excavated, and that it is thus possible that parts of the image are still to be discovered within the mithraeum (or outside it). However, all of the relevant section of the central nave, which has yielded all of the large fragments, has been excavated; it seems thus highly probable that also the majority or all of the surviving fragments have been recovered. It will come as no surprise that no trace of the head of Mithras was found at Koenigshoffen. Despite the uncertainty resulting from the incomplete excavation of the temple, it seems highly probable that it was singled out for special treatment in antiquity rather than being in the smaller area which has not been excavated and at some distance from all the other fragments. Interestingly, one of the torchbearers standing beside the bull-slaying Mithras escaped destruction; he might have been overlooked amongst the large array of stone blocks scattered over the temple nave floor.

The Sarrebourg relief fared slightly better, but here, in contrast to Koenigshoffen (where we cannot be absolutely certain whether the absence of the head indicates its complete destruction, removal or, possibly, deposition in an unexcavated part of the temple), there can be no doubt that Mithras's head was condemned to obliteration. A few fragments only retained enough detail to reveal themselves to the eye of the archaeologist: parts of the upper eye-lids, eye-brows, nose and hair curls as well of the oriental cap the god once wore. This proved that the relief was hacked to pieces on site rather than being partially re-used elsewhere. Vulfilaicus's method of using iron tools to reduce stone images to powder has, undoubtedly, been applied widely, by others as well as himself.

Not only the degree of fragmentation, but also the manner in which it was achieved reveal the action of determined and insistent characters rather than the result of a quick eruption of destructive impulse. Both the Sarrebourg and Koenigshoffen relief stood at the back wall within their respective sanctuaries. There was no easy way to turn them by 180 degrees and thus if pulled down they would have fallen on their face. The Koenigshoffen mithraeum had a clay floor, possibly covered by wooden planks; the nave of the Sarrebourg mithraeum by contrast appears to have been paved in sandstone slabs. By the time of destruction of the Koenigshoffen relief some debris had already built up on the floor and the stone relief thus will have had a comparatively soft landing. The impact, even on a fairly soft surface, will undoubtedly have resulted in some fracturing, but most of the images should have survived. Robert Forrer, the excavator of the Mithras temple at Koenigshoffen, produced a detailed distribution map of the larger fragments of the cult relief within the sanctuary. Neither the degree of fragmentation nor the wide distribution (**44**) can be explained by simple collapse; some of the fragments were found at a distance of 10m or more from the original base (no. 9 on **44**), including parts of the frame (no. 48 on **44**) whose oblong shape suggests that it was carried rather than naturally hurled to this position. The distribution pattern and level of fragmentation is easiest explained by the assumption that the big relief once lying face down on the temple floor was further fragmented into parts light enough to be turned around; the comparatively wide spatial distribution of parts may well be the result of deliberate spreading of the fragments to facilitate further fragmentation of the central parts of the image; the smaller fragments could, of course, also have been flung away during the process of destruction. A wide dispersal

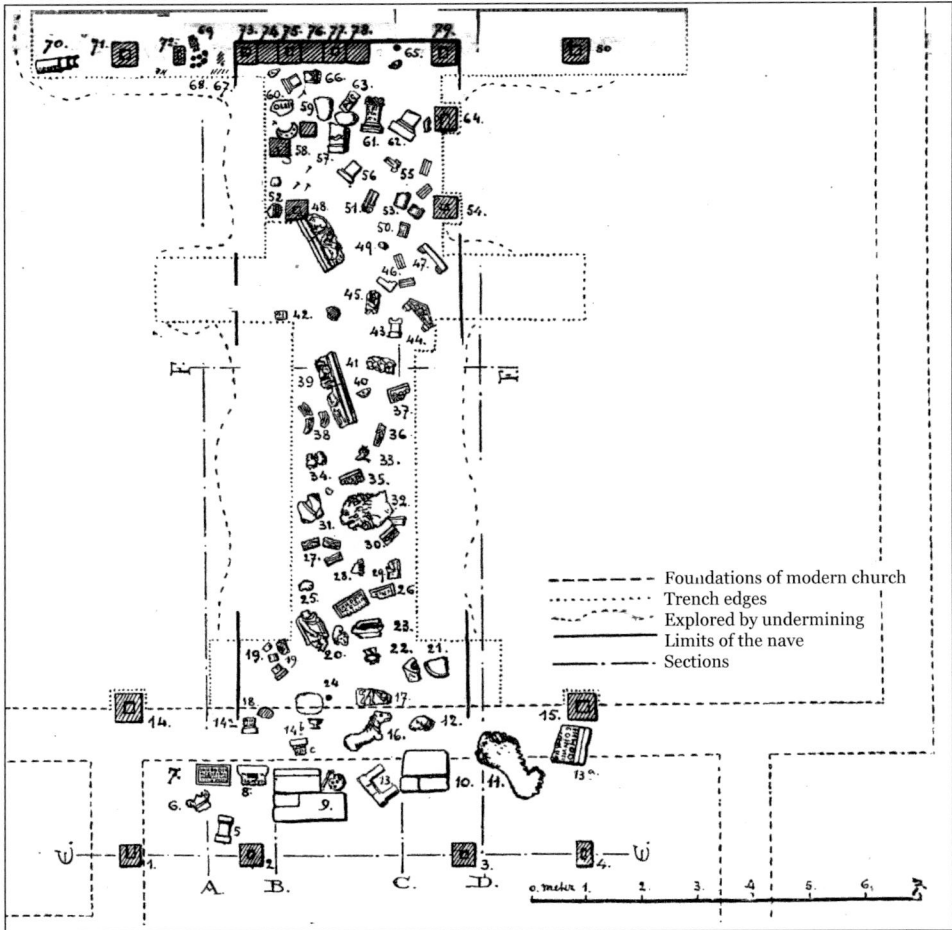

44 *Most (though not all) of the remains of the mutilated images were found in the western half of the temple at Strasbourg-Koenigshoffen. This section of the excavator's plan gives an idea to what extent the larger fragments were found scattered over the temple floor*

of the fragments has equally been observed at Sarrebourg even though we are less well informed about their precise spatial distribution. Yet some fragments were used here for an unusual purpose, namely to build a stone cist for the body of a man with his hands chained behind his back. We will come back to this macabre burial in a later chapter.

The iconoclasts also found in both Koenigshoffen and Sarrebourg a series of other images and altars. At Sarrebourg altars were smashed and some images presumably beheaded as is suggested by the fact that a small number of isolated heads and fragments of headless torsos in stone were found. At Koenigshoffen all five altars dedicated to Mithras and still identifiable as such were thoroughly destroyed. While the altar dedicated to the eastern god Attis was quite well preserved, it had been broken into two fragments, which were

found 1m apart. The altar to the native god Cissonius bears little damage and does not appear to have been deliberately targeted. This suggests that those responsible for the destruction at Koenigshoffen felt particular hatred against Mithras. They must have been literate, and the destruction presumably took place in the fourth or fifth century while the cult was still practised elsewhere or its memory still alive. Both the sculpture of the rock-born Mithras (**45**) and the depiction of a torchbearer in an *aedicula*, a small model of a temple (**46**), had their head or face chopped off while the moon goddess whose bust decorated the tympanum (the triangular part of the façade underneath the roof) of the same temple model was spared. The targeted anti-Mithraic procedure at Koenigshoffen and the sparing of other deities reminds one of the targeted destruction of Mithraic art in the military zone behind Hadrian's Wall in the earlier fourth century. There, similarly, Mithraic cult images were smashed in the first half of the fourth century while no action against other deities was taken at the time. As at Hadrian's Wall care was equally taken not to obliterate inscriptions naming military units. The explanation for this specific anti-Mithraic hatred has to be sought in similarities between

45 (Opposite) *The headless Mithras from Koenigshoffen born out of a rock*

46 (Right) *Temple model from Koenigshoffen with mutilated Mithraic torchbearer and unharmed moon goddess*

Christianity and Mithraism, to which we will come back later, such as ceremonies similar to Holy Communion, baptism, the promise of an afterlife etc. It ought to be stressed, however, that while there are some instances in which Mithraic cult objects were specifically targeted, in the majority of cases of late Roman or early medieval iconoclasm monuments dedicated to a variety of pagan cults were subjected to indiscriminate destruction. This is by no means surprising; the written evidence leaves little doubt that a multitude of individuals and groups were responsible, and that their action spanned centuries. It is unsurprising that not all of them acted in a uniform manner. Whatever the precise reason for sparing the non-Mithraic images at Koenigshoffen, be it a specifically anti-Mithraic attitude or sensitivity towards the adherents of other cults while these were still locally strong, such a selective procedure would be hard to reconcile with the assumption of an attack by invaders from across the borders of the Empire. These, one would have thought, would not have been intimate with the subtle differences between different deities or would have had any particular animosities or reasons for selective constraint.

One of the most crucial factors in assessing whether we are dealing with Christian or pagan image destruction is, of course, the date of the events. In the case of Sarrebourg a series of coins proves that the sanctuary was in use until at least AD 394. For reasons to be given in chapter 13, it seems likely that the destruction occurred some time between AD 394 and the fifth century. The chronology of Koenigshoffen is less well known. Only 13 coins were recovered as opposed to the 274 at Sarrebourg, and nine amongst these 13 coins belong to an early silver hoard. The latest of the remaining four specimens was a plated silver coin modelled on an original minted under Septimius Severus (AD 193-211). On two inscriptions the honorific epithet of the eighth legion, which had been named after emperor Alexander Severus, had been chiselled out. This proves that the mithraeum in any case continued to exist beyond the death of this emperor in AD 235. Comparatively few coins entered circulation in Germany between the early third century and the AD 260s, and the coin spectrum would be perfectly typical both in size and chronology for a temple abandoned some time between AD 235 and the AD 260s. Most temples in Gaul and Germany west of the Rhine, which were still used in the fourth century, by contrast, have yielded a fairly large number of coins. Even if the temple should have been plundered, it seems hard to believe that this was done in such a systematic manner that not a single specimen was overlooked. One is thus tempted to assume that the temple at Koenigshoffen was abandoned as such within the third century. This does not come as a great surprise as the adjacent village of Koenigshoffen, a suburb which depended on the nearby legionary fortress of Strasbourg, seems to have been largely abandoned as well by the later third century.

There is, however, no need to assume that abandonment and image destruction occurred necessarily at the same time. In fact, while the stratigraphy of the lower levels in the fill of the nave is not described in as much detail as one would wish, the indications given in the excavation report by Robert Forrer provide a strong indication that the destruction post-dated the abandonment by a considerable span of time. Astonishingly, the fate of the western half of the building (which contained the remains of the main cult relief) was, according to Forrer, substantially different from the eastern half. In the western half the fragments appear to have been partially embedded in a charcoal-rich layer with fragments of burnt clay, which was immediately on top of the floor. They were covered by parts of the collapsed roof. In the east of the temple the floor had been artificially raised and even the well within the building had been filled in. Forrer attributes these structural changes to the third and last building phase of the temple. This phase also saw the re-use of some smashed altars as post bases which poses the question as to whether we are dealing with an earlier partial destruction or, more probably, whether the third phase post-dates the abandonment of the mithraeum as a temple. The fragments of smashed sculpture, which included the beheaded sculpture of the rock-birth of Mithras, were deposited on top of this level. In both west and east the eventual collapse of the roof post-dates the destruction of the monuments.

The eastern half of the building had been re-used prior to the collapse of the roof as early medieval Merovingian artefacts clearly prove. A spindle whorl and loom weight attest that it was no longer a temple, but was re-used for domestic purposes, including the production of textiles. Pottery with a stamp design characteristic for the early medieval Merovingian period, especially of the sixth and seventh century, provides the date for this period of re-use. The distinct burnt layer in the west made Forrer think that the western half of the building had been burnt down on the occasion of the image destruction which he places around AD 395, more on historical considerations than on observations from the excavations. The roof in the eastern half by contrast had remained intact until the early medieval period. Yet is this likely? It certainly would not have been possible to deliberately burn down half of a 31m-long building short of demolishing the central part first as a firebreak. It seems unlikely that such a partial destruction could have occurred accidentally while the temple was still structurally intact: should we really think that a fire catastrophe fierce enough to destroy the western half was suddenly extinguished by a downpour before it had caused any significant structural damage to the eastern half? Nor is it probable that we are dealing with two separate instances of iconoclasm, the first being confined to one half of the building while avoiding inflicting any damage upon the images in the other half. It seems much more likely that we are dealing with a single instance of iconoclasm immediately before or during the re-occupation of the building in the late Roman to early medieval period. Possible models include that the whole of the building had burnt down, yet only in the east had the debris been removed and the building re-roofed. Alternatively, if the conflagration post-dated the abandonment by a considerable period of time, then it is indeed conceivable that part of the roof had collapsed which would have rendered a partial destruction by fire possible. After the destruction the ground was raised in the west by artificially depositing 0.75m of sterile soil on top of the debris. This artificial make-up was covered by several layers containing late Roman and Merovingian pottery, suggesting that the destruction occurred no later than at the beginning rather than towards the end of the period of re-occupation.

There is yet another indication that the iconoclasm also in the west of the building occurred long after its abandonment as a temple. Every field archaeologist knows that an underground feature with vertical sides, such as the central nave of a mithraeum, will, if allowed to decay and silt up naturally, almost always be slowly transformed from a feature with an inverted Π-shaped profile into one with a U-shaped profile by sedimentation and side-erosion. Strikingly, 27 of 29 plotted fragments within the nave lie within the central 2m of the 4m wide nave; all 29 are at least 0.75m away from the side walls of the benches. This was the case despite the fact that the whole width of the nave had been excavated either completely or by undermining the profiles in the relevant layers. The inescapable conclusion is that by the time the main cult relief was destroyed the central nave had already partially silted up to form a gentle U-shaped profile, no matter whether the iconoclasts specifically chose the flat bottom in the centre of the nave for further destruction of the fragments or whether natural gravity resulted in the fragments hurling or sliding towards the centre subsequently. Had destruction immediately followed abandonment while the nave still had a level floor, then we could not easily explain why all the fragments cluster in the centre. Certainly, by the time the roof had collapsed after the destruction of the Mithraic monuments the nave's floor had a U-shaped profile as one of Forrer's section drawings clearly demonstrates, and the absence of any smashed sculpture from the side strips within the nave proves that this had already been the case beforehand. Even if the temple was abandoned as such in its original function in the third century, all the evidence suggests that its cult inventory was hacked into pieces at a much later date.

Sarrebourg probably functioned as a temple up to the time of its destruction; Koenigshoffen did not. The question arises what would have motivated invaders to a thorough destruction of images in a visibly abandoned building. Ardent Christians, by contrast, would have found pagan images, especially if depicting an animal sacrifice, as in the case of the bull-slaying scene, very offensive even if the temple was no longer a place of worship. This observation as well as the likely date of the acts of destruction after the Christianisation of the Empire shifts the balance of probability distinctly from pagan invaders towards the Christians.

The thorough and laborious manner in which both the Sarrebourg and Koenigshoffen reliefs were destroyed, totally removing or pulverising the head of the central deity provides further circumstantial evidence to support such a conclusion. It is worth stressing that strong fragmentation of pagan monuments features repeatedly in Christian reports on image destruction. The methods of Vulfilaicus were not exceptional; for example, Sulpicius Severus (14,6), St Martin's biographer, informs us that the saint pulverised not only the images in a rural temple in fourth-century Gaul, but even the altars. Of course we cannot be sure whether thorough and laborious modes of destruction were the sole monopoly of religious zealots, but it would probably be fair to conclude that the likelihood of Christian responsibility increases with the amount of effort invested in a particular act. Singling out the head for special treatment, as had been done at both temples, is equally not without literary parallel. According to the church history written by the Syrian Theodoret (5,22) in the fifth century, the monumental wooden statue of the god Serapis in his temple in Alexandria, Egypt suffered such a fate in AD 391 at the hands of Christians. It was cut into small pieces, which were thrown in the fire, yet the god's big head was dragged right through the whole city. It was paraded like a trophy of a slaughtered enemy (which in a way he was) in front of those who had worshipped him before. If, in addition to the arduous and thorough manner of the destruction, we take into account the selective procedure at Koenigshoffen (suggestive of knowledge and local sensitivities only provincials are likely to have been intimate with) and the fact that hundreds of coins were left behind at Sarrebourg (the significance of which will be discussed below), Christian responsibility in both cases is, in my view, a near certainty.

7

DESTRUCTION AT DENDARA: A COLOSSAL TASK

If the fragmentation of over life-sized images and cult reliefs north of the Alps involved sustained efforts by iconoclasts, it was nothing in comparison with what awaited determined zealots in Egypt. Had the cult relief of Strasbourg-Koenigshoffen as one of the largest images north of the Alps been about 4m high with its base, the entrance hall (*pronaos*) to the main temple at Dendara was 17.2m high, the temple covered over 3,200m² and the walls, columns and ceilings of its numerous halls, chambers, passageways and crypts were densely decorated with thousands and thousands of elaborately carved images, as was the exterior (**47**). It may give some idea of the scale that the edition of its sacred hieroglyphic texts (without translation) including photographs of some of these texts and some of the images fill so far eleven large-folio volumes with over 2,700 pages and a total of 1,356 plates. It ought to be stressed that the plates are highly selective and depict significantly less than half of the images at a vastly reduced scale. Two more volumes are in preparation, and these thirteen volumes cover merely the main temple and not the smaller sanctuaries located in the same sacred precinct. The main temple was dedicated to Hathor, the Egyptian goddess of love and fertility. Dendara, some 75km north of Luxor on the left bank of the Nile, was her main cult centre. Construction works at the temple had started in 54 BC under Ptolemy XII, Cleopatra's father, yet the shell of the entrance hall was only completed under Tiberius in the AD 30s, and some of its images and hieroglyphic inscriptions date to the time of Emperor Nero (AD 54-68), the latest to AD 64. It had taken 117 years to complete this marvel of Egyptian temple architecture.

Yet, those who came centuries later to destroy had no sentiments to waste on the efforts of generations invested in carving the reliefs, on their artistic or historical value or on their sheer beauty (**colour plate 14**). It was only the massive size of the monument which saved the artwork from complete obliteration. The numerous pictorial representations of deities were attacked in an astonishingly uniform manner suggesting that we are dealing with iconoclasm in a specific period of history and certainly not with separate episodes of iconoclasm spread over centuries. It ought to be stressed that my description of the

*47 Columns in the vast entrance hall to the main temple with mutilated reliefs. The defaced heads with cow-ears are those of Hathor, the divine mistress of the temple. (See **colour plate 14**: artist's impression of possible techniques used in the destruction of the images)*

damage is based on the scrutiny of many hundreds of good photographs, yet not on a study of the original reliefs; indeed the height of the walls would make such a study very difficult short of using scaffolding. The targeted divinities and divine rulers are strewn with a multitude of small hack marks, normally several hundreds per figure (**48** & **49**). The marks are small in diameter, only about one centimetre across in the majority of cases. Most are roundish, but there are also some oblong marks; at least some of the oblong marks were inflicted by blows at an oblique angle from above, presumably with the same sort of pointed blade as the round ones (**50**). The occurrence of a series of parallel marks next to each other indicates that blows often followed in quick succession and suggests eager and vigorous action rather than unenthusiastic and slow fulfilment of an unpleasant duty. This is all the more remarkable as mutilating image after image in the same manner (**colour plates 15** & **16**) with, at a rough estimate, 300-500 blows each would rather seem a monotonous and dull task. There was nothing like the dramatic cracking apart which would have rewarded the iconoclast who smashed a smaller free-standing statue or relief with some primitive sense of achievement. In Dendara, by contrast, each blow merely resulted in a small punctual mutilation. It was the cumulative effect of enduring efforts which increasingly defaced the images. Multiple scratch marks occur as well, but are rather rare; they could have been inflicted with the same sort of small pointed tool. We can almost see in our minds the iconoclast whose arms are beginning to ache from persistent hammering; not yet prepared to give up, he is trying a different technique of image destruction to shift the strain to a different group of arm and shoulder muscles.

Only the images low on the wall could be destroyed by persons standing on the ground. Sometimes just the lower bodies of figures in the second row above the ground are mutilated, and the damage stops just slightly over 2m above the ground (**51**); this was presumably the height a person standing on the ground could reach when swinging a tool above the head. Frequently, however, even the images at the upper sections of the walls and columns were subjected to the same treatment. The type of damage is identical to that suffered by the images in the lowest panels. The deities and rulers are again brutally mutilated by a volley of blows with a smallish pick. Interestingly, however, we sometimes observe a figure who escaped entirely unscathed despite standing between other figures whose bodies are strewn with the usual pick marks without any obvious reasons why it attracted less rage than its bystanders (**52** & **53**). We may thus conclude that those responsible used ladders rather than scaffolding to carry out their not entirely systematic work. The uppermost reliefs on the walls often escaped destruction.

The question arises as to how we ought to explain the contrast between the massive scale of the decorated walls of the Dendara temple and the use of tools, which left marks barely more than a centimetre across. One wonders whether the employment of larger and cruder tools would not have resulted

48 *The king (left) and queen (far left) in front of the deities Harsomatus (right) and Isis (far right). The iconoclasts at Dendara did not or could not differentiate between different deities and god-like rulers*

49 *The king (left) offering aromatic oil and other gifts to Hathor sitting on a throne in front of her son, the divine Ihy. The image-haters spared only hieroglyphs and objects*

in a quicker and more thorough work of destruction. The temple was certainly of sound architecture, and there would hardly have been a risk of collapse even if such tools would have left deeper holes in the walls. As far as the upper panels are concerned, however, this would hardly have been possible for those standing on high ladders. Nobody could have swung a pickaxe or similar tool with both hands standing several meters above the ground without sooner or later losing his balance, thus risking life and limb. However, the fact that no marks of big tools spoil the reliefs within striking height of a person standing on the ground may suggest that big iron tools simply had not been available to those labouring in their plight to purge the building from detestable imagery. We thus have to visualise them standing frequently over 4, sometimes 10m above the ground, grasping with one hand the ladder and with the other their smallish iron tool, which is raining down on the images at the wall with monotonous regularity.

From our point of view this method of destruction shows much more clearly which pictures the iconoclasts found particularly repugnant, offensive or dangerous (if thought to represent demons) than in the case of the destruc-

50 Presumably because of their height at some 4.25–5.20m above the ground, figures on this panel in an inner chamber of the temple (once the storeroom for precious votive gifts) were only partially destroyed. The king on the left was attacked from the front, suggesting that the ladder was positioned nearby. The iconoclast could probably only just reach Hathor, accounting for the oblong marks on her body. The god Horus escaped, whether because of his appearance in the guise of a falcon (though falcon images were attacked elsewhere) or because he was beyond reach. The mutilation of the lion goddess Bastet (on the far right) proves, however, that the ladder was moved

51 *No ladders were used when attacking this image in a chapel dedicated to Hathor at the very back of the temple. The damage stops just slightly over two metres above the ground, saving the youthful face of the goddess Nekhbet who stands between Hathor and the king*

tion of smaller free-standing images. Each and every one of the thousands of figures in the Dendara temple will have required more blows than were needed to mutilate the pictorial inventory of the average temple in the North of the Empire beyond recognition. The efforts involved made the iconoclasts at Dendara select carefully what to spare and what to target.

It is a universal phenomenon in image destruction, whether for religious, political or personal reasons, that the face as the most individual part of the human (even if not always of the divine) anatomy tends to be the main target. This can also be observed at Dendara. Each of the massive columns, 24 in the entrance hall, six in the inner hall of apparition, two in an inner court and 12

THE ARCHAEOLOGY OF RELIGIOUS HATRED

52 *The queen in the centre of the picture escaped erasure, presumably because she could not easily be reached from ladders on either side; the other four figures next to her, by contrast, were thoroughly destroyed. Note that the figure on the far left was mutilated by scratching rather than by direct blows. The images are c.4.35-5.30m above ground in a chamber which once served for the storage of ceremonial garments*

of the roof chapel was crowned by a capital, the upper half of which rested on four colossal heads of Hathor looking in every direction. On the reliefs decorating the walls Hathor, the mistress of the temple, is often depicted as a young woman of great beauty, often wearing a crown consisting of cow horns and the sun disk, yet she could also appear in the guise of various animals, notably in that of a cow. The 176 representations of her head in superhuman size on the column capitals combine different aspects of her divinity by depicting her with a human face, yet with the ears of a cow. These massive ears as well as her hair were spared, while the faces were thoroughly attacked with few only being spared, sometimes leaving her human traits recognisable, sometimes leaving no more than a flattish rough surface where once her face had been. These massive quadruple-headed column capitals offered the most arduous and the most dangerous challenge; in contrast to the thousands of bas-reliefs, they were three-dimensional, thus requiring much more stone to be chiselled off, presumably with the same basic tools used to disfigure the reliefs.

1 *St Columbanus and St Gallus on Lake Constance as envisaged around AD 1460*

2 Ireland was thoroughly Christianised between the fourth and sixth century and then became one of the most proactive centres of Christianity, providing missionaries for the Continent, like Columbanus and Gallus. Even small settlements, like Kilcolman on the Dingle peninsula, bear witness to the thorough Christianisation of the island: this boulder bears an early Christian cross with an ogham inscription probably naming a pilgrim called Colman

3 Artist's impression of the destruction of the main cult relief in the Dieburg mithraeum.
Deborah Miles-Williams

4 *Some temples were transformed into churches or cathedrals, such as the Athena temples at Syracuse in Sicily, whether to re-use existing architecture or to prevent pagan worship. While being a powerful symbol for Christian victory, this phenomenon is not discussed here, as normally no traces of pagan images survive. We may assume, however, that they were removed and probably destroyed*

5 *A 3.5m-high lion sculpture, re-assembled (and partially restored) out of fragments re-used in the walls of c.AD 300, the latest pagan phase of the temple of Allat at Palmyra*

6 *The Mithras temple at Capua is one of several such buildings whose images escaped destruction as the interior was filled with debris*

7 *A replica of the Jupiter giant column from Ladenburg whose remains were found in a well (see **31**)*

8 *Dura-Europos in Syria was taken by the Persians in AD 256. Despite its capture in war, the town provides no certain examples for deliberately mutilated images amongst its abundant pagan monuments. It was a ghost town and no longer part of the Empire after the victory of Christianity*

9 *A Christian cross above an erased Mithraic cult relief in a natural cave at Doliche*

10 Mosaics in San Marco at Venice: a winged demon, dark and evil, appears when St Simon destroys the innocently looking image of the sun god (left). A demon equally inhabits the statue of the moon goddess and tries to resist her annihilation by St Jude (right)

11 Mosaic in San Marco at Venice: a dragon exemplifies the evil powers of Mars, here pulled down at the instigation of St Philip

12 *Carefully laid to rest rather than disfigured: the fate of the head of Mercury at Uley, symptomatic of the more gentle pagan to Christian transition in Britain?*

13 *The hilltop sanctuary at Tawern, now reconstructed, has been subject to an iconoclastic attack. A series of pagan stone monuments were thrown into the over-14m-deep temple well near the entrance in the background*

14 *The sheer size of the Dendara temple made image destruction an arduous and dangerous task. Artist's impression by Deborah Miles-Williams*

15 *Emperor Nero in the guise of a pharaoh (right) offers to Hathor (left) and her son, the child god Ihy, a birth-house (another temple in the same precinct). Relief in the entrance hall of the main temple destroyed by image-haters*

16 *Reliefs in the entrance hall of the Dendara temple: the pagan figures were painstakingly destroyed panel by panel*

17 The main temple at Dendara (centre) was in immediate vicinity of a, now ruined, sixth-century church (foreground)

18 Because of the soot on columns, walls and ceilings, it has been suggested that people lived in the former temple after its abandonment as a religious building, quite possibly even in the Christian period

19 Many temples of Mithras, and all which have yielded numerous coins, continued to be visited until the late fourth century or beyond, a strong argument against an early collapse of the religion without force

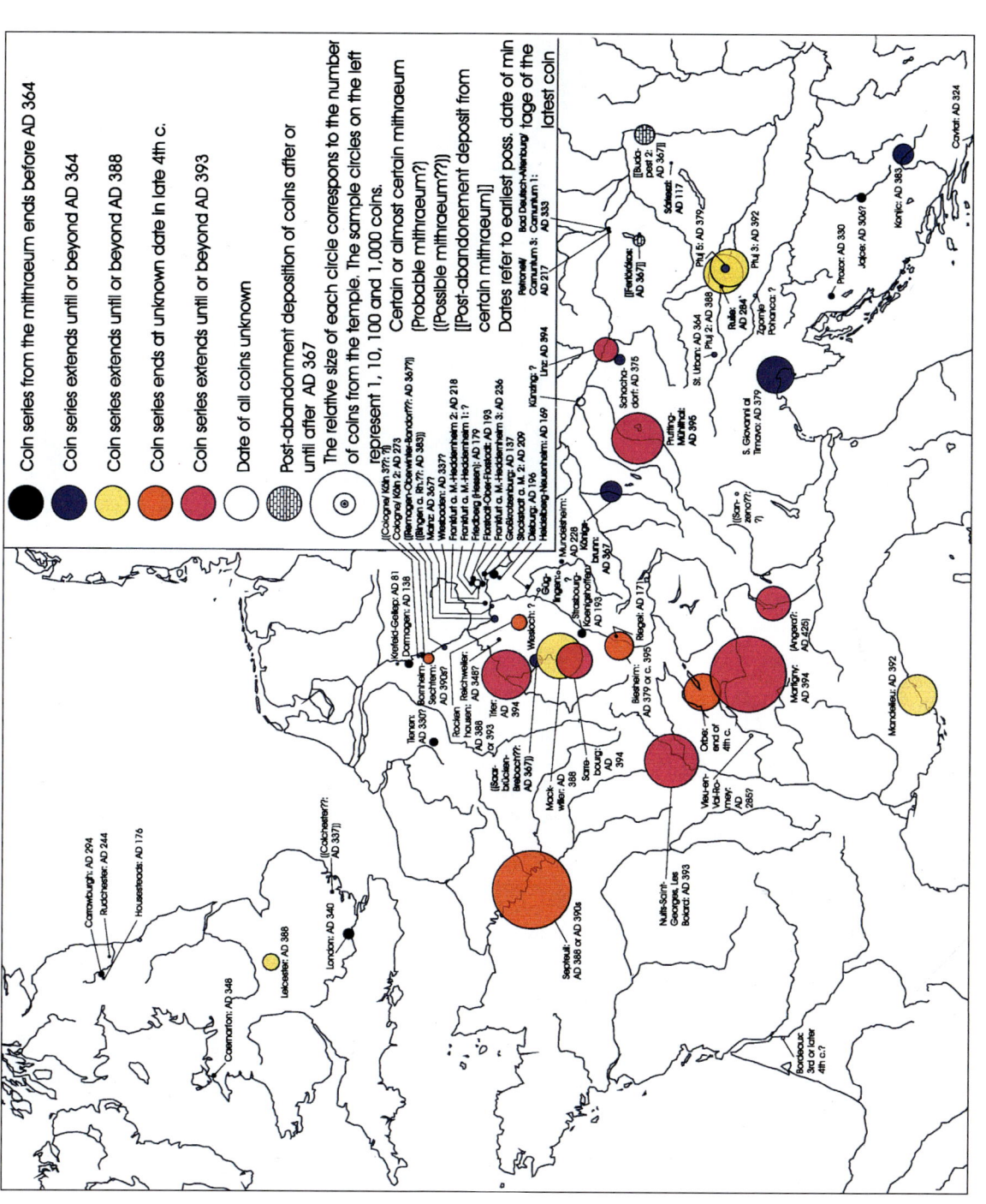

20 Parts of the spring sanctuary at Septeuil near Paris were transformed into a temple of Mithras as late as AD 355/365. The cult images were destroyed violently in the late fourth or fifth century: one of many testimonies for the vibrant nature of paganism under Christian rule

21 & 22 A lion statue and a small column decorated with an oak branch with leaves and acorns escaped the violent destruction of the rest of the temple inventory at Nuits-Saint-Georges, Les Bolards: because the iconoclasts saw nothing offensive in representations of nature in art?

23 *This rock-carved image of three mother goddesses and one other pagan figure on the left and two on the right never seems to have been touched by iconoclasts despite being on open display at Kindsbach for almost two millennia*

24 *A second rock next to the previous one and adjacent to a healing spring (on the right), had been deliberately turned over despite its massive size. It depicts a mother goddess on the left, three pagan worshippers, one of which is making an offering on an altar (top centre) and three further figures underneath who wear armour; the central one is the war god Mars*

25 *The most recent victim of religious iconoclasm: the larger of the two colossal Buddha statues at Bamiyan (54m high) in 1974, now destroyed by Taliban and Al-Qaeda explosives*

DESTRUCTION AT DENDARA

In the case of the columns in the *pronaos* the quadruple-head of Hathor was (to judge by photographs and general information about the dimensions of the temple; no scale drawings appear to be published) some 9-11.5m above ground, the colossal heads being no less than about 2.5m high (**47**). Thus the heads were bigger and at greater height than virtually all other mutilated images. While the gigantic size of the Hathor heads and practical considerations (the massive ears might have offered support for the ladders) forced the iconoclasts to be selective here and to concentrate their efforts on the face, less discriminate procedures predominated in the treatment of the bas-reliefs. While it is not difficult to find examples of figures in relief whose faces were selected for more thorough destruction than other parts of their bodies, the majority of deities and rulers had the whole of their bodies disfigured with pick marks in similar density. What is noticeable, however, is that the crowns were usually not considered to be a worthwhile target (though there are exceptions to the rule) nor were images, which did not depict deities or those involved in their worship. Several pictorial representations of a huge water lily (lotus) from which emerged a serpent (**54**) were not targeted, in complete contrast to the deities which surrounded the floral image. This may be the result of the plant and animal being regarded as forming part of a harmless scene from nature, while in reality the serpent was meant to represent an apparition of Harsomatus, the divine son of Hathor and Horus, and the water lily a symbol of regeneration and rebirth often associated with him. Much more noticeable than the occasional sparing of non-offensive images is the fact that

53 *The images of deities and the king on top of this door lintel inside a side chapel were destroyed, while the queen (standing far left) and the divine falcon (in the centre) escaped the attack*

54 The image of the god Harsomatus emerging in the guise of a serpent out of a lily in the same chapel was spared, presumably because it was not recognised as a pagan image while all by-standing figures, including the same god, Harsomatus, as a falcon were destroyed

the extensive hieroglyphic texts which accompany and provide the religious context for the images were in most instances not attacked.

During the era of the Graeco-Egyptian Ptolemaic dynasty (323-30 BC) and in the subsequent period of Roman rule, the use of hieroglyphs had become restricted to sacred texts. Only a small circle of priests still commanded this script with its repertoire of c.7,000 characters, and between the last dated hieroglyphic text of AD 394 and the decipherment in the nineteenth century the meaning of the mysterious pictorial symbols had fallen into complete oblivion. Incidentally, it is interesting to note that this latest hieroglyphic inscription of AD 394, from Philae in southernmost Egypt, is equally just next to a mutilated pagan relief, one of many such examples from this late pagan stronghold. Whether the texts were spared because they could no longer be read by the iconoclasts or, indeed, anybody else or whether the small pictorial symbols were not regarded as being as dangerous or offensive as the images, is open to debate.

The question arises who was responsible for image destruction on such a massive scale. It seems safe to acquit pagan invaders without religious motivation from any responsibility. Egypt over the long period of Roman rule (30 BC-AD 642) was on average affected by invasion and warfare to a far lesser scale than Rome's northern territories. More importantly, it seems unimaginable that such extensive and laborious destructions could be the result of a burst of 'vandalism' or even of hatred towards the culture of a hostile power. The sheer effort and perseverance, and the sparing of some seemingly non-religious images and of the indecipherable texts, clearly points to religiously motivated iconoclasm. Two religions, Christianity and Islam, have dominated Egypt in the period since the millennia-old tradition of Egyptian paganism had ceased to be tolerated. The uniform style of the iconoclasm renders it highly unlikely that destruction spanned a long period of time, and that we can apportion blame to followers of both religions. The question thus arises in the name of which faith these acts were carried out. Hack marks in stone, unfortunately, do not allow independent dating. A modern excavation of the interior in the temple may well have found small sandstone and granite splinters of the relief-decorated walls and columns fallen on the ground, associated with artefacts of a specific period in a distinct layer. Yet Dendara was, like so many other ancient monuments in Egypt and the Mediterranean, cleared of the debris which had accumulated over the centuries and millennia in typically mid-nineteenth-century manner without any records of what artefacts were found embedded in them, let alone any description of the different layers which must have existed. It seems likely that such layers were sealed by later sediments and thus well protected and preserved: when the artist David Roberts visited Egypt before the start of the clearance operations, in December 1838, the entrance hall (*pronaos*) of the temple was half buried in sand. The very fact that so much sand had accumulated is in itself an indication, even though an imprecise one, of an early date of iconoclasm. Since some of the reliefs near the bottom of the entrance hall columns were mutilated, the attack must have taken place before any significant layer of sand or other debris had been allowed to build up. The phase of intensive image destruction does not appear to have been preceded by any significant period of abandonment when sand was no longer cleared out.

While this observation in itself renders iconoclasm during the three centuries of Christian domination more likely than in the subsequent period of Islamic rule, so do the signs for a strong Christian presence at the site. Dendara was already a diocesan town in the early fourth century, and a church was installed in one of the smaller temples at Dendara, the Mammisi (birth-house) of Nero or Trajan. It comes as no surprise that the reliefs which once had decorated this temple were disfigured in a manner very similar to the one familiar to us from the Hathor temple. Another church was built next to it, possibly in the early sixth century (**colour plate 17**). Both churches were within a 100m radius of the entrance to the Hathor temple. Was the latter an abandoned building at the time when imagery was considered to be so offensive or dangerous that it merited nevertheless arduous destruction? Auguste Mariette-Pacha (1880, 38), a nineteenth-century scholar to whom we owe one of the earliest treatises on the temple, explained the sticky black soot which covers walls and ceilings (**colour plate 18**) with the smoke of fires and lamps of Christians Copts who lived in the temple at the time. In the absence of a proper excavation we cannot test his theory; yet, it is attractive and in the light of the circumstantial evidence, perfectly possible. The gigantic scale of the temple ensured that some images escaped destruction, yet the only part of the temple spared in its entirety appear to have been the crypts with their concealed entrances. They might have been sealed off, whether by pagans to avoid their profanation or by Christians to prevent image worship. Interestingly, the innermost sanctuary of one of the smaller temples at Dendara, the Mammisi of Nectanebo, appears to have escaped destruction as well since it was sealed off with a brick wall at an unknown date, perhaps following the laws to close the temples in the late Roman period.

It would be far beyond the scope of this book to provide a complete list of deliberately disfigured images in Egypt, but it ought to be stressed that the temples at Dendara and Philae form no isolated cases of image destruction in the Nile valley. The Opet temple at Karnak, to quote just one more building, provides examples for similar forms of image destruction, here more often concentrated on the heads (**55**). As in many other parts of the Empire, the archaeological evidence for image destruction does not stand on its own. To judge by the written sources, Christian image destruction was no less prevalent in Egpyt than elsewhere. A whole series of factors accounts for the

55 *In contrast to Dendara, at the Opet temple at Karnak the faces of deities were particularly targeted by iconoclasts*

fact that it is not normally possible to link specific reports on image destruction with cases detected by archaeologists, neither in Egypt nor elsewhere: the coincidences involved in what came to the attention of ecclesiastical writers, what they considered worth reporting and what manuscripts have survived as well as the frequent lack of topographical information in the description of sites which came under attack and the scanty nature of archaeological exploration. It is, nevertheless, worth noting that the activities of one of the most well-known iconoclasts in late Roman Egypt, the Abbot Shenoute, were centred on his monastery, just a little over 110km downstream from Dendara as the crow flies and somewhat further following the winding course of the Nile. The glorious deeds of the abbot and his monastic companions in the fifth century comprised the incineration of a temple in a settlement near their so-called 'White Monastery', the re-dedication of a temple as a church, multiple image destruction in a village temple, a nightly raid on the idols kept in a private house in the nearby town of Panopolis, smashed and thrown into the Nile on their way back to the monastery, and other incidences of temple and image destruction. Shenoute's anti-pagan image raids are reported to have extended until Coptos, a town some 25km beyond Dendara following the Nile valley from the vicinity of the 'White Monastery' southwards. While Dendara thus appears to have been still within the sphere of activity of Abbot Shenoute and his monastic following, the time-consuming and systematic manner of image destruction makes one rather suspect that local Christians in Dendara itself were responsible. There seems little doubt that there were numerous likeminded men who found no hagiographer to create a permanent record of their deeds. It is not because Shenoute himself is likely to have had a hand in the image destruction at Dendara that his example is interesting here, but because literature provides us with an insight into the mindset and scale of operations of an iconoclast active in the same area. Those who destroyed the reliefs at Dendara so thoroughly remain incognito; yet, their very deeds carry the signature of religious extremism.

8
DESTRUCTION AND RE-USE IN EGYPT AND PALESTINE

The Abbot Shenoute is of interest to us not only as an Egyptian iconoclast whose deeds were propagated by literature; his own monastery, sometimes called the 'White Monastery' because of the white limestone its church (**56**) was built of, bears witness to the dramatic change in the religious landscape which unveiled itself at the time. The destroyed temples provided convenient quarries for the monastery. Columns, capitals, fragments of the temple entablature and dissected stone plaques with reliefs and hieroglyphic texts were re-used in the construction of the church of the monastic complex. Part of the stone derives from the temple of King Ptolemy XII in the town Athribis, merely three kilometres to the south-east of the monastery as the famous Egyptologist Flinders Petrie already had suggested. Petrie and his team had cleared the massive temple in as little as seven weeks in 1908. This temple covered an even larger area than the roughly contemporary Dendara temple. Petrie noted that figures of the gods decorating the walls in the inside were chopped away (though by no means all of them) and the walls then whitewashed. He interpreted this rightly or wrongly as a sign that the building had been converted into a church. Later the building provided a stone quarry. Then it was apparently transformed into a cattle pen, served for a second time as a quarry and was finally filled with rubbish and sand. What Petrie had suspected was confirmed in 1996 during restoration works at the 'White Monastery' (i.e. at the church of the monastic complex) when a considerable number of stone blocks from this temple as well as spoils from other temples were found. Unfortunately, despite renewed excavations in the temple in the 1980s and 1990s, no small finds or details of the stratigraphy have been published. The recycling of building stone, stone reliefs and inscriptions (religious and non-religious alike), already referred to above, was a widespread practice in the late Roman Empire and can be observed with particular frequency in late defences. Could the re-use of old building material from temples at the 'White Monastery' similarly have had purely practical purposes?

DESTRUCTION AND RE-USE IN EGYPT AND PALESTINE

56 The fifth-century church in the monastery of Shenoute, one of Egypt's most famous iconoclasts

The Christian archaeologist Friedrich Wilhelm Deichmann (1975, 54-60) observed a large granite slab amongst the paving stones of the central nave of Shenoute's church whose hieroglyphs are still visible despite 1,500 years of wear. Two of the church's portals re-use parts of votive reliefs, dissected in such a manner that, if left exposed, any church-goer could see the cut off legs and torsos of the figures (**57**) which had once been the object of religious veneration. Why were they not turned round to show the undecorated backsides? Was it to propagate the Christian victory?

Yet, the pagan art on display was by no means so dominant that one can be certain about such an interpretation. Surely, there would have been no difficulty in finding more pagan images to cut apart and to incorporate in the walls in inverted and undignified positions had there been a strong desire to do so. In the light of the widespread fear of demons, perhaps a compromise had to be negotiated between powerful symbolism and anxiety about the evil powers embodied by pagan images. Maybe the 'offensive' relief fragments were even once concealed beneath plaster and they were only re-used as their oblong shape predestined them as suitable material for a doorframe. Indeed, Deichmann observed that other building stones carried traces of reliefs, but that these presumably had been initially concealed. The hieroglyphs need not be relevant either. The iconoclasts at Dendara at least had not considered the systematic erasure of hieroglyphic texts, by then presumably indecipherable, worth their efforts. Yet, it may not have needed numerous dissected images on display or once sacred texts on the floor of the church trodden with the bare feet of the congregation to remind people of Christian victory. There

57 Spoils from demolished pagan temples were re-used in the church, presumably still built in Shenoute's lifetime

can be no doubt that the church in Shenoute's monastery was either partially or even entirely built of materials robbed from demolished temples presumably including the columns and capitals, even if the display of overtly pagan monuments was the exception rather than the rule. While we can develop some idea of what once happened on the basis of the spoils, how much more must contemporary people have been conscious of this? They had witnessed the dramatic events, how the centres of religious life from time immemorial were reduced to rubble or purged of their sacred art and rededicated while the monuments of the new religion rose up. They did not need reminders of what must have been the most radical revolution anyone could remember.

The deeds of Bishop Porphyrios of Gaza in Palestine, outside, but at the border of the Egyptian provinces, spring to mind. Pagan religion in Egypt and Palestine was distinctively different; yet, it is permissible to compare the manner of its eradication. Porphyrios had become bishop of the populous town while Christians still only constituted a small minority: as few as 280 men, women and children in the mid-AD 390s we are told by his biographer, the Deacon Mark (chapter 19). Whether this figure is accurate or whether it was a slight understatement to emphasize how groundbreaking the later missionary work of Porphyrios was, there can be little doubt that the pagan population still vastly outnumbered the members of the Christian congregation. The biography was written within living memory of the events and numerous people would have been aware as to whether Christians or pagans constituted the majority at the time; any obvious lie would have undermined the credibility of the whole biography. Furthermore, as we shall see, the bishop and his following were far too weak to enforce the eradication of pagan monuments without outside support. The aim of iconoclasm was, quite explicitly, to suppress vibrant paganism, not to achieve symbolic closure of a bygone chapter of history. By petition to the emperor, Porphyrios succeeded first in ensuring that anti-pagan laws were enforced, the temples, partially at least, closed and the images therein destroyed. Later, after a renewed personal petition and with military support, the temples of Gaza were against the resistance of the population either demolished or burnt to the ground. The outburst of religious zeal culminated in the incineration of the temple of the city's chief god, Marnas, which burnt for several days. The idols' images in the sanctuaries had already, as we have seen, suffered the same fate at an earlier date while their domiciles had still enjoyed a short stay of execution. Now, however, private houses were searched and numerous images requisitioned which were either thrown in the fire or refuse deposits (we may presume after sufficient mutilation to prevent recovery and re-use). It is worth noting that these most easily identifiable pagan monuments were not singled out for re-use, but the marble slabs from the holiest of the holies of the temple of Marnas. These were either undecorated or, at least, we are not informed about any votive reliefs or inscriptions. As it had not normally been allowed to enter the holiest of the holies, and as there had been a special ritual ban on women, the bishop ordered the plaques to be used to pave the street outside the burnt out temple and building site for a church. The plaques, he hoped, would thus not only be trodden on by men and women, but even by dogs, pigs and other beasts. Yet, with this wilful act of desecration Porphyrios achieved only a partial success. Long after the events, we hear from his biographer Mark (in chapter 76), that the majority of pagans, and, in particular, the women, still refused to walk on the marble plaques; religious respect for Marnas outlived the annihilation of all visible remnants of his former glory. What is important for us here is the power of memory. The pagans, as far as we can tell, did not avoid stepping on the marble plaques, because there were inscriptions or artwork, which reminded them that this was holy material, but because they could not forget.

Similarly, the re-use of sheer undecorated pagan building materials at the 'White Monastery' was a powerful reminder of the dramatic change, whether intentional or a by-product of purpose-orientated quarrying of closed temples, as was the disappearance of temples and the creation of new places of worship. Both textual evidence in the case of Porphyrios and archaeological evidence in the case of Shenoute suggest that pagan artwork was re-used selectively, if at all, in prominent and visible places in ecclesiastical buildings, partially at least, we may assume, because of the pervasive fear of demons thought to inhabit the idols' images. And there was no need to create symbols for the obvious.

9

THE SPEED OF CHRISTIANISATION IN EGYPT

Paganism apparently remained strong at Gaza until and beyond Bishop Porphyrios had dealt a death-blow to its visible manifestations. Gaza, of course, was in Palestine not Egypt, and the question arises whether the deeds of Porphyrios at Gaza and those of Shenoute in Egypt can reasonably be compared. While paganism clearly appears to have been dominant in Gaza into the early fifth century, it is widely believed that it shrank to insignificance at a much earlier date in Egypt. De Lacy O'Leary (1938), for example, introduced his article on 'The destruction of temples in Egypt' with the following words: 'Soon after Constantine [who ruled over Egypt AD 324-37] granted toleration to the Christian religion the pagan temples of Egypt began to be deserted and before long became ruinous.' This conclusion does not appear to derive from any material evidence for the abandonment of temples at the time, but from a study of Christian sources which 'seem to imply that Egypt generally was Christian at the beginning of the IVth cent.' even though it is claimed elsewhere that 'During those two centuries [the time between the early fourth and the sixth centuries] paganism lingered still and expired slowly.' Such seemingly contradictory statements must represent an attempt to square the irreconcilable words of Christian authors implying both an early triumph of Christian mission and an enduring struggle against paganism. In a later response to De Lacy O'Leary, Labib Habachi (1972) expressed doubts about O'Leary's theory that there was widespread demolishment of temples by Christians even though he conceded some Christian image destruction. Yet he was happy to accept O'Leary's hypothesis that temples were deserted prior to their re-dedication as churches or before any stones were re-used in churches or monasteries. These views are by no means only expressed in old publications. Roger Bagnall claimed as recently as 2001 that temples and traditional religion declined already in the first 250 years of Roman rule (i.e. between 30 BC and the AD 220s) and implied an accelerated pace of decline thereafter. Yet, while the view that Egyptian paganism largely collapsed in itself is widely held, there is no agreement as to when the process of decline started. Steven Snape (1996, 58), for example, postulates that the pagan cults of ancient Egypt died out over a period of no less than seven centuries, starting as early as the third century BC. Who then were the pagans Shenoute combated as late as the late fourth and the first half of the fifth century by destroying their temples and images, should it indeed be true that paganism in Egypt had already reached a stage of advanced decline well before the government began to profess Christianity? The last few survivors of a dying breed whose days were numbered irrespective of whether or not there was direct Christian intervention? Perhaps even figures invented for the purpose of making Shenoute fit the stereotype of the saint struggling against image worshippers?

Whether or not paganism indeed collapsed on itself at an early date is of crucial interest here. It would not affect our assessment of the circle of suspects for the systematic image destruction at Dendara. Even if committed pagans in Egypt had dwindled to insignificant numbers before the Empire came under Christian government (and there is no strong evidence to suggest that there was Christian image destruction anywhere in the Empire on any noteworthy scale before), there still would have been good motives for committed Christians to do what God had commanded on numerous occasions in the Old Testament, namely to destroy pagan images: the resulting deep-felt repugnance towards anything pagan, the pervasive fear of demons, the wish to make a symbolic statement or the desire to prevent any potential future pagan backlash. Still, ecclesiastical literature almost uniformly claims that the aims of such interventions went in most instances beyond principle and symbolism. They were thought to be instrumental in preventing the continuation of pagan practices – just as digging out the roots of a lushly growing plant was in destroying it for good. The annihilation of the nuclei of pagan communities, like temples, images and other sacred monuments, made a continuation of object-centred religious rituals simply impossible.

The speed of the postulated disaffection with paganism and of Christianisation in Egypt are thus indeed central to the subject under investigation here. While all too often scholars' claims about the early decline of paganism and the explosive spread of Christianity in Egypt remain unsubstantiated or are solely based on odd passages in ecclesiastical literature, one notable exception is Roger Bagnall, one of the most renowned specialists on the history of Egypt in the Hellenistic and Roman periods who has meticulously compiled evidence for the phenomenon. It is thus worthwhile to examine his arguments. Bagnall (1993, 261-73) bases his assessment on the decline in written testimonies for various forms of cult-related activities and on the decline in building temples. These are, undoubtedly, correct observations; yet, whether the decline in documents and building activity can be translated into a decline of temple visits and religious devotion amongst the masses is quite a different question. Can we exclude the possibility that we are merely dealing with a

THE ARCHAEOLOGY OF RELIGIOUS HATRED

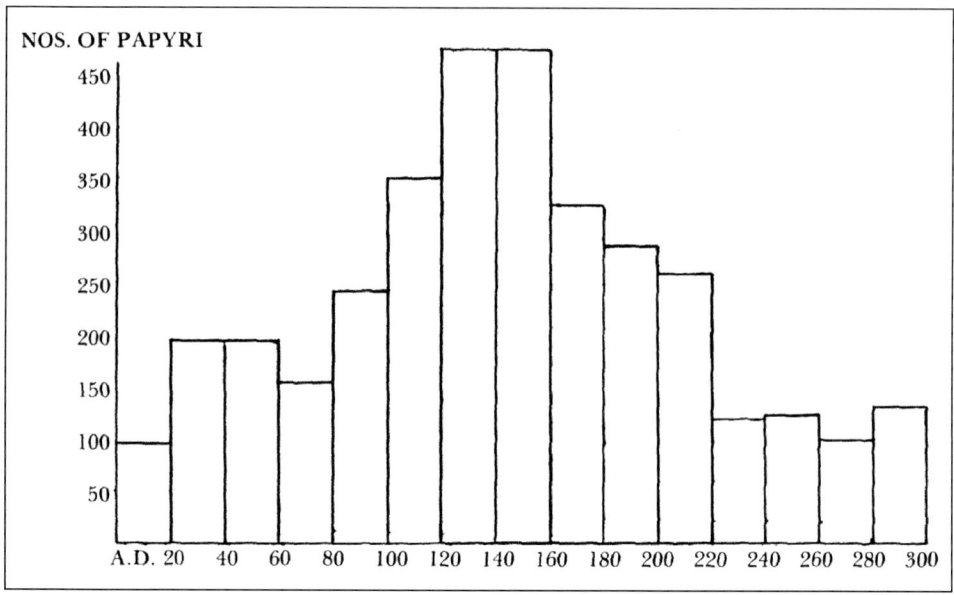

58 *Ramsay MacMullen compiled over 3,500 texts on a wide range of subjects from Roman Egypt written on papyrus and pottery sherds (ostraca). They generally peak in the mid-second century and have significantly diminished in number by the third. This renders it dangerous to read too much into the decline of textual information for pagan practice, as secular texts decline likewise*

decline in sponsorship and a transformation of cult to a new form in which the erection of monuments and scripture played no longer a decisive role? This question will be explored further in the following chapter in an Empire-wide context. Suffice it to say here that Ramsay MacMullen has been able to show that the output of papyri and, in particular, public papyri in Egypt declined sharply during the period in question (**58**). The number of documents datable to a given period in the middle and second half of the third century amounted to merely some 40 per cent of those datable to the same length of time at the beginning of the century and less than 30 per cent in relation to the mid-second century. There is no doubt that the role of writing declined markedly in third-century Egypt as well as elsewhere in the Empire. The question must thus be allowed whether the decline of written evidence for pagan cults allows us to say any more than that religious written documentation also lost ground, but not necessarily religion itself.

Yet, it is also archaeological evidence, which, according to Bagnall, supports the general decline in paganism. The temple at Luxor, for example, was famously incorporated before the victory of Christianity, at the very beginning of the fourth century, into a Roman fortress and its cult inventory ritually buried. Votive reliefs were used in its construction (as in some other contemporary fortifications elsewhere in the Empire). Parts of the temple were even transformed into a regimental shrine. Does the incorporation of the Luxor temple into a fortress indicate that it had been abandoned previously and does it thus signal that Egyptian religion in general had fallen into decline despite a vociferously pagan government at the time? The other cases Bagnall (1993, 263-4) cites as examples for the third-century abandonment of temples are less convincing. Judging them solely by the literature quoted by Bagnall himself, the precise dating of the abandonment of the temples in Karnak appears to rely on an unsubstantiated claim, that of a temple at Karanis on a circular argument: the excavators had no firm dating evidence for the abandonment; yet in the light of economic decline elsewhere in the settlement in the third century and in the light of their assumption that the population of Karanis was thoroughly Christianised by the beginning of the fourth century, they placed the abandonment around the middle of the third century. The indications for a third-century abandonment of a temple at Herakleopolis seem to be somewhat stronger, yet they are merely based on the hypothesis that it would have taken at least a century for several feet of rubbish and earth to accumulate on the dilapidated ruins and that quarry pits with fourth-century pottery belong to a second phase of robbing a century later. No evidence is provided for the postulated separation of stone robbing into two phases a century apart. Furthermore, we are not told how much or how little fourth-century pottery came from the pits. In urban sites quarry pits tend to fill up with eroded material from the sides, and the pottery does not even necessarily give certainty that stone robbing took place within the fourth century and not at a later date. It is possible that the temple was robbed of its stones in the third century, but the published archaeological evidence is by no means conclusive and would equally be perfectly consistent with the assumption of a fourth- or even fifth-century stone robbing.

This is not to deny that temples could have been abandoned in the third century in Egypt, as some were also in other parts of the Empire, but the quoted cases are dubious and, even if accepted, do not permit us to conclude that this was a general trend. Even if, however, future archaeological work should establish that a certain proportion of Egyptian temples was abandoned prior to the victory of Christianity, the question will have to be asked, to what extent would such a hypothetical decline reflect a loss of piety and to what extent a loss in population. There appears to have been significant loss of life as a result of epidemics in Alexandria at least by AD 261. Bagnall (1993, 265) himself quotes a heroine account of a couple who stayed behind to guard a temple in the village of Theadelpheia in the Fayum oasis in the early fourth century after the whole village had been abandoned by its population. A demographic decline could have resulted in the abandonment of temples even if there was no decline in temple visits per head of the population.

While it is fair to conclude that paganism underwent a transformation prior to the victory of Christianity, and that the period of ostentatious display was over, there is no way to tell on the basis of the above-mentioned arguments whether or not the use of existing facilities per head of the population declined.

More fruitful is a new approach, also pioneered by Bagnall (1982), to estimate the numerical growth of the proportion of Christians amongst the population of Egypt. Bagnall analysed the proportion of persons with Christian names in various dated administrative documents and observed a steady rise. Some 12 per cent of children born in the earlier fourth century bore Christian names as opposed to 52 per cent born some time later – the date shall be discussed below. The proportion rises to 18-19 per cent and 66 per cent respectively if we add the children whose fathers bore Christian names even though they themselves did not. Allowing for some Christians without Christian names (and at no later point in time does the proportion of Egyptians with Christian names ever appear to have surpassed a maximum of about two thirds of the population) Bagnall argues that the real percentage of Christians amongst the Egyptian population in the latter case was even probably as high as 78 per cent (i.e. one and a half times the percentage of names with some leeway in either direction). We seem to be tracing a truly explosive growth after the early fourth century: the proportion of Christians seems to have increased by over 400 per cent; yet, how quickly did this happen?

Bagnall's stimulating paper has provoked a lively debate. There is no space here to discuss the minutiae of the arguments pro and contra his hypothesis which rests on the precise date of specific documents, the average age of the persons listed, the classification of individual names, the question of what proportion of people without Christian names were Christians, and whether or not we can be sure that all of those who bore Christian names were indeed Christians. The most crucial problems lie in the apparent scarcity of suitable documents and the difficulty to date them. Originally Bagnall had postulated that the papyrus document with 52 per cent of the listed 222 men (excluding their fathers) bearing Christian names, dated to AD 388. Obviously, the time when the men, by then paying taxes, had been given names was somewhat earlier, and Bagnall thus concluded that the document reflected on average circumstances around AD 353. Had the proportion of Christians indeed risen to 78 per cent of the population and, consequently, that of pagans plummeted to less than 22 per cent as early as the mid-fourth century? A similar conclusion had, incidentally, already been reached by Adolf von Harnack (1924, 726), who thought that the majority of Egyptians were Christians by the middle of the fourth century. If so, the destruction of places of worship to prevent the continuation of pagan cults cannot have played a determinant role in transforming Egypt from a pagan into a Christian country. (Cases of Christian image destruction, while already occurring in the mid-fourth century, spiralled out of control only towards the end of the century.) Had paganism declined to insignificance well before the time when Abbot Shenoute is alleged (by Christian sources it ought to be stressed) to have carried out his anti-pagan raids in the late fourth and the first half of the fifth century?

Remarkably, Bagnall (1987) himself proved his earlier hypothesis about the rapid spread of Christianity to be wrong. He shifted the estimated date of the document with 52 per cent Christian names, one of the cornerstones of his statistics, by as much as 75 years from *c*.AD 388 to *c*.AD 463 between 1982 and 1987. As already pointed out, the time when children were given names was somewhat earlier, and Bagnall thus concludes that the document reflects circumstances around AD 428 instead of, as he had originally assumed, AD 353. It hardly needs emphasising that it makes a crucial difference as to whether the proportion of pagans had dropped to below a quarter of the population as early as the mid-fourth century, less than a generation after Constantine's baptism in AD 337 or only after Roman emperors had professed Christianity for almost a century. Bagnall (1987, 248-9) claims that the later date of around AD 428 in itself makes it likely that the real proportion of Christians then was actually close to 100 per cent and that we therefore might have to multiply the 52 per cent of Christian names by 1.9 to arrive at nearly 100 per cent, a circular argument which surprises, given his otherwise lucid reasoning.

Notwithstanding the difficulties in trying to deduce from Bagnall's statistics the precise percentage of Christians amongst Egypt's population at a given time, he is undoubtedly right in claiming that the increasing proportion of Christian names mirrors a rising proportion of Christians in the population, no matter what multipliers we need to use at different times to translate the percentage of Christian names into the percentage of Christians. It also should be pointed out that the document in question refers to a single village, which might well, but need not, necessarily reflect the fact that the proportion of Christians was equally high all over Egypt. It is perfectly possible that the proportion of pagans had indeed dropped to some ($\pm$)22 per cent of the population by the late AD 420s. However, this was long after the process of eliminating centres of pagan cults had started in earnest, and we thus have no right to conclude that temple destruction in Egypt was no more than the removal of ruins the people had long lost interest in. Ecclesiastical sources confirm that image destruction was instrumental in eliminating paganism and did not merely mark a *fait accompli*. Furthermore, 20-25 per cent would still constitute a very significant minority. Several different religions flourish in the UK today whose members extensively use their places of worship despite the fact that they constitute significantly less than 20 per cent of the overall population. The proportion of regular church-goers has dropped well below this figure. Nevertheless, if a radical government came to power and declared all except one of the UK's major religions illegal, surely nobody would assume that the adherents of all other religions would just quietly and without force abandon their places of worship out of opportunism or a longing for change; and neither is there any logical justification to assume that, even if pagans had been reduced to a committed core in Egypt by the AD 420s, that their religion just collapsed in itself. Bagnall's stimulating research into the speed of the Christianisation of Egypt does in no way disprove that the significant degree of pagan resistance (amongst all classes of society) against the eradication of their heritage as portrayed in early Christian literature was a real phenomenon. It ought to be stressed that Bagnall, unlike others who believe in a rapid decline of paganism in Egypt to be replaced effortlessly by Christianity, does not explicitly claim that it did.

Even if Christians had reached some 80 per cent of the Egyptian population only some decades into the fifth century, it would still be no exaggeration to describe the spread of the new religion as rapid. Yet, in contrast to a hypothetical growth to 80 per cent as early as the mid-fourth century, it is no longer possible to rule out that pressure and destruction of cult centres was one major factor in achieving this, even if it was by no means the only one. It is in any case interesting to compare the process of Christianisation in Egypt with its southern neighbours, the Nubian kingdoms. In Qasr Ibrim, just outside the southern boundary of Roman Egypt, coins continued to be deposited on the floor of one temple from the second to the beginning of the fifth century, a ritual practice imported from the Roman Empire. A different temple in the same town was probably constructed as late as the fifth or early sixth century (and in case not before the mid-fourth at the very earliest: it sealed a grave with pottery of c.AD 350-450 under its walls). Most interesting in our context, however, is a third temple; already 1,000 years old when Christianity gained state support in nearby Egypt, it continued to be used for another 200 years until religious life was brought to a violent and sudden halt in the sixth century. In the inner hall of this mudbrick temple, just outside the sanctuary, a pile of broken statuary was found. The excavators suggest that they had been thrown out of the sanctuary through the doorway for further fragmentation. Significant parts of the statues, such as a bird's head and upper body of Horus in the guise of a falcon, have never been found, and may have been removed or pulverised. Various small cult objects appear to have been shattered and then strewn over the temple floor, and some of the wooden objects burnt. Even three small curtains, preserved because of the desert climate, were torn into 15, 23 and 32 recognisable pieces respectively and scattered in the temple. A fourth temple was converted into a church in the sixth century as well, while the above-mentioned temple in which coins had been offered into the fifth century presumably served as a quarry when a five-aisled Christian stone basilica was built in the seventh century.

Were the climactic events of the sixth century the result of popular groundswell from paganism to Christianity? The excavators of the destroyed temple point to cult objects, especially statues, statuettes, offering tables etc. being covered in dirt and oil and interpret the squalid conditions as a sign of the temple having fallen into neglect prior to its destruction. Yet, perhaps it is precisely the opposite, and we are dealing with the residues of ritual ointments of the cult images attesting to vibrant ritual activity, even if far removed from modern notions of cleanliness. It is worth noting, however, that the temple had been reduced in size prior to its violent end. Burial practices suggest that Christianity began to spread into the area in the fifth century, yet how quickly the new religion dominated the area is still unclear. It is in any case remarkable that pottery evidence for the conversion and destruction of temples in Qasr Ibrim seems to coincide with the historically attested conversion of the northern Nubian kingdom, in whose territory the town lay, in the mid-sixth century.

As in Egypt, the conversion of northern Nubia was probably neither an entirely voluntary popular movement nor a change enforced from above on an exclusively pagan population. Despite occasional warfare, there was intensive contact across the Empire's southern boundary in Egypt. The fact that Christianity spread so much slower just outside the borders of the Empire is no doubt largely due to the fact that there was no compulsion and destruction until the king himself had converted in the mid-sixth century. Yet, even in Egypt itself paganism remained remarkably resilient. Not only did the Isis temple in Philae remain an important pilgrimage centre for Rome's southern neighbours, open until the AD 530s, we even hear of a case of secret image worship and sacrifices within walking distance of Alexandria, Egypt's largest city, as late as the AD 480s, almost a century after such practices had been made a capital crime. Unsurprisingly, the fate that awaited the deities seized from the site of the 'crime' was ridicule, mutilation and partial incineration. Archaeology and written sources corroborate each other: Christianity was remarkably successful in Egypt, but force was amongst several important reasons for its success.

10

A WORLD WAITING FOR CHRISTIANITY?

Egypt had always formed a distinct geographic and cultural unity. Even after it had been incorporated into the Empire in 30 BC, its religion and art still retained more independent elements than was the case anywhere else in the Roman world. Embalmment, certain animal cults, its peculiar temple architecture and the depiction of emperors as pharaohs are just some of the phenomena which gave Egyptian culture a certain uniqueness which was only lost once it became part of the Christian world. Furthermore, Egypt's desert climate preserved more extensive administrative documents for the period (which lend themselves to a study of the spread of Christian names, for example) than are available for any other area within the ancient world. It thus seemed justified to deal with the Christianisation of the Nile valley in a separate chapter. Yet, in terms of ancient and modern claims that Christian proselytism resulted in a rapid spread of the new religion, Egypt is by no means an isolated case. In this chapter we shall explore whether in the remainder of the Roman Empire Christianity progressed so rapidly that iconoclasm mainly entailed the removal of meaningless remnants of a past age or whether it was instrumental in crushing vibrant but object-dependent paganism into oblivion.

Early Christian sources are seldom modest in proclaiming the success of mission. As early as the AD 50s the new religion had taken the province of Asia, the western part of modern Turkey, by storm if we follow the *Acts of the Apostles* (19, 23-27). The silversmith Demetrios from Ephesus who made votive models of the famous temple of the goddess Artemis, fearing for his business, is alleged to have spoken the following words to local fellow craftsmen:

> And you see and hear that not only at Ephesus, but in the whole of Asia, this Paul has won over and converted a substantial mass of people, saying that images made with hands are no gods. But not only is there a risk that our work will fall into disrepute, even that the sanctuary of the great goddess Artemis will count for nothing, the destiny of her majesty being to be dethroned, she who is worshipped by the whole of Asia and the world . . .

Yet, if we follow Christian sources, not only had the new religion spread so rapidly in the west of Asia Minor as to threaten businesses associated with pagan cults within one generation of Jesus's crucifixion, it continued to grow at a truly astonishing pace in territories across the ancient world. Towards the end of the second century, less than 150 years after St Paul's missionary activity at Ephesus, the Christian writer Tertullian of Carthage in northern Africa made even bolder claims when addressing in a book the pagans involved in capital trials against Christians (*Apology* 37, 4-8).

> We have only just come into being and yet we have already flooded all that is yours, the towns, the islands, small fortified places, self-governing communities, administrative centres, even military bases, the ranks of the citizens entitled to vote, the (higher class) jury panels, the imperial palace, the senate and the forum; we have only left the temples to you.

Yet, Christians were not only omnipresent, they were so numerous that the state depended on them. Tertullian asks his pagan readers to imagine the hypothetical scenario of what it would be like if all Christians, 'such a great number of people', had united and left the Empire to go to some hiding place in a remote part of the world:

> Doubtlessly you would have become terrified at your loneliness, at the silence all around you, at the true numbness of a world almost without any life; you would have searched for people to rule; you would have been left with more enemies than citizens. For now, because of the multitude of Christians, you have fewer enemies, since nearly all the citizens you have in nearly all the communities are Christians.

According to Tertullian his religion had thus become the majority religion, at least in parts of the Empire, well over a century before Constantine's conversion and despite bloody persecutions.

Scholars of our time frequently follow a similar line. The prolific writer and ancient historian Michael Grant (1968, 163) paints a picture of people losing enthusiasm for pagan deities and increasingly abandoning temples in the wake of war and disaster between the second and the fourth century. 'Another reason for waning interest in the old religion was the growth of monotheistic feeling.' According to Grant the only exceptions from this rule were mystery religions promising individual salvation and deities concerned with the protection of the state. The opinion that paganism was in severe decline long before the victory of Christianity is widespread, as we have already seen in the case of Egypt. One of the most outspoken representatives of the school of thought that it did not need Christian intervention for paganism, including the oriental cults, to collapse is Robert Turcan. His views on the subject are unequivocal as the following passage from his book *The Cults of the Roman Empire* (1996, 329) demonstrates:

> The gods formerly domiciled on the Rhine frontier had been swept away in the third century in the turbulence of the first invasions, at the same time as the fortresses then abandoned by the legionaries; and on the banks of the Danube, the few Persian or Syrian sanctuaries did not hold out for long after the Tetrarchy [i.e. not long after AD 293/311].
>
> Christianity first made progress in the urbanized centres where in other times the oriental cults had recruited the best part of their clientele, and the anti-pagan laws of Theodosius [AD 379-395] often did no more than ratify what had already taken place. The scattered survivals in rural paganism had more to do with variations on a naturist and 'neolithic' religion than with the lasting signs of oriental idolatry properly speaking.

This is a crucial point for us. Had the majority indeed turned away from paganism long before Christian image destruction started? Were many temples then abandoned old buildings without function or deeper meaning for the people who were either already Christians or, at least, thoroughly dissatisfied with the old religion? Was image destruction thus more motivated by principle than by the desire to prevent pagan worship, which was in severe decline anyway? Did violence against pagan monuments have no relevant role in converting the ancient pagan into a Christian society? Such a hypothetical course of events would appear to be in sharp contrast to the string of laws issued in the fourth, fifth and sixth centuries against various form of pagan ritual. Furthermore, the majority of cases of image destruction recorded in the biographies of saints were allegedly carried out against fierce pagan resistance. Was some of this resistance just invented for the purposes of dramatic effect and to heroise the main characters, or are we perhaps dealing with a few isolated pockets of pagan survival, considered worth reporting even though this was the exception rather than the rule?

If we concede that Christian sources may be biased in emphasising the success rate of early missionary activity, can we test their accuracy by comparing them with pagan testimonies? Pagan literary sources tend to be more concerned with state religion or minority movements amongst the educated elite (such as the philosophical movement of Neoplatonism) than with the religious life of the masses. They do not offer any statistics of temple visits or other expressions of religiosity. Yet, they do provide occasional insights. One of the most remarkable testimonies, also cited by Michael Grant in support of the postulated decline of paganism, is a famous letter the younger Pliny (10,96) wrote to the emperor Trajan in the early second century. In this letter he sought advice and assurance from the emperor as to whether or not his treatment of persons accused of being Christians was right. Pliny was then governor of Bithynia and Pontus, a province in the north-west of modern Turkey. He had the unrepentant ones executed, but spared those who were prepared to offer wine and incense to the images and to revile Christ. This procedure was approved by Trajan, as long as it was limited to openly accused persons and did not escalate into an actively pursued hunt for members of the outlawed religion. Pliny lamented the spread of this 'epidemic of superstition' not only in the towns, but also in the villages and the countryside. Temples had been almost abandoned, religious ceremonies had ceased to be celebrated for a long time, and it had been nearly impossible to sell the meat of sacrificed animals. All these dramatic changes were, according to Pliny, a pagan author without any interest in glorifying the success of Christian mission (but with a good motive for stressing the appropriateness and effectiveness of his measures), the result of the spread of Christianity. Yet, he was pleased to be able to report to the emperor that his salutary interventions had reversed the decline of a pagan cult.

However, if paganism as a result of the rapid spread of the new religion had indeed already lost much ground in Asia Minor as early as the time of Pliny or even that of the missionary journeys of St Paul, it proved remarkably resilient. The testimonies in literature and inscriptions for the vibrant nature of pagan cult in the area in the subsequent centuries are too numerous to list them here. However, it is worth noting that some 300 years after Pliny had written his famous letter to Emperor Trajan, Hypatios, the abbot of a monastery at Rouphinianai in Bithynia just 10km from Constantinople on the opposite shore of the Sea of Marmara, still did not find himself in a province in which paganism had paled into insignificance. At least not, if we follow his biographer, Callinicos (*Life of Hypatios* 30,1):

> He had a zeal for God, and he cleared many places in the land of the Bithynians from the error of idol worship. If he heard that people venerated anywhere a tree or some other object, he went there immediately, taking the monks, his disciples, with him, cut it down and burnt it completely. And so, finally, a part of them became Christians.

Another century later, after emperors residing in the nearby Constantinople had professed their Christian faith for over 200 years, paganism was still strong in the Anatolian countryside. It was in AD 542 that John from Diyarbakır (ancient Amida) in Mesopotamia, later to become Bishop of Ephesus, embarked upon a mission of converting the pagans in the west and south-west of Asia Minor (modern Turkey). If we can trust the figures in his own church history (3,36), paganism was still rampant at the time. Many thousands of pagans living in the mountainous territory of Tralles, some 45km east of Ephesus, were then converted. John also destroyed a mountain temple to its foundations and replaced it with a monastery. This pagan shrine was said by the old men living there to be the ritual centre for no less than 1,500 other temples spread over an extensive area in the late Roman provinces of Asia, Caria, Lydia and either or both of the two Phrygian provinces; all these temples were apparently still open and the hearts of pagan communities who sent delegates to an annual gathering at the shrine near Tralles as late as the sixth century.

The long survival of paganism need not necessarily disprove the validity of Pliny's observations. It is perfectly possible that Pliny and the *Acts of the Apostles* have a true core and that Christianity very rapidly gained a significant number of followers. There is no doubt that there were numerous elements in the new religion, which made it very attractive: the promise of an afterlife, mutual love and charity, the appeal of the secret and forbidden etc. Even the severe laws would hardly have formed a sufficient deterrent. Converts did not necessarily risk their lives as in most periods of Roman history Christianity was not systematically persecuted. Before the episodes of large-scale persecutions between the mid-third and early fourth centuries the risk of denunciation was presumably quite small. Acquittal was always guaranteed if one simply renounced one's faith and performed some formal pagan rituals as, indeed, many did during periods of persecution. Surely, acquittal in such circumstances was bought for the price of possible eternal damnation, but even this was no worse a prospect than one would have faced if not converting to Christianity in the first place; and some of the repentant fallen Christians were even re-admitted into the church. Even if there was incontrovertible evidence that a person was a Christian or even in case of a confession to such 'guilt', it was still possible to renounce one's faith and go unpunished and, indeed, the authorities sometimes pleaded with Christians to do so. The risk was thus not boundless, and it was only a small minority of the most committed Christians (and by no means all of them) who were tortured to death. The physical risk for one's earthly life lay not in conversion, but in strong conviction; even if only some were prepared to die for their faith, this does by no means disprove that there could have been large numbers of Christians.

Yet could they have constituted the majority, in parts or all of the Empire, as Tertullian claims as early as the end of the second century? The North-African writer had good motives for exaggeration, yet, would he have committed the sin of telling a deliberate lie? If so, he could be sure that it was not easy to disprove his claim. As it would be impossible in a modern dictatorship, in which political opponents face torture and death, to carry out a reliable opinion poll of what part of the population opposes the government, so would it have been very difficult for anybody in the Roman Empire to conduct a survey of who was member of the outlawed religion. One even wonders whether Christians themselves normally knew what part of the population they constituted while meetings had to be conducted in house circles and a degree of secrecy was essential. It is, nevertheless, difficult to believe that Tertullian's claims are based on fact or even that he himself genuinely thought they were. Cornelius, the Bishop of Rome claimed, according to Eusebius's church history (6,43,11-12), that the church in the capital supported over 1,500 widows and other needy people in the year AD 251 (i.e. half a century after Tertullian). Adolf von Harnack (1924, 806), to whom we owe the first systematic compilation of evidence for the early spread of Christianity, has identified this as the most important statistic we possess for the first three centuries of church history. He estimates the Christian lay community of the city of Rome (described by Cornelius himself as 'extremely large and countless') on the basis of the number of widows at some 30,000-50,000, roughly 3-5 per cent of the city's population. Robin Lane Fox (1986, 268-9) shares this estimate, and considers it to be well above the imperial average. However, whether these figures are reliable and representative is very hard to assess, considering that they are unique. Furthermore, Cornelius had become Bishop of Rome in the immediate aftermath of the first Empire-wide persecution of the Christians, which might have reduced the size of the community to a committed core. There are, incidentally, no signs that the Emperor Decius's (AD 249-251) edict that everybody had to take part in a sacrifice or face severe punishment, involved the execution of more than a minute fraction of the Empire's population. This, however, merely proves that the number of committed Christians prepared to die for their religion (and some managed to hide) was comparatively small. The proportion of 'weak' Christians, some of whom were re-admitted if they showed genuine remorse, cannot be gauged from such a drastic measure.

Since positive evidence for the numbers of Christians may not have been available in Roman antiquity and certainly cannot be reconstructed today, we will have to concentrate on negative evidence as Pliny already had done; namely whether or not there are reliable indications for a decline in paganism, be it due to the spread of Christianity or to growing disaffection from pagan deities and irreligiousness.

Here it is worth examining the arguments of those who believe that paganism sank to insignificance for reasons other than Christian intervention, and largely already before Christianity had gained imperial support. It ought to be stressed that there is by no means universal agreement on this matter. The list of scholars who have argued for and against this proposition is long, and a detailed scrutiny of their views and arguments would go beyond the scope of this book. Frank Trombley (1993 & 1994), Ramsay MacMullen (1984 & 1997), Karl-Leo Noethlichs (1971 & 1986) and Robin Lane Fox (1986, 669), to name but four, have argued that paganism remained strong in the late Roman period and that a series of suppressive measures was needed to ensure Christian domination. They rely, in common with most other scholars who have examined this subject, to a great extent on written evidence whereas it is the aim of this book to evaluate what contribution the inclusion of the largely neglected archaeological evidence can make to settle the dispute (without, of course, trying to pretend that it is desirable or even possible to study the material remains in isolation from the documentary sources). There seems little point in compiling statistics to establish whether the belief in an early decline of paganism largely without Christian pressure or the reverse is currently majority opinion. It is clear, however, that both views are voiced frequently and with similar conviction. The proponents of the former opinion include, as we have seen, such well known and widely read scholars as Professor Grant and Professor Turcan. This is not to say that there is a uniformity of views amongst them. Grant believes that despite the general early decline of paganism the mystery religions, which promised individual salvation, were still powerful as were the deities concerned with the protection of the state. Turcan, by contrast, argues that mystery religions and the deities, which had proven to be unable to protect state or individuals shared the general collapse of paganism and makes an exception only for nature cults. Such a diversity of opinions, all claimed to be based largely on the written evidence, gives grounds to doubt as to whether inscriptions and literature taken on their own will ever have the capacity to unite scholars behind one accepted version of events.

Turcan, as we have seen, is convinced that pagan gods were already 'swept away' on the Rhine frontier during the first invasions in the third century. This refers presumably to oriental deities, like Mithras, Isis, Attis, Cybele and other gods and goddesses with a universal sphere of influence as opposed to local cults; a later passage (Turcan 1996, 336) makes clear that Turcan believes that stone, mountain, tree and spring cults held their ground. It is unclear from the context whether this was due to people losing their belief as a result of the 'turbulence of the first invasions' or due to the postulated departure of legionaries. Turcan's logic and factual basis for his claims are indeed difficult to follow. Since legionaries constituted, at a rough estimate, only a quarter of a per cent of the Empire's population (and only half of the army), though, obviously a somewhat higher proportion in Rome's frontier provinces, it seems hardly conceivable that they would have constituted the majority of the pagan community. Turcan is thus probably implying that the postulated departure resulted in a total breakdown of law and order and that people lost their beliefs as a result of this. Later he paints a vivid picture of the military disaster and the resulting hardship for the population. He concludes (1996, 336): 'For people no longer believed in gods who did not protect them . . .' His statement that legionaries abandoned their fortresses in the third century is, incidentally, hard to reconcile with the evidence. At least three, but probably all four, of the legions on the Rhine still occupied their old fortresses or new installations nearby in the first half of the fourth century. The sizes of garrisons are likely to have dwindled during the Third-Century Crisis (AD

A WORLD WAITING FOR CHRISTIANITY?

235-284/5) and were certainly reduced towards the end of the century. There were presumably shorter phases of temporary abandonment of individual bases, especially after the devastating invasions of AD 275/76. Nevertheless, the army was always able to re-establish control (with the exception of most territories beyond the Rhine and Danube which were abandoned for good). This is not to deny that the Third-Century Crisis was a terrible time for people living in the northern frontier provinces of the Empire, as shall be discussed below. Yet, that this would have automatically resulted in people losing their faith in the power of their old deities is no more than an unsubstantiated and unlikely assumption. Indeed, numerous parallels could be quoted for episodes in the history of Christian, Muslim or Hindu societies in the last millennium, during which devotees suffered terrible hardship as a result of war and war-related events. However, such catastrophes have hardly ever resulted in large numbers of humans immediately deserting their faith. The reverse is normally the case, and humans seek divine protection most desperately when their lives are at risk. Where is the logic in believing that Christianity could survive the most extreme periods of hardship unscathed, or even strengthened, while precisely the same phenomena should have led to the instant collapse of all pagan cults with the possible exception of nature worship? The answer may have to be sought in Turcan's own belief (1996, 340-1) that Christian theology was infinitely superior to anything else on offer to a person seeking religious fulfilment.

What then is Turcan's evidence for the postulated decline of paganism (except for the veneration of nature) in the second half of the third century? It is based on a survey of the epigraphic, iconographic and archaeological finds all over the Empire, not to mention the literary evidence (1996, 328), some of which we have already discussed here. This seemingly impressive body of evidence is used to reconstruct the developments. There was, according to Turcan, an irresistible and overwhelming rise in the popularity of the oriental cults in the Roman Empire, which reached their apogee in the Severan period (AD 193-235) only to descend into freefall in the second half of the century. It is true that inscriptions dedicated to oriental deities indeed reach their peak under the Severans and sharply decline thereafter. Yet, virtually the same observation can be made for inscriptions in general (**59**), the sole notable exception being milestones, which are increasingly often just manifestations of political loyalty to the reigning emperor. If inscriptions in general first rise in number and then sharply decline then this is certainly evidence for a major cultural change, but is it evidence that the oriental religions or paganism as a whole was in decline? The argument is as flawed as it would be claim that the age of cathedrals in the high Middle Ages marks the apogee of European Christianity as opposed to periods of religious doubt and crisis before and after – or that today the religiosity of a country can be measured in the number or scale of religious monuments recently erected, totally irrespective of the economic resources and

THE ARCHAEOLOGY OF RELIGIOUS HATRED

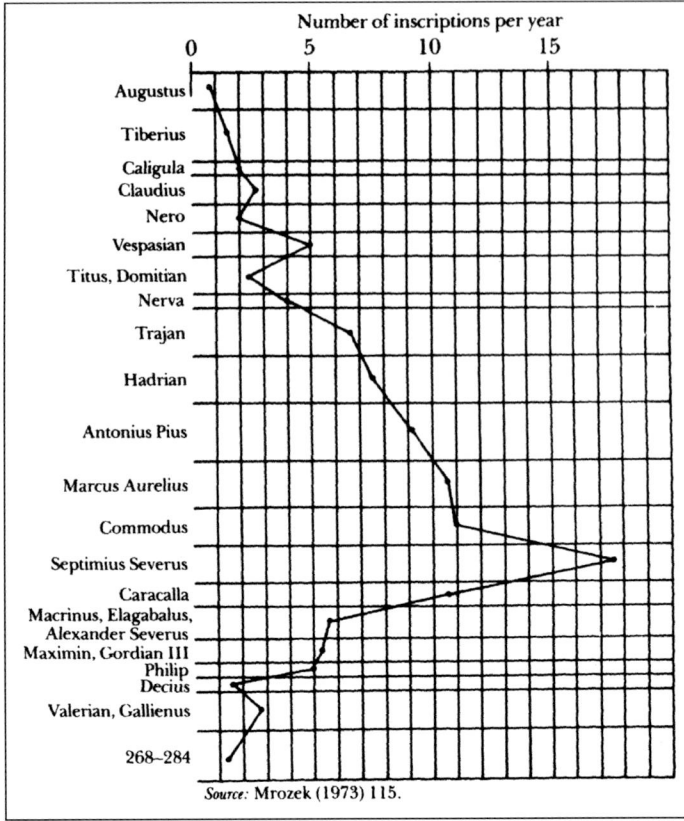

59 The Polish scholar Stanislaw Mrozek recognised that there were substantial fluctuations in the number of Latin inscriptions per year dedicated in different periods. Under emperor Septimius Severus (AD 193-211) this habit reached its peak. The output of most types of inscriptions, not just votive monuments, declined dramatically in the mid-third century

irrespective of whether there is peace or war. There are, incidentally, still some fourth-century pagan inscriptions, such as an altar dedicated to the native god Erudinus in Ongayo in northern Spain, dedicated as late as AD 399. Yet, at least in the west of the Empire, such inscriptions have long ceased to be a reliable yardstick for the popularity of pagan deities.

There can be no doubt that a major change in the history of pagan culture occurred during the Third Century Crisis. Regional armies became increasingly conscious of their power to make emperors. A string of successful generals were proclaimed emperors only to have to fight against pretenders for the throne supported by rival units elsewhere in the Empire. These 50 years saw no less than 48 emperors and usurpers (excluding their co-emperors or probably fictitious personalities). The frontiers were again and again depleted of soldiers needed in civil war. Such weakness did not remain unnoticed by Rome's neighbours who easily broke through the weakened defences and helped themselves to whatever was worth taking, not only in the frontier provinces, but even in the central regions, some of them not affected by invasions for centuries. Besides the northern tribes which attacked territories ranging from Britain, Gaul, Germany, Italy, the Danube lands and Greece to the area of modern Turkey and even Spain and Morocco, Rome had a powerful and aggressive neighbour in the Persian Empire. This led to a severe economic crisis as manifested by a sharp reduction in non-defensive building and in the production of many non-essential items, such as samian ware (fine pottery with a slip in characteristic red colour, previously produced in abundant quantities). The precious metal content of the silver currency was reduced from *c.*45 per cent at the beginning of the crisis to around 2 per cent by AD 270. In the light of this monetary devaluation and the circumstances, the previously comparatively fair taxation system was increasingly substituted by local requisition, placing excessive burden on the population in the frontier zones which had already more than their fair share of suffering to bear. To make matters worse, parts or all of the Empire were affected by epidemics in the AD 250s and 260s. Archaeological evidence suggests that, for whatever combination of reasons, in eastern Gaul, for example, population density decreased, especially in marginal land. While one of the trademarks of Roman civilisation had previously been to establish settlements at convenient locations in the traffic network and without much regard to natural defences, numerous hills over the frontier territories and their hinterland in north-western Continental Europe were now used as hilltop refuges.

It can come as no surprise that in a time of such a catastrophic economic downturn and seemingly omnipresent risks for one's physical survival, people (even the few who still would have been able to afford making generous donations) lost the belief that there was much sense in erecting monuments, be they impressive buildings, works of art or stone inscriptions. Furthermore, financing such monuments tended to be the preserve of the wealthy; while the dedicators could include ordinary soldiers or successful craftsmen, inscriptions are hardly a medium which tells us much, if anything, about any trends towards greater or lower levels of religious dedication amongst the majority of the population. It is fair to conclude that the Third-Century Crisis marks, by and large, the end of private self-aggrandizement in buildings and stone inscriptions. Yet, this equally affected religious monuments and secular utilitarian undertakings. Here lies Turcan's fundamental error. He is right that there was a sharp numerical decline in both inscriptions and works of art produced after the apogee under the Severan emperors. However, since this decline affected religious and profane spheres alike, how can he be so confident that we are observing a decline in paganism rather a decline in the habit of monumental display? The inscriptions taken on their own do, of course, neither prove nor disprove Turcan's supposition; while psychological and economic changes would be sufficient to explain the decline in the dedication of monuments, we cannot exclude, one might argue, the possibility that this went hand in hand with the postulated widespread loss of pagan religious beliefs. Yet, a different field of research may allow us to establish whether Turcan's claim is merely based on shaky foundations, but is, nevertheless, a correct guess or whether it is wrong. It is the examination of the material evidence for temple visits and minor ritual acts. If people simply could no longer afford to dedicate stone inscriptions or works of art or no longer saw the point in leaving memorials for themselves in such an unstable and rapidly changing world, but still felt they depended on the support of their old gods, one would expect that temple visits continued throughout and beyond the crisis. Analogies with more recent crises indeed show that what we should expect, if religious devotion endured during such periods of destitution and despair, are not grand monuments and masterpieces of art, no headline events considered worthy of commemoration by the educated literary figures of the time, but signs of simple religious perseverance amongst ordinary people, detectable only by careful excavation if at all.

A good analogy is provided by the Thirty Years' War (1618-48). In southwest Germany, for example, no other event in recorded history had similarly devastating repercussions on the population. As a result of various related factors, some of them quite possibly very similar to the less well documented Third-Century Crisis in the Roman Empire, the population in some regions of central Europe was decimated to less than a third of pre-war levels. There was, of course, loss of human life as a direct result of combat and atrocities; worse, however, were the losses suffered as a result of epidemics while the population was weakened by hunger, since war often impedes the regular cultivation of fields. Prosperity and living standards plummeted to hitherto unimaginable levels. In the small village of Tamm in south-west Germany, for example, the church was burnt down and the poverty-stricken villagers assembled for many years in a windowless and roofless building whose repair they could not afford. Surely, any scholar who thought that religiosity can be measured in the number of religious monuments erected or aggrandized or in the number of works of art created during a given period would have as little difficulty in 'proving' a 'decline' in Christianity during the Thirty Years' War as a 'decline' of paganism during the Third-Century Crisis. The only difference is that there are vastly more documents dealing with the lives of ordinary people in the seventeenth century than there are in the third century. Such documents firmly disprove this theory in the case of the Thirty Years' War while scholars continue to maintain such a hypothesis based on the same weak arguments in the case of the Third-Century Crisis, safe in the knowledge that it cannot be tested against a representative body of written documents with relevant information.

While Turcan claims to have taken archaeological testimonies into account, in reality what he accepts as archaeological evidence is confined to the grand monuments already discussed. Coins found in temples, he argues elsewhere (Turcan 1984), referring specifically to those dedicated to the god Mithras, do not allow us to establish whether a temple was still used as such at the time of their deposition. Late pottery or other small finds do not feature in Turcan's treatises of the subject either. He thus excludes per definition all evidence which is likely to illuminate the scale of rituals associated with temple visits in the mid-third to fourth century. Essentially we thus have to ask ourselves whether or not Turcan is justified in excluding closely datable finds from the interior of temples, which do not carry purpose-made images or inscriptions associated with the specific cult in question; are his concerns that the acceptance of such objects as evidence could mislead well founded? Might small finds indeed have been deposited or lost when the building was re-used for a different purpose? Even if his cautious approach should be justified, it would not support his conclusions. If virtually all traces which we can reasonably expect to survive from rituals carried out within a temple are indeed inadmissible as evidence, then this does not prove an early end of paganism, but merely that we have no way of telling one way or the other.

Turcan's argument that coins from the temples of Mithras are merely re-deposited since their chronology does not mirror that of votive inscriptions deserves closer scrutiny. Turcan first voiced this view in 1979 and it has to be conceded that indeed most coin series known from temples of Mithras were un-stratified. Even then, however, a significant number of temples were known which had yielded considerable quantities of late coins. While a small number of late coins in the odd temple, particularly in urban contexts, could conceivably be re-deposited or derive from some profane re-use, the presence of numerous late coins in a large proportion of temples in Gaul and the Danube lands, urban and rural alike, certainly would have sounded a note of alarm against such an interpretation in the mind of any scholar with basic understanding of statistics and with knowledge of the ancient monetary economy. What was to be expected has been confirmed in the light of recent and more careful excavations. Many mithraea have yielded a high number of coins, most of them minted between the mid-third and the second half of the fourth century (**colour plate 19**), and the idea that such an exceptional concentration of coins in small buildings could be a post-abandonment phenomenon occurring coincidentally in a series of ruined temples over extensive territories at the same time is too absurd to merit serious consideration. There is in any case no parallel for any type of profane building of similarly small size, which has yielded large numbers of coins in a comparable proportion of cases. These coins can only be interpreted as firm proof for continued offerings by Mithraic communities. Stratified coins even prove that temples were constructed and modified as late as the AD 360s (as shall be further discussed below). Late pottery, as published from the interior of some temples, such as at Septeuil and Mandelieu in Gaul, further invalidates Turcan's scepticism. Turcan's claim, echoed by other scholars, such as Ladislav Vidman (1977) and Luther Martin (1989), that Mithraism collapsed on itself and was dead well before the end of the fourth century, is a prime example of misinterpretation. It is the result of an unwillingness to engage with unfamiliar methodologies and categories of evidence where they stand in the way of preconceived ideas.

It would be wrong to assume that material evidence allows us to trace the 'rise and fall' of ancient paganism with mathematical precision. Stone buildings are easier to detect than wooden structures, and statistics are thus biased towards prosperous periods when the largest number of temples were built of durable materials. Rituals often change over time. The deposition of weapons reached its peak in the early imperial period while the custom of coin offerings was most widely practised in the late Roman period, at least in the north-west of the Empire. Small-scale or old excavations are particularly prone to have missed late phases during which a temple was in use. Not every period during which a temple was visited need have involved the loss or deposition of datable artefacts anyway. This is particularly true for the fifth, sixth and seventh centuries when, as we have seen, according to the biographies of saints still a number of temples attracted religious visitors while virtually no easily datable objects of lower value and made of non-perishable materials were in circulation in north-western Europe making it exceptionally difficult to trace any continued ritual activity in those late centuries. Despite all these caveats, at least during the period of a rich material culture, i.e. until the late fourth century, a careful scrutiny of the archaeological evidence is our best hope to gain a realistic idea of the developments.

Unfortunately, most of the well excavated pagan shrines are located in the north-west of the Empire, while most of the passages in classical texts and church literature on the spread of Christianity refer to Mediterranean provinces. This renders it difficult to compare and contrast written and material evidence. Do Pliny's almost abandoned temples comprise all shrines in his province? Were developments in neighbouring territories in Asia Minor similar, such as those visited by St Paul in the previous century? In this case we have to assume that Christianity after an almost explosive initial success suffered a substantial backlash later from which it had not yet fully recovered as late as the sixth century. This seems unlikely, and it seems more plausible that Pliny, who probably exaggerated anyway, thought mainly of public cults, which may indeed have lost popularity with the masses. Or should we indeed assume that even rural shrines were almost abandoned in the early second century only to flourish again by the AD 540s? Archaeology might be able to provide the answer in the future, yet as far as Asia Minor is concerned, the architectural and art-historical bias of many past excavators has led to the destruction, non-recovery or non-recording of crucial evidence in the majority of instances. Firstly, excavations mainly focused on major urban centres, more likely to yield art-historical delights than on peripheral rural sites. To quote Stephen Mitchell (1993, 16): 'Archaeology has virtually nothing to say about rural shrines in Anatolia, for none has been excavated.' Even though this is no longer strictly true, there is, to my knowledge, virtually no published information on how long rural sanctuaries remained in use. Can the magnificent urban Greek and Roman temples known to tourists of western Turkey give us at least some idea of the developments? Here again we find that the majority of lavish publications of the architecture of these monuments lack any information on small finds. Much effort has been devoted to establish a chronology of phases of construction of these temples, based on architectural style and, if available, inscriptions and literary evidence. Yet, pottery and coins which would have helped to refine this chronology and, more importantly in our context, give an idea of the intensity of usage during various periods of history after the original construction, were often not considered worth mentioning, if recorded at all.

A similar bias dominates publications, even recent ones, of the coinage from Asia Minor. Coins are mainly seen as isolated objects of historical and artistic interest, and the majority of publications focuses on those aspects or on the history of provincial coin production. The provenance of individual pieces is seldom indicated. Statements on the speed of Christianisation in any part of the ancient world where no representative sample of well excavated and published temples is available thus have to be treated with great caution. They may be consciously or unconsciously influenced by the assumption that a decline in number, scale or even architectural sophistication of pagan monuments constructed in a specific period directly reflects a decline in pagan religiosity. Such changes could, however, be solely due to economic changes, and do not prove that the masses were any less religious than before. Fortunately, much more attention is paid to small finds in recent excavations and once these will be published, we should have a much clearer idea as to whether paganism declined in Asia Minor quicker than in the north-west of the Empire with its multitude of well excavated temples.

It is, indeed, the north-west of the Empire where sufficient data are available to follow the changing intensity of various cult-related activities over the centuries in some detail. There, as elsewhere in the Roman Empire, paganism was not a static phenomenon. Some temples remained centres of worship from pre-Roman times to the Christianisation of the Empire, new temples were built and some old ones abandoned. In Gaul most Gallo-Roman temples in indigenous tradition were established in the first century BC or the first century AD (**60**). In the second century the number of new foundations seems to have dropped to less than half of first-century levels and in the third

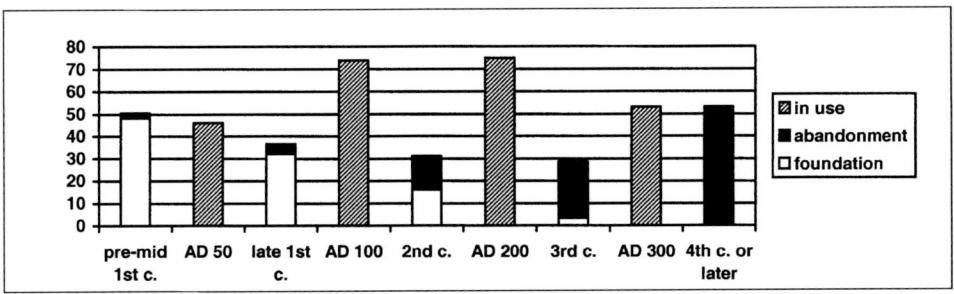

60 *Foundation, abandonment and use of Gallo-Roman temples in Gaul. The values are in per cent.*
Source: Fauduet 1993, 119-20

century to less than a tenth. This dramatic decline in the foundation rate in Gaul, interestingly, seems to mirror similar developments in Egypt. Is this evidence for the widely postulated decline in paganism or simply of public munificence? Might the number of sanctuaries have reached saturation point in Gaul by the second century, when the number of temples in use appears to have reached its peak? In the third century the number of foundations sank markedly, while the abandonment rate shot up. Yet, even during the third century less than a third of the temples in indigenous tradition visited at the beginning of the century had gone out of use by the end. The number

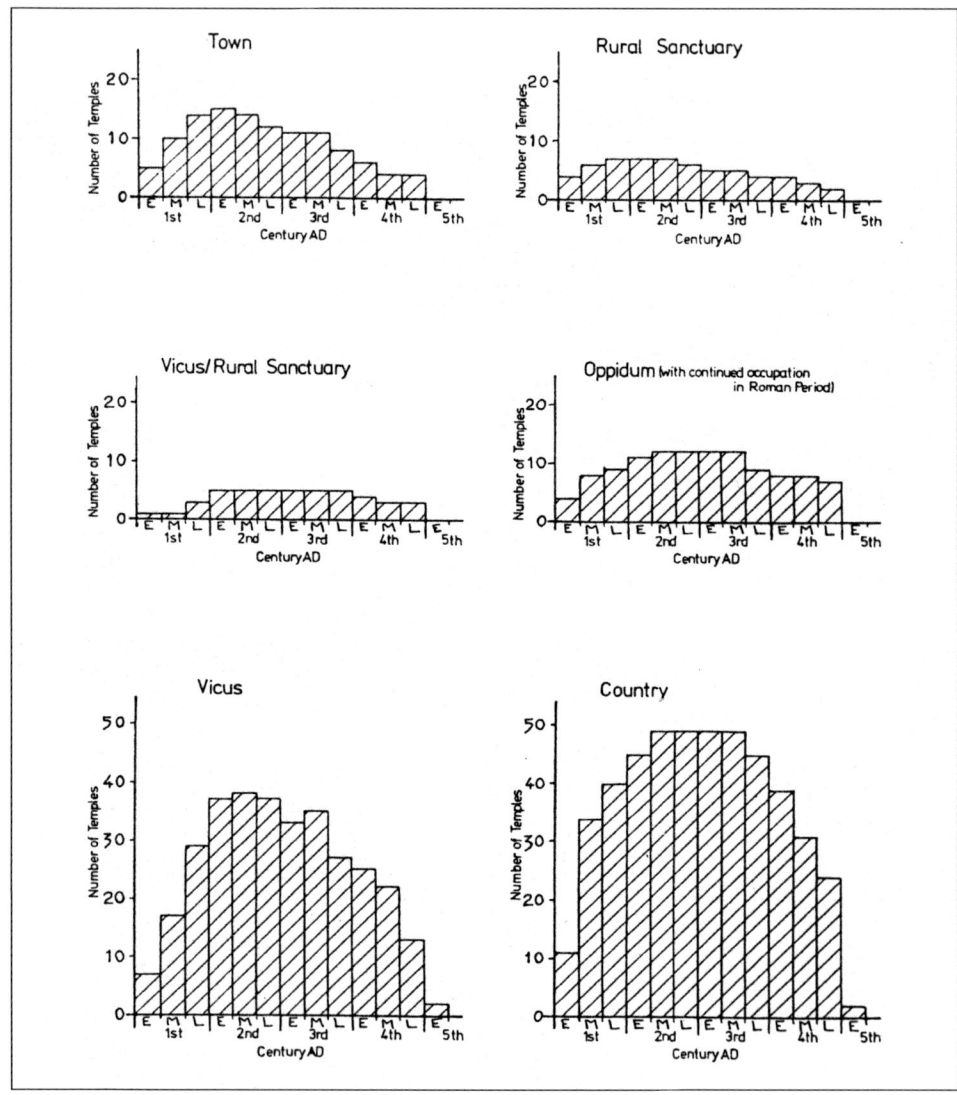

61 *The use of Gallo-Roman Temples in different periods in Continental Europe, according to their location. E = early, M = middle, L = late.* Peter Horne

of shrines visited in the countryside decreased more slowly than those in towns (**61**). Whether the general downwards trend indicates a decline in religiosity prior to Christian oppression of paganism is uncertain. It ought to be borne in mind that there are strong indications for a population decline in the third century. Karl-Josef Gilles (1987) has been able to show that, as far as hill temples in eastern Gaul are concerned, those in remote regions were abandoned while those in vicinity of the imperial capital at Trier, for example, still flourished in the first half of the fourth century. In the later AD 340s coin deposition at a series of temples in Trier itself and in its surroundings declined much sharper than coin loss at secular sites, an observation which Gilles plausibly explains with the increasingly anti-pagan policy of the sons of Constantine. However, the coins prove that most temples in this area again attracted pilgrims in the period of religious tolerance in the AD 360s and 370s and many even beyond. In Roman Britain the peak period of temple use falls, remarkably, even later than in Gaul, namely in the middle of the fourth century (**62**). The fourth-century peak is particularly marked in rural shrines while the period when most urban temples were in use had been in the century before. That Britain forms a special case, not only in its particularly late pagan peak, but also in a seemingly gentler and less destructive transition from paganism to Christianity, has been pointed out above.

On the whole, it would probably be true to say that all over the north-western provinces of the Empire temple construction and the dedication of stone inscriptions and images had declined markedly well before the Empire had turned from pagan to Christian. Undoubtedly, this reflects the end of a period of ostentatious monumental display which affected not only religious, but also secular buildings. To argue that this proves a decline in religiosity is like arguing that people in the Iron Age had been less religious than in the first and second centuries, since we know fewer Iron Age than Roman temples. The number of shrines in use decreased in most areas during the third century, but at a much slower pace than new foundations. Whether economic and demographic developments fully account for this phenomenon, or whether there was indeed some moderate decline in pagan worship, is impossible to establish. It is, however, remarkable that the majority of those temples which survived the changes of the third century continued to be visited for much of the fourth century and, to judge by the quantity of datable artefacts, pagan ritual activity was on the whole as vibrant in the first three quarters of the fourth century as it had ever been. Pilgrims tenaciously continued to visit their rural shrines, people threw coins into sacred springs in undiminished and often even increased numbers and many Mithraic temples flourished often right until the time when they and other destructible religious sites met their violent end or were emptied of their religious inventory in the late fourth century and thereafter. A comprehensive approach which takes into account the large-scale deposition of coins at religious sites in the fourth century, corroborated by the recurring theme of pagan resistance in the biography of saints, leaves no doubt that popular pagan belief was alive and well when iconoclasm struck. Counting pagan inscriptions and works of art per century may suggest otherwise, but only to those who fail to see the difference between a decline of belief and a decline of a culture of privately financed monumental display.

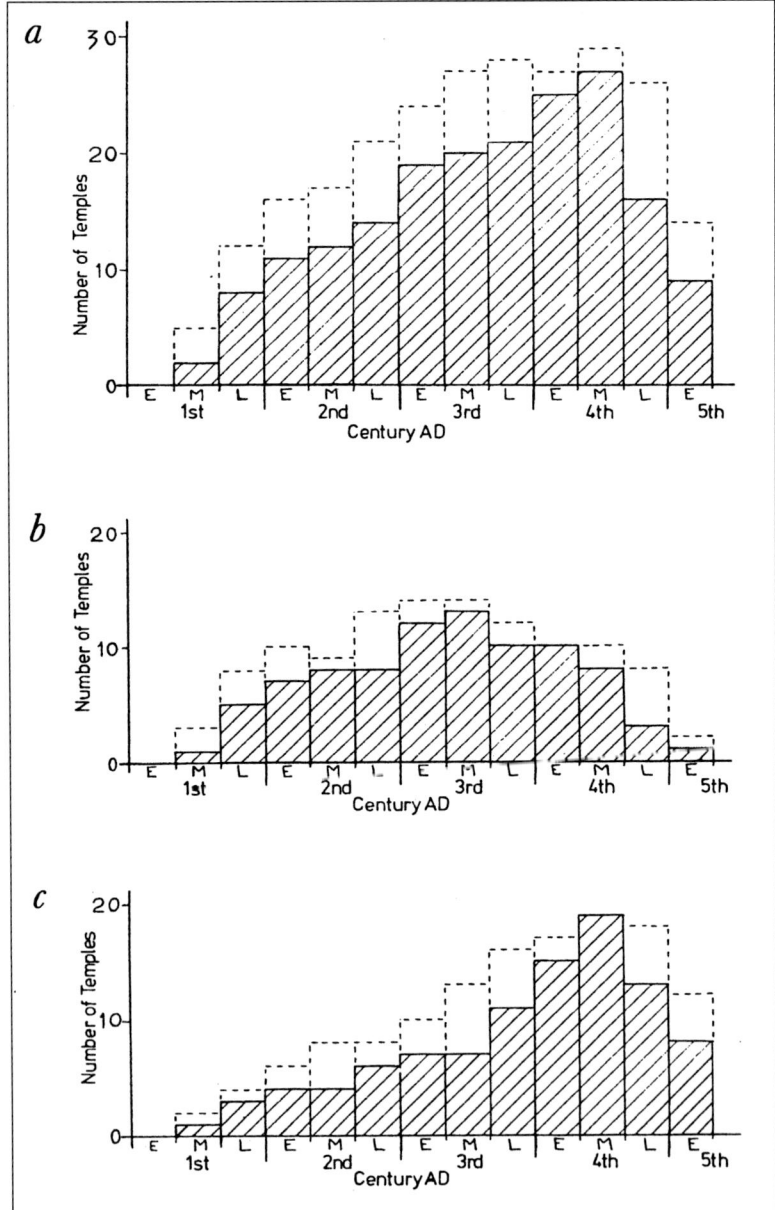

62 The use of Gallo-Roman Temples in different periods in Roman Britain. a: all, b: in towns, c: in the country. E = early, M = middle, L = late. Dotted line = possible. Peter Horne

11

AFTERLIFE AND ORIENTAL CULTS: SERIOUS COMPETITION FOR CHRISTIANITY?

Not every aspect of Roman paganism was necessarily as attractive as those Christianity had to offer. There is no need to go as far as Turcan (1989, 337) who praises the superiority of Christian theology, both from the point of view of the individual and the state:

> Never had any of the religions of ancient Africa or Asia, even when they were hand in glove with the imperial cult, benefited from a theology so effectively coherent and appropriate to the conflicting demands of humanity, but which also singularly matched those of an absolute monarchy and God-given right as the Christian Empire.

It is not the purpose of this study to examine the widely discussed subject of how well suited Christian theology was to the demands of an absolute monarchy. The claim, however, seems somewhat doubtful if we think of the numerous and often contradictory doctrines which have been based on the Bible and the conflict between papacy and worldly rulers which emerged in later centuries; no question that the authority of any priest was superior to that of the emperor who himself was supreme priest (*pontifex maximus*) responsible for public religion had ever arisen in pagan Rome. Turcan's former claim that Christianity had been better suited to the demands of humanity than any other eastern religion is no more than opinion. Undoubtedly, it would be possible to find representatives of every living religion who would make similar claims about the superiority of their own religion without any objective way available to us to pass judgement on the (mutually exclusive) validity of such claims. The eastern mystery religions or Roman paganism as a whole have, of course, no longer any representative to speak for them.

While it is an academically futile exercise to assess the comparative merits of different religions, most would agree that elements in different religions and philosophies differ in their attractiveness. The shadowy world of Hades will hardly have had the same mass appeal as the Christian promise of paradise.

Yet, one of the reasons for the success of Roman paganism was its openness. Those dissatisfied with the prospect of descending to Hades or other gloomy religious or philosophical notions of what, if anything, was to come after death, had the option of joining an eastern salvation religion without any need to abandon their other traditional practices. The individual could freely combine deities, beliefs and ritual practices of the most diverse origins. The system was dynamic, retained attractive traditions while abandoning unattractive ones, and remained relevant by constantly adding new elements depending on the demands of the time. Pliny's observations that some pagan ceremonies as well as visits to some temples were in decline need not necessarily signal that paganism as a whole was going downhill. His formulation does not make clear whether all temples had been almost abandoned or perhaps no more than some prominent examples. It is quite possible that some public cults lost ground, yet this could have been the result of a shift to other forms of pagan worship. The elements of paganism which register most prominently in the archaeological record in the later fourth century are rural sanctuaries, including natural places of worship, such as a sacred springs. These must have been deeply rooted in local consciousness and, presumably, gave people a sense of being connected with the landscape and the divine forces thought to inhabit it.

Another religion which features strongly in the later fourth century was Mithraism. While mithraea with sizeable deposits of late coins cluster in an area stretching from eastern Gaul to the northern Adriatic and adjacent territories east of the Alps, it was probably not just a regional phenomenon, but the result of a more thorough archaeological investigation of those areas. Votive inscriptions of the later fourth century for Mithras are in any case also known from Rome, Constantine in Algeria and Sidon in Lebanon. Dedications from Naples and Lavinium in Italy probably date to the same period. Late coins attest the continued use of mithraea in Rome, Hawarte in Syria and, possibly, Sofia in Bulgaria. In numerical terms mithraea are, nevertheless, infinitely fewer than rural sanctuaries dedicated to other deities. Yet in terms of the high relative proportion of the temples of Mithras, which were still visited in the late fourth century, they feature no less strongly. The question thus arises what Mithraism had to offer which ensured that its sanctuaries remained vibrant centres of cult long after secular opportunists had lost any incentive to join the cult. It is difficult to tell whether the widespread late popularity of Mithraism, in much of the northern provinces at least, was a phenomenon peculiar to this specific cult or whether it might have extended to some other oriental cults. Far more well excavated mithraea are known than sanctuaries in use by any other eastern mystery religion. There are signs that the cult of Isis still held ground in fourth-century Germany, for example, but there is insufficient data to tell how widespread her worship was then, and how long it continued.

The cult of the enigmatic god Jupiter Dolichenus, by contrast, who had a higher proportion of soldiers amongst his votaries than any other eastern religion, seems to have largely disappeared in the third century with the possible exception of Rome itself (at least on the basis of our present knowledge). We do not know what the god had to promise to his devotees to attract a following spread all over the Empire, since no document shedding deeper light on the theology has come to us (except for a few vague hints provided by inscriptions), and thus it is difficult to be certain about the reasons for its possible early disappearance. Tóth's (1973) view that the emperor Maximinus Thrax (AD 235-38) was responsible for a significant degree of destruction since several temples end with coins of the AD 230s seems doubtful, since there is clear evidence for a continuation of the cult thereafter, and it is difficult to see why such a measure should have been limited to some provinces only. The absence of coins of the AD 240s or 250s is, incidentally, not necessarily proof that a temple was abandoned before then, since few coins of this period reached some of Rome's frontier territories. Speidel (1978, 74-5) contemplates the possibility that the temporary capture of the god's hometown at Doliche (Dülük in modern south-east Turkey) in the AD 250s by the Persians might have dealt the final death-blow to the cult. The end of a geographically widespread religion in the Roman Empire as a result of the misfortunes of one particular site would, however, be without parallel, as far as I am aware, and Speidel himself considers it as no more than a working hypothesis. The fact that a large proportion of Jupiter Dolichenus's known sanctuaries was located in territories abandoned between AD 250s and 270s makes one wonder whether our database is sufficient, and I would not be surprised if in future a sanctuary was found west of the Rhine or south of the Danube which provided evidence for continued use into the fourth century.

To what extent we can base a judgement on the strength of individual cults on a few isolated references in late Roman sources or the absence of them is open to debate, yet, on the whole the impression is that Isis features more prominently than Mithras while Jupiter Dolichenus does not feature at all. While it thus would be daring to claim that all oriental cults shared a similar fate (and there is no space to examine all of them here), it is still interesting to ask what had made some of them so popular in the first place and ensured that at least the Mithras and Isis cult still appear to have been strong during the first few decades of Christian rule.

All of the oriental cults originated in or were based on models from the East of the Empire. Our knowledge about their theology is limited to the odd passage in literature, divine qualities and interventions summarised in a few keywords on inscriptions and the often encoded messages provided by works of art. Not even for a single cult do we possess anything near a complete and coherent treatise of the belief system. One of the better-known cults is that of Isis, and particularly famous are the words the Roman novelist Apuleius makes the Egyptian goddess speak to Lucius, the fictional hero of his *Metamorphoses* (11,5-6) during a nightly apparition. The goddess concludes her divine revelations to the prospective initiate into her mysteries with the following words:

But you will be a happy man, you will have my protection and live in glory, and when, after the end of your pre-determined lifetime, you are brought down to the dead, you will even there, in the subterranean hemisphere, frequently worship me, whom you see now, as the one who is kind to you, as the one who shines over the darkness of the Acheron [the river flowing around the edge of the underworld] and who rules over the [river] Styx in the innermost part of the underworld while you will live in the Elysian Fields. Because if through unremitting obedience, devout services and persistent purity of morals you will have gained the favour of our divine majesty, then you will know that I alone have the power to preserve your life, even beyond the length of time fixed by your destiny.

It is no less than eternal life in the Elysian Fields, the classical pagan equivalent to the paradise, which was on offer to the Isis devotee, a prospect which did not fall short of the afterlife promised to Christians. The belief in bodily resurrection of those judged to be worthy of it had a long tradition in ancient Egyptian religion, as is shown by texts, art and burial rites, notably mummification. Isis, who resurrected her murdered brother and husband, the god Osiris, and restored him to eternal life, was one of the key deities in the Egyptian belief in an afterlife. While all oriental religions which spread in the West of the Roman Empire underwent a substantial transformation incor-

63 *Subject to an axe attack: the wall paintings in the Mithras temple under the Christian church of St Prisca at Rome*

porating elements of diverse religious (and sometimes also astrological and philosophical) tradition, they (or at least the better known ones) also retained core elements of the original religion and by no means just an exotic façade as some modern scholars mistakenly think. It can thus hardly come as a great surprise that the Roman Isis cult preserved what was probably the most attractive element in the old Egyptian religion, namely the belief in an afterlife.

The same is true for the cult of Mithras, which equally, despite reconstitution as a separate mystery religion and notwithstanding other changes in the theology, still preserved key parts of ideas of the afterlife in Persian and Indian tradition. 'And you have saved us by shedding the eternal blood' wrote the Mithraists on the wall of one of their temples in Rome. This mithraeum is now named after the church of Santa Prisca built on top of the former temple after it had been deliberately filled up with sand around AD 400. It is worthwhile to digress shortly from the subject of the afterlife to take a closer look at an incident of image destruction within the temple (**63**). The same wall, which carried this graffito, was later covered with a new layer of paintings depicting a procession advancing towards the sun god, Sol and Mithras. At some stage before the building was filled in, the sharp blade of an axe, about 14cm wide to judge by the photographs, mutilated the scene. The axe attack left deep marks on the bodies of several figures. Sometimes the target was narrowly missed, suggesting that the instrument was swung at considerable speed. Anybody with practice in using an axe for cutting wood

will know that it requires a level of experience to always hit a target just a few centimetres across without fail. The most forceful blows are most likely to leave a well defined mark in material which does not splinter or crack apart. As wall plaster is comparatively soft and the paint no more than a thin film on top of it, less vigorous, but sustained hammering at an oblique angle to the wall would probably have resulted in a more thorough and better targeted destruction. Yet, would it have been as satisfying for a person motivated by passionate hate? Indeed, in this specific example we are probably seeing the material traces of an eruption of hatred (whether built up or spontaneous) rather than of calculated and rational action. The later filling up of the temple and its replacement by a church are an entirely different matter. Images, made both of stone and stucco, including the central cult image with the bull-slaying scene, were equally attacked in a violent manner and smashed to pieces. As far as the wall paintings are concerned the heads of the sun god and of Mithras himself were undoubtedly amongst the main foci of hatred and bore direct hits. The light blue halos surrounding their divine heads were signs of sanctity they soon shared with Christian saints and Jesus himself.

Yet, the similarities between some of the Eastern cults, notably Mithraism, and Christianity, were not confined to artistic symbolism. Here we come back to what the votaries had written on the wall of the temple. The above-mentioned graffito did not spark the eruption of violence. In fact, since it was written on the earlier layer of wall plaster, it would have been concealed at the time of the attack. Yet it provides us with an insight into the nature of the cult. Mithras was considered to be a personal saviour. The eternal blood spilled must undoubtedly refer to Mithras's great act of salvation, the slaying of the divine bull. The death of this divine being is as central in temples of Mithras as the crucifixion much later in Christian churches. The son of God equally had to spill his blood to save humanity; salvation required in both cases the bloody sacrifice of a divine being, the main difference being that in Mithraism the saviour and the victim were two different deities. This act of salvation is commemorated in Christianity with Holy Communion. On the testimony of the Christian writer Justinus (1,66), the same rite was practised in the Mithras mysteries, using bread and a drink of water (instead of wine). He specifically stresses the essentially identical nature of the ceremony in Christianity and Mithraism. Three separate cult reliefs from the first mithraeum at Frankfurt am Main-Heddernheim (**18**) and from Ladenburg in Germany as well as from Konjic in Bosnia (**64**) allude to such a sacred meal. The one from Konjic represents the votaries of different grades with drinking horns and four small loaves of bread on a table. The two German reliefs depict Mithras and the sun god taking the holy meal themselves, both of them showing loaves of bread and grapes. The Ladenburg relief shows in addition both deities holding a drinking horn. This implies that the sacred meal included bread and wine as its two essential components, just as in Christianity. In all three cases either the

64 *The sacred meal in the Mithras mysteries involved the consumption of bread loaves (on the table) and of a drink, probably wine or water. (The votaries hold drinking horns.) Cult relief from Konjic in Bosnia*

slain bull or its skin is depicted. Tertullian in a context, which almost certainly refers to Mithraism, even associates the offering of bread with the idea of an afterlife. Other images of the bull-slaying scene show ears of grain growing out of the tail of the dying divine bull or even out of the stab wound, undoubtedly symbolising that life comes out of death, out of the act of salvation performed by Mithras. This is closely mirrored in the Persian and Indian tradition where equally the slaughter of a divine bull, even if in the early texts not associated with Mithras, results in the creation of new life. It is commemorated by the consumption of an intoxicating liquid, *haoma*. The parallels are far too close to permit any doubts that Mithraism inherited essential parts of its notion of an afterlife from the East.

There is no space here to discuss in great detail the treatise by Richard Gordon (1975), which is erudite yet unconvincing in this specific respect. Gordon was able to show that the Belgian scholar Franz Cumont, whose views had dominated research into the cult of Mithras for several decades, had strongly overemphasised the oriental elements in the Roman form of Mithras worship. Yet he succumbed to the temptation of going from one extreme to the other. Instead of an exclusively oriental cult, Mithraism was suddenly an exclusive Western creation with no traceable elements of its Eastern origins surviving in the theology. Gordon was undoubtedly right that Mithraism as a mystery religion was a newly created cult which incorporated elements of diverse origin, though it was by no means necessarily founded in the West of the Empire as he believes. When Gordon discussed the passages in Justinus and Tertullian, and claimed that there could not be any connection between the consumption of *haoma* in the Eastern religion of Zoroastrianism and the sacred meal in the Mithras mysteries, no mention was made of the above-mentioned works of art. Yet in both Eastern tradition and in the Roman Mithras mysteries the sacrifice of a divine bull is a central element of the theology, in both cases life springs from this act of salvation, and in both cases this was commemorated with a sacred meal involving the consumption of an intoxicating liquid. By denying that there is a connection Gordon undoubtedly overshot his target. Gordon's idea (1975, 245 no. 119) that Mithraism was invented only in the second century has, incidentally, been disproved. The latest research at Doliche in Commagene (in modern south-east Turkey) has revealed a typical temple of Mithras in use by the early first century, if not before. This might provide the missing link between East and West as first correctly pointed out by the Canadian scholar Roger Beck (1998). It is precisely because Christianity did not have a monopoly on the promise of salvation and heavenly life after death that Eastern mystery cults, notably those of Isis and Mithras, were serious competition, even though the exclusion of women put Mithraism at a major competitive disadvantage.

We have seen in the case of differential treatment of monuments dedicated to different deities in the mithraeum of Strasbourg-Koenigshoffen and in case of the early end of mithraea at Hadrian's Wall that occasionally Mithras seems to have been the object of particular hatred and either more intensive, exclusive or earlier destruction. There was more than one possible reason for this occasional 'special treatment': the 'devilish' similarities observed by Justinus and Tertullian, the competition in terms of the promise of an afterlife, the depiction of an outlawed animal sacrifice, and the dark windowless meeting places probably gave rise to suspicion. Nevertheless, the widespread fear in the late Roman period of secret rites and evil magic was probably not the main factor since Mithraism, to judge by coin evidence, reached its final peak precisely when the 'witch hunt' against those suspected of involvement in such black arts reached its climax under the reign of Valens (AD 364-78) and his brother Valentinian I (AD 364-78). In part this was mere superstition, however attempts to discover the future fate of reigning emperors via evil magic could, of course, be a real threat, since predictions might give potential conspirators the courage to act. It is in the spirit of the fear of such magical practices that the otherwise tolerant imperial brothers issued a law that anybody who conducted certain ceremonies at night, namely wicked prayers, magical acts or sinister sacrifices, should be executed. The law, issued in AD 364, pre-dates the final peak in coin deposition at many temples of Mithras and thus cannot have anything to do with their demise.

Other Eastern deities could equally attract intense hatred. At Sarsina, Italy, a series of cult statues belonging to the Isis and the Attis and Cybele cult were found fragmented in a particularly thorough manner. The imposing sculpture of the Graeco-Egyptian god Serapis, 6ft 1in (1.85m) tall while seated, had been hacked into over 300 pieces (**65** & **66**), the great mother goddess Cybele into 260 (**67**), excluding her head, neck and substantial parts of her body, which have never been found. Other monuments, which included two statues of Attis and probably both Isis and her infant son Harpocrates, fared little better. The architectural elements found with the fragments during building works in the 1920s suggest that they derive from a temple or two, though no finds are recorded which give any clue to the date of destruction. The extreme and purposeful fragmentation of the cult images with particular destructive energy concentrated on the heads and faces has, nevertheless, been plausibly attributed to Christians because of the thoroughness of the destruction. This interpretation gains additional credence if we consider the remote location of the site in a side valley in the north-eastern Apennines away from the main roads and invasion routes.

Notwithstanding such attempts at virtual annihilation of any traces of oriental deities, these examples are the exception rather than the rule. In most instances iconoclasm directed against Mithras, other oriental deities or indigenous or classical divine beings, seems to have been of similar intensity (even if the 'offensiveness' of some images, especially naked ones, could occasionally be an aggravating factor). This need not come as a great surprise. Written sources leave no doubt that violent intervention against pagan monuments stretched over centuries and that a multitude of individuals was involved whose knowledge (or lack of it) on individual cults will have differed. Furthermore, the Bible campaigned quite indiscriminately against all other religions since they were all in opposition to the one true religion. There could be no acceptable pagan deities, none which could be pardoned or granted kinder treatment; pagan image worship was just one phenomenon which demanded one response: complete annihilation.

Ultimately the oriental mystery religions and, indeed, most other forms of worship which depended on elaborate and destructible temples or images, were condemned to death. The most enduring forms of paganism were those which were invulnerable to iron tools and fire. The power of holy men against powerful natural phenomena, like rivers, springs, lakes, bogs, rock formations, hills or mountains which enjoyed religious veneration, was far more limited than it was against manmade votive objects, images or temples. While humanity has never created anything which is indestructible, major natural landmarks and phenomena could not normally be destroyed by the means of contemporary technology nor was there a desire to do so. St Augustine (*letters* 47,4) aptly points out that 'we [Christians] certainly do not refuse to enjoy the light of the sun, because sacrilegious persons do not cease to make sacrifices to it wherever they can.'

65 (Opposite) *Hacked into over 300 pieces: the fate of the god Serapis from Sarsina in Italy (here after restoration)*

66 (Above) *The god's mutilated head after reconstruction*

67 *The fragmented remains of the goddess Cybele from the same religious complex*

Individual sacred trees were the only widely venerated creation by nature which could be effectively attacked with the axe of the missionary. Examples for the felling of holy trees range from Gaul to Egypt. The ubiquity or remote location of numerous other indestructible religiously venerated natural phenomena made it impossible to control them effectively so that no pagan ceremonies could take place, and their sheer presence formed a permanent reminder of the pagan traditions and beliefs associated with them. Such magnets for pagan worship had to be accommodated into the new system for there was no way to annihilate this link with the past. Sacred springs, often re-dedicated to saints, were amongst the most enduring sites of pagan worship, which, in superficially Christianised or Islamised form, continued to attract visitors. Yet, enough is known about the persistence of spring and nature worship that it would merit a separate book, and it falls outside the subject of *The Archaeology of Religious Hatred*.

12
MONEY AND MITHRAISM

And Jesus said to his disciples: truly I tell you it will be difficult for a rich man to enter the heavenly kingdom.

(*Matthew* 19, 23)

This followed an episode when he had suggested to a wealthy admirer to sell his possessions and to donate the proceeds to beggars in order to have treasures in heaven. The wealthy man, as is well known, could not bring himself to make such a great sacrifice and went away still rich, but sad. It has often been stressed how many Christians in history have not heeded Jesus's advice either. Yet, considering human nature, it is perhaps more remarkable and seldom emphasised how many have. We have already seen that the ascetic movement gained a wide following in early Christianity. Amongst the multifarious chastisements Christian ascetics inflicted upon themselves was living in poverty. It is, of course, not always easy to tell whether biographers of holy men did not make them even holier than they were by using the usual stereotypes of the way saints were meant to behave. We may have our doubts whether St Germanus from Auxerre indeed asked for all the money in his travel purse to be given to the poor on his journey through northern Italy, trusting that God would pay him back one hundred-fold whatever he gave (as indeed he did through the agency of a rich family) to have even more money for charitable purposes. Yet, even allowing for some invented demonstrations of selflessness, the evidence for the lack of interest in acquiring non-essential earthly possessions amongst early Christian ascetics is overwhelming. The migratory lifestyle of saints like St Columbanus or the drive amongst certain monastic communities (including that of Columbanus) or hermits to settle in places where it was hard to live, whether in the desert or in densely forested mountain ranges, cannot be rationally explained with any interest in acquiring financial riches. Such domiciles were specifically chosen to shun the temptations of the world.

The non-materialistic aims were also reflected in the ways Christians dealt with temple property. During the above-mentioned wave of temple destruction in AD 402 at Gaza, Porphyrios cursed in a church service any member of the congregation who would dare to take anything out of the idols' temples for personal profit. If we can trust his biographer Mark (chapters 65, 69 & 70), he succeeded indeed in making sure that this occasion was not abused for personal enrichment by members of his congregation, even though he did not have the power and influence to bring the soldiers and foreigners involved in the destruction to act likewise. Severus, bishop on the western Mediterranean island of Minorca, proceeded similarly. The building assaulted was in this case a Jewish synagogue. The bishop enjoyed the support of a crowd, numerically superior to the Jews and burnt the synagogue in AD 417 to the ground. The bishop was content for all ritual objects to perish in the flames or to be buried under the rubble except for the holy books and the silver. The scriptures were recovered prior to setting the building alight, as they were sacred to Jews and Christians alike; the silver, by contrast, in order to be able to hand it back demonstratively to the Jewish community. No suspicion should arise that the deed had been motivated by greed.

That this was indeed the 'proper' way for a Christian to conduct himself when burning or smashing to pieces what was sacred to others, is confirmed by the north-African bishop and Christian thinker St Augustine (*letters* 46-47) even though St Augustine refers in this context to pagan temples only and not to synagogues. There was more to it than just arousing suspicion of greed; there was also the fear of contamination in case of any object, valuable or otherwise, dedicated to a pagan deity.

> If a Christian on a journey suffers from a need for nourishment, if he has been hungry for one day, two days or, indeed, many days, so that he has reached the stage when he can endure it no longer, if it then happens, while he suffers from such desperate hunger and knows he is about to die, that he finds food in an idol-temple at a place where there is no human being and where he cannot find any other food, does he have to die or may he eat from it?

This was just one amongst 18 questions, most of them on how to avoid contamination from anything pagan, which preoccupied the pious north-African estate owner Publicola so much that he felt he had to write a letter and seek the advice of the bishop. To take advantage of anything related to pagan cults was anything but a laughing matter. Even an emergency did not form an excuse as is confirmed by the bishop's response (*letters* 46-7): it was better for the Christian traveller to reject the food if he knew that it had been offered to a pagan deity, even if this meant certain death; only if there were doubts about whether or not it had been offered or if there was certainty that it had not (e.g. if it was left behind by other travellers) was is permissible to eat it in such an otherwise hopeless situation.

If even in such an emergency a true Christian should die rather than using anything sacred to a pagan deity for personal advantage, how much more did it apply to non-emergency situations where no Christian's life depended on taking possession of any pagan votive object. A passage in *Deuteronomy* (7,25-6) provided guidance here to St Augustine and his correspondent. It is written there that the carved images of pagan gods in the Promised Land should be burnt. The Israelites should not desire the silver and gold, which covered the wooden images; they must not take the metal or be trapped in evil, for it was an abomination to God. They should not bring such abominable pagan material into their house or they would be cursed themselves; instead they should utterly detest and abhor such cursed objects. St Augustine thought that this passage provided both ample justification for temple destruction and the theological foundation on how it should be done. It was not permissible for a Christian engaged in destroying temples, images or sacred groves to take possession of any votive object, since it should be obvious that piety and not greed was the motive of such laudable interventions. Even though St Augustine had no objections against communal or ecclesiastical re-use of items recovered from pagan sanctuaries, it is quite obvious that Christian iconoclasts were careful to avoid any possible accusation of greed.

If such a clear non-materialistic ideology underpinned Christian acts of destruction, might we be able to differentiate between the archaeological traces of pagan and Christian outbursts of violence by the amount of valuable items left behind? In summary: on the basis of the textual evidence it appears that committed Christian iconoclasts combined a zeal for destroying anything pagan as thoroughly as possible with a strong reluctance to take any temple property and, in particular, any items of value for themselves. As we have seen, it is a much more difficult question to decide the extent to which invaders engaged in temple and image destruction. Even if they should indeed have caused extensive damage to religious monuments, there is no good logical motive why they should have behaved in a similarly non-materialistic manner. Indeed, there is strong evidence to the contrary. One hundred and twenty-eight silver votive plaques, about half of them bundled up to facilitate transport, have been dredged from the River Rhine near Hagenbach. Inscriptions revealed that they presumably derived from a shrine dedicated to Mars in the south-west of Gaul, modern France. A second hoard, equally dredged from the Rhine, at Neupotz, also contained some votive objects besides numerous utilitarian items. Quite apparently they were lost by Germanic invaders as well, when trying to cross the Rhine with their booty plundered from both temples and secular buildings. Considering the wide range of objects in either hoard which include, in case of Neupotz, a high proportion of wagon parts made of iron, it makes little sense to speculate that we may be dealing with an offering to the river; but even if so, it would change little about they way the items had been acquired in the first place. There are no isolated examples for the theft of cult objects by enemies; a wide range of votive objects have found their way beyond the boundaries of the

Empire, sometimes cut up with an intention of melting them down. We may assume that a considerable part of such items have been pillaged from temples.

While there can be little doubt that invaders normally had materialistic motives and a significant proportion of Christian iconoclasts had not, we certainly must not conclude that every temple whose artwork suffered deliberate destruction while no valuable items were left behind was ransacked by enemies. A series of alternative explanations for the absence of valuable items present themselves:

- they might have been absent in the first place,
- they could have been ritually buried by the votaries themselves (whether or not they had reason to fear profanation), a common practice in antiquity or
- they might even have been taken by nominal Christians who took advantage of anti-pagan measures (as in the case of Gaza) or
- by Christians for communal purposes if this could be done without arousing suspicion of greed, not to mention the seizure of large temple treasures by Christian and already pagan emperors short of cash.

For all those reasons, it is impossible to draw any sensible and meaningful conclusion from the absence of valuable items. Highly significant, however, is their presence, especially if the temple was violently destroyed and if there is reason to believe that the items would have been visible at the time of the destruction.

Only a very minor proportion of cult centres ever contained, as far as we can tell, rich temple treasures and these were, for obvious reasons, neither overlooked nor left behind. Coin assemblages are, however, frequently found. These scarcely comprise a significant number of precious metal coins, but, in the majority of cases, exclusively or almost exclusively copper alloy coins or very debased silver pieces whose precious metal content amounted to no more than single-digit percentage figures. For this very reason little significance has been attributed to such 'small change' in most scholarly work on late Roman religion. The average diameter of the average late antique coin (obviously, with some variation) was similar to that of one Euro cent and smaller than a one-penny coin. Surely, common sense alone would tell that such a minute piece was worthless small change rather than a valuable item a plunderer could have been bothered to pick up?

The temple of Mithras at Mühlthal in Bavaria, for example, presented a scene of utter devastation after a violent intrusion, presumably not before the early fifth century. Besides scattered fragments of sculpture and inscriptions, in excess of 500 coins were left behind by those who had hacked the cult inventory to pieces. Can we be sure that they were Christians? Not if we follow the excavator, Jochen Garbsch. Garbsch (1985, 445) postulates that it is by no means beyond doubt that we are dealing with Christians: perhaps they were looters who came because they thought there was treasure to be found in the temple? Might their disappointment about the low value of the coins have manifested itself in unrestrained 'vandalism' (even if the substantial force was need to break the altars)?

The assumption that such coins would not have been worth collecting is shared by Richard Gordon (1999, 687):

> Of course there are some cases in which violent destruction of a mithraeum by Christians is the likeliest explanation – though, in the case of, say, Mackwiller or Sarrebourg, the extremely low intrinsic value of the coins found might just as well be taken to suggest that the Alamanni, Franks or whoever could not be bothered to collect them as that Christians scorned pagan offerings.

While Gordon cited coin assemblages in different Mithraic temples, there was little difference between them and Mühlthal in terms of average intrinsic (i.e. metal) value per piece.

Yet, Gordon and Garbsch and, indeed, several other scholars who stress the low value of such late Roman base metal coins appear to argue solely on the basis of gut instinct and, in any case, offer no evidence whatsoever that these coins were indeed as worthless as they claim they were. In antiquity, it ought to be borne in mind, the value of coins closely corresponded to the metal they contained. The Roman state never had any lasting success on the few occasions when it tried to force the population to accept coins at an artificially inflated value (unless it was merely by a small percentage). This is in complete contrast to our own time when the value of means of payment, notably banknotes, is merely confidence-based and can exceed their material value by more than a thousand-fold. This observation may, at first sight, seem to add strength to Gordon's and Garbsch's views. We have seen that the majority of these pieces consisted of nothing more than base metal and were worth no more or, at least, not significantly more than their raw material. Yet, the cardinal error of Gordon is the implicit assumption that the copper was of similarly low value at a time of manual extraction methods and very high demand as it is today.

The value ratio between different metals in antiquity is well known. A law (Theodosian Code 11,21,2) issued in AD 396, in the same decade when temple visits had been outlawed, informs us that minted gold was 1,800 times more valuable than raw copper. No figures are available for the weight of the pieces found in the mithraeum at Mühlthal, but, since the weight and metal proportion of Roman coins tended to be fairly standardised, we can calculate the total weight of the 570 pieces at roughly 1.7 kg of copper or copper alloy and $c.16$ g of silver. (Silver was 125 times more valuable than copper and 14.4

times less valuable than gold at the time.) It is thus a simple calculation that the sheer metal value of the coins from the mithraeum amounted to as much as 2g of minted gold, a third more than the smallest gold denomination, the *tremissis*, which weighed merely 1.5g. Yet, how much was this worth? Two grams of minted gold were the equivalent to the pay and allowances of a soldier in the fifth or sixth century for the period of a fortnight. A manual labourer paid normal rates would have had to work for ten to twenty days (if being in the fortunate position of having constant employment) to earn that much. The same amount would have paid for the basic maintenance of a child for over five months. Few thieves today would deliberately leave the equivalent in modern currency behind. And this, it ought to be borne in mind, was the sheer metal value of the coins from the Mühlthal mithraeum. Furthermore, in the whole of Roman antiquity the value of copper never fell below one 1,800th of gold. Thus the above cannot possibly represent an overestimate; if anything the value of the coins from Mühlthal is slightly underestimated.

As a simple rule of thumb, we may assume that about 50 base metal coins of average dimensions found in late antique temples had enough value to pay for the maintenance of a child for one week, even if there were no pure silver coins (in Mühlthal there were three pure silver coins amongst 570) and if we disregard the silver content of the debased silver coins. The calculation is simple: we know that about 4.5g of minted gold paid for the maintenance of a child for a year and, at a ratio of 1:1,800 this corresponds to 8.1kg of copper. The weight of base metal coins found in a late antique temple varied considerably and could be as low as 1g, but was roughly 3g on average. (This is the average of the types represented at Mühlthal; the average amongst the 362 coins of the mithraeum of Mandelieu in southern France was 2.6g, but includes many pieces which have lost a substantial proportion of their weight as a result of corrosion.) Fifty coins thus equal roughly 150g, one 54th of 8.1kg and the 54th of the value of the money required to cover the basic needs of a child for a whole year. The 54th part of a year is just marginally less than a week. It thus does not require as many as 570 coins as at Mühlthal to allow us to argue that those who deliberately left the money behind had no financial interests. Even as few as 50 coins gives sufficient grounds to draw such a conclusion, unless we want to assume that the wealthiest members of society carried out the destructions unaided. It makes infinitely more sense to argue that the decision to leave money behind was borne out of religious conviction, the fear of contamination with cursed votive objects, and the fear of divine punishment.

Yet, there is one possible objection: if those responsible came not from within provincial society, but from beyond the northern frontier, they would not have been involved in monetary economy. However, the metal-value argument is no less valid. The systematic nature in which objects and coins made of all metals were collected during raids, as indicated by the deposits of Neupotz and Hagenbach, indicates strongly that metal was by no means

68 *The hack marks in the face of the rock-born Mithras from Septeuil near Paris attest to the violent end of the temple*

in lower demand in the unconquered parts of northern, central and eastern Europe. Those who lost the Neupotz deposit when crossing the Rhine had not considered it pointless to hoard base metal coins in addition to over 10kg of silver and over 400kg of other metals (excluding parts of wagons, probably used for transport); we cannot tell how many there were originally since the finds were dredged out of the Rhine during commercial gravel extraction and a disproportionate part of the small finds will have been lost. The very fact, however, that base metal coins were even present in the largest deposit of robbed metal ever recovered from the German frontier zone, suggests that copper was at least as valuable for Rome's northern neighbours as it was within the Empire.

The number of temples of Mithras where iconoclasts left large quantities of coins behind is impressive (**colour plate 19**). We have already discussed the cases of Sarrebourg and Mühlthal, but many others can be added: in the area of modern France there is Septeuil, a spring sanctuary transformed into a temple of Mithras around AD 360 (**colour plate 20**). Over 1,300 coins were found, the latest minted towards the end of the century; only the central parts of the central cult image survive, but neither the head of Mithras nor that of the bull. On the relief showing Mithras's birth out of a rock, the god's face is disfigured by a series of deep hack marks (**68**). In the mithraeum of Les Bolards, the whole cult inventory, images and altars alike, was shattered to pieces. Only a 55cm-long lion statuette (**colour plate 21**) and a 45cm-high small column decorated with oak leaves and acorns (**colour plate 22**) survived

THE ARCHAEOLOGY OF RELIGIOUS HATRED

69 *The heads and much of the bodies of Mithras and the bull have been crushed to powder or removed by the iconoclasts who attacked the inventory of a temple at Timavo in northern Italy*

unscathed. Was it because of the small size that the monuments were spared or rather because Christians could not see anything offensive in naturalistic representations of a wild animal and plants (in parallel to Dendara, for example)? Whoever it was, they left over 600 coins behind, the latest of which was minted in AD 393 at the earliest. In the administrative centre of Trier in modern Germany the images in a mithraeum fell prey to a violent attack while over 500 coins remained. Cult activity ended at some point after AD 394. At Rockenhausen there are equally traces of iconoclasm and a series of at least 55 coins running down to the last years of the fourth century was left in the ruins. In Martigny in Switzerland altars were smashed though stone images, if ever present, had been removed. As many as 1,261 coins were found, apparently deliberately deposited by the votaries in the nave. Ceremonies did not cease to be celebrated before AD 394 at the very earliest. In Linz, Austria, the cult image had been deliberately destroyed, yet 128 coins left behind, the latest again no earlier than AD 394. In Timavo, northern Italy, two bull-slaying reliefs were hacked into pieces and the heads of Mithras and the bull in either case removed or crushed until no recognisable parts survived (**69**). Three-hundred coins attest that those responsible had no financial motives and perpetrated their act of destruction not before the late fourth century at the earliest. In Konjic in Bosnia 91 coins attest that Mithras worship continued at least into the AD 380s culminating once again in a violent end. The town of Ptuj, Slovenia, contained no less than five known mithraea. One of these may have been abandoned at an early date and another one is insufficiently explored, yet the images of all the remaining three were thoroughly destroyed. We know that two of them have yielded in excess of 300 coins each, while the coin series in all three mithraea runs into the last quarter of the fourth century.

We need to exercise some caution in interpreting these findings since we do not always possess sufficient records as to where precisely within the mithraea the coins were found. Where information on the distribution of the coins is available, it appears that they were frequently widely scattered, presumably by the votaries themselves as offerings. Some coins could be buried in earlier layers if a succession of trodden earth floors built up (as, for example, the case at Martigny), but many, if not most, would have been visible at the time of destruction. It ought to be pointed out that fresh base metal coins by and large ceased to be supplied to the northern territories in the AD 390s. If a coin series ends with an issue minted no earlier than AD 393 or 394, we can only conclude that ritual activity came to an end no earlier than then, but quite possibly decades later.

It is not my intention here to give the false impression that mithraea invariably yield smashed sculpture in combination with large numbers of coins. A considerable number of temples dedicated to Mithras have yielded no coins or only a small number. Such temples cluster in particular in those territories east of the Rhine abandoned by Rome around AD 260 and in Britain where the cult appears to have enjoyed less broad support, never spread into the countryside and appears to have disappeared earlier than on the Continent. By contrast, in wide stretches of the Continent, from the central parts of modern France to the Alps and adjacent regions the majority of well excavated temples has yielded a substantial number of coins attesting to a vibrant cult even in the second half of the fourth century. Mithraism seems to have flourished particularly in the AD 360s and 370s, probably already under the pagan Emperor Julian (AD 360/361-363) and certainly under his tolerant Christian successors, notably Valentinian I (AD 364-75) and Valens (AD 364-78). Not only do coin finds of the Valentinianic period cluster in many Mithraea, even structural improvements were carried out: the temple at Martigny in Switzerland received a new mortar floor, some of the elaborate paintings in the recently discovered mithraeum in Hawarte, Syria (to be destroyed and built over by a church at the turn of the century) date to this period, even two new mithraea were erected: at Septeuil near Paris and at Constantine, Algeria. The only part of the Empire where there is firm evidence for widespread intervention against the cult prior to the last quarter of the century is Britain. All four known mithraea in the military zone fell prey to iconoclastic attacks: Carrawburgh, Housesteads and Rudchester on Hadrian's Wall in the earlier fourth century, and Caernarfon towards the middle of the century. While the mithraea in those territories beyond the Rhine and Danube abandoned by Rome around AD 260 must have ceased to function as temples (as, presumably, did the little known temples in Dacia, modern Romania), there is no certainty as to when precisely the artwork in these temples was destroyed. The only two temples in territories which remained under Roman control where we can prove extensive destruction prior to the last quarter of the fourth century are Mackwiller and Biesheim in eastern France. In Biesheim the destruction is not well dated, but, in any case, seems to be later than AD 270. In Mackwiller systematic destruction appears to date to the AD 350s. We cannot know whether this was the direct result of the devastating Germanic incursions, which affected the area in these years or whether committed Christians used the power vacuum to eradicate some visible manifestations of paganism. While a small proportion of Mithraic temples on the Continent suffered wilful destruction during the first two thirds of the fourth century, the vast majority of excavated temples, at least in those territories then still under Roman control, did not. Even the two temples whose artworks was devastated at an early date, Biesheim and Mackwiller, whether at the hands of Germanic invaders or Christians, were re-occupied and continued to receive coin offerings until the closing quarter of the century, a remarkable sign of the strength and persistence of pagan faith. It was only between the AD 380s or 390s and the fifth century that catastrophe overtook Mithraism, and the artwork in the vast majority of devastated temples was smashed then. Even though the first half of the fifth century was anything but a peaceful period, and major invasions affected most parts of the Empire, it ought to be borne in mind that there had been periods of large-scale invasion before. It can hardly be coincidental that the archaeological evidence for destruction on a hitherto unparalleled scale coincides precisely with the period from the AD 380s onwards when written sources also attest that the destruction of pagan art was, with increasing frequency, tolerated and soon even sanctioned, encouraged and actively supported by the imperial government.

It is worth stressing that by no means all mithraea were violently destroyed, and there are even many which have yielded numerous coins, but no signs of destruction. This, however, need not surprise us. Even if Christians were responsible for the majority of destructions, as all the indications seem to suggest, there was no well co-ordinated 'cultural revolution' throughout the Empire. When temples were destroyed in a particular region appears to have depended largely on the initiative of charismatic Christian leaders in the area.

The wealth of literary evidence for temple and image destruction as late as the sixth and seventh century proves clearly that not all of the immensely rich material culture of Roman paganism was hacked to pieces in the first wave, but that it was wave after wave over centuries, affecting some areas earlier and more thoroughly than others. Yet, it would be a fallacy to assume that those temples which have yielded numerous coins, but no artwork, attest that people voluntarily abandoned their religion as they had lost interest in it. When no stone monuments were left then this was probably in most cases the result of their careful concealment outside the temple, unless there is reason to believe that it could be the result of much later re-use of the stones. This implies that those who did it feared that the sacred monuments were at an acute risk of falling prey to an iconoclastic attack, that they still cared enough about their religion to undertake the laborious task to carry away the heavy monuments and that they did not commit the sacrilege of stealing the votive coins despite the fact that, as we have seen, they were not of negligible value.

Mithraism forms a good case study since the temples, often partially dug in the ground, are easy to identify as such. Yet, as we have seen, one does not get the impression that Mithraism, despite a few exceptions, suffered on the whole an earlier or more violent attack than other monuments of similar complex religious systems.

Furthermore, the practise of coin offerings seems to have been adopted by a very high proportion of Mithraic communities in central and eastern Gaul, Germany and the Alpine region by the fourth century. There is far greater variation in the case of sanctuaries in indigenous tradition, for example, where, depending on local cult practise, the ritual of coin deposition on the floor of sanctuaries was practised in the case of a few temples, but apparently not in the case of many others. It is thus far more difficult to establish whether or not those responsible for destruction had non-materialistic motives. Where coins have been found outside temples in votive pits or scattered over a wider area, it is normally impossible to establish whether or not those responsible for any destruction would have know about them. At Lux near Dijon in eastern France, for example, a small shrine dedicated to the god Mercury attracted worshippers at least until the year AD 392 when the series of 175 coins ends. No less than 25 stone monuments were smashed, the remains scattered and the temple, probably deliberately, burnt to the ground. Since 161 of the coins derive from a votive pit 9m east of the temple, we cannot be sure whether those responsible deliberately left them behind or simply did not know about their presence. It is the difference in ritual, namely the widespread large-scale deposition of coins within a limited space indoors, which makes the non-materialistic motives visible in the case of those who destroyed many Mithraic temples. The period and the modes of destruction seem to be strikingly similar in case of many temples dedicated to other deities, only large-scale coin deposition at visible places appears to be less common. It thus seems more likely that

70 *The offertory box immediately in front of the entrance to the Gallo-Roman temple at Crain in Gaul had been forced open*

mithraea are exceptional in that we can prove the non-financial interests of those who destroyed them, rather than that there was any difference in greed or lack of it between those who destroyed mithraea and those who destroyed most other temples in the late fourth or fifth century.

Despite the remarkable fact that coins were left behind in most mithraea in the north-west of the Christian Empire, it would be simplistic to assume that all Christian iconoclasts acted in precisely the same manner (if the theory is accepted that they were indeed responsible for the majority of cases). Undoubtedly, there must have been weak or opportunist Christians, as is confirmed by the above-mentioned case of temple destruction at Gaza (if reliable in detail). Even firm believers, such as St Augustine, could make a case for re-using temple property for the public good or whatever they saw as such. St Gregory, the 'illuminator', the founder father of the Armenian Church, is reported to have given the treasures found in a temple he destroyed to the poor. Whether or not the passage in the work of a later author who wrote under the pseudonym Agathangelos (chapter 134) is reliable, it certainly confirms that it seemed a perfectly acceptable course of action and probably not just in an Armenian context.

Interesting in this context is the fate of a small Gallo-Roman temple with ambulatory at Crain, some 120km west of Lux. An offertory stock buried outside the temple and near its entrance (**70**) contained 207 coins, ending with an issue of AD 186. The sculpture in the temple was once again violently destroyed and fragmented to such an extent that it was impossible to identify a single deity, though a broken spear probably belonged to a war deity, either Mars or Minerva. The fire-reddened sculpture debris and an ash layer on the temple floor suggest that here also iconoclasm was followed by arson. The small number of coins found within the temple (merely 11) does not allow any reliable estimate how soon or long after AD 367, the earliest possible date of mintage of the latest two, this happened, but it was presumably in the late fourth century or later (pottery seems to confirm the date). The procedure is strikingly similar to that observed at many other religious sites and the likely date of destruction in or after the late fourth century coincides with the explosion of Christian image destruction. Interestingly, in this case the votive money was not disregarded, and the offertory box was forced open. It consisted of heavy stone blocks and was almost entirely buried. This and its hour-glass-shaped receptacle (**71**) for coins made plundering a difficult task and probably accounts for the fact that over 200 coins were left behind, 90 per cent of them in the bottom of the 'hour-glass'. The perpetrators first hacked a hole in the top stone, they lifted it and eventually even tried (with little success) to enlarge the narrow passage between the two parts of the hour-glass-shaped receptacle. The coins were totally mixed, and the earliest and latest pieces occurred both, at the bottom of the receptacle and in higher layers. This suggests that the pieces were mixed up when the plunderers 'fished out' as much as they could. It seems inconceivable that all late coins could have been removed had they been present in any significant proportion. We have to conclude that offering

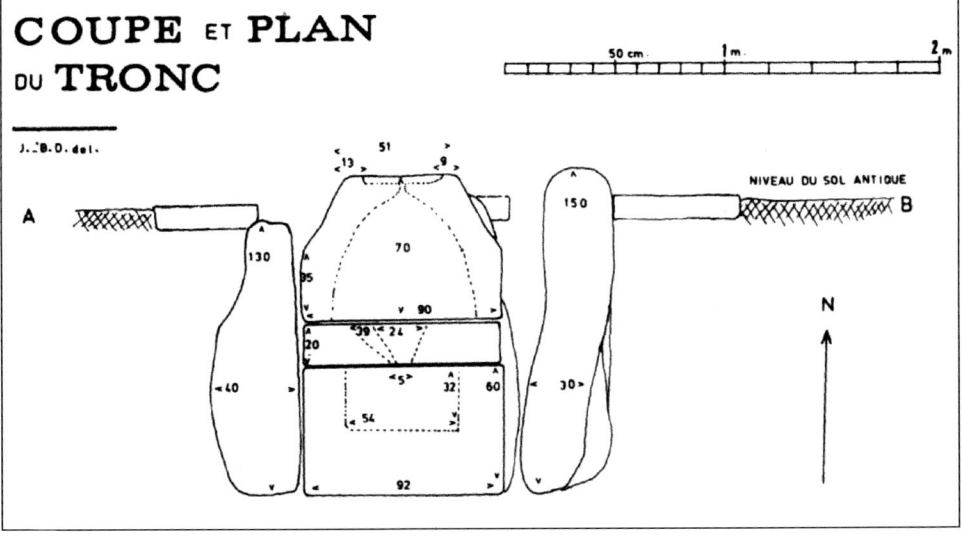

71 *Coins were inserted through a slot at the top of the interred offertory box. The hour-glass-shaped interior contained two receptacles for the donations*

came to an end in the late second century, two centuries before the temple was abandoned and destroyed. Maybe the offertory box had been sealed for ritual reasons in the late second century. This makes one wonder whether the plundering of the offertory box and the temple destruction are contemporary at all. Late pottery (though we do not know how late) mixed with the coins renders it likely that the iconoclasts or somebody else who took advantage of the situation robbed the votive money whether for personal enrichment or the 'public good'. The first- and second-century coin types were no longer in circulation in the fourth century, but they still retained their metal value. Base metal coinage (and there was not a single gold or silver piece amongst the 207 coins) was worth plundering even long after it had gone out of circulation. All we can conclude from the Mithraic example and other comparative evidence is that there was a tendency amongst Christian iconoclasts to leave temple property of smaller or medium value, up to the equivalent of several weeks work, behind. This applied presumably to cases of iconoclasm carried out in areas where paganism was still strong at the time in particular. Needless to say that there were exceptions to the rule, and Crain may well have presented such an exception.

13
CHRISTIANISATION AND BLOODSHED

There can be no doubt on the basis of the written and archaeological evidence that the Christianisation of the Roman Empire and early medieval Europe involved the destruction of works of art on a scale never before seen in human history. Yet, did it go a step further: were not only objects of pagan veneration, but also those who persisted in worshipping them, condemned to perish? An interesting observation in this context has been made in the Mithras temple at Sarrebourg. This sanctuary has undoubtedly, as we have already seen, been the site of a sustained iconoclastic attack which reduced the large cult relief into a multitude of fragments, over 300 of which could still be recognised. A different purpose was found for some of the smashed remains of this hated pagan image; they were to form a stone cist as a grave for a small man in his thirties buried without any grave-goods (**72**). This was not a burial of some later time; it presumably followed immediately on the destruction of the image. The body had been buried lying directly on a part of the base of the cult image which had been broken and inverted. The hands of the skeleton were chained behind his back. We can hardly be wrong in concluding that this macabre discovery marks a deliberate contamination of the ransacked sanctuary, presumably by the same people responsible for the destruction.

One would not expect prisoners to be kept in the Roman small town of Sarrebourg, and it would be a strange coincidence for him to be a captive who happened to die a natural death at the time. It seems more likely that he was put to death and buried in the temple, presumably because of some association with the cult. Yet, if so, the fact that he was chained probably indicates organised action rather than a spontaneous act by itinerant religious zealots. Why was the chain not removed prior to burial despite the fact that iron was precious and sought-after in Late Antiquity and the early Middle Ages? One possible explanation is that those responsible for the burial and quite possibly death of the man had no strong materialistic interests (a hypothesis also supported by the observation that 274 coins were deliberately left behind). Considering that the burial was covered with larger stone

72 A victim of religious hatred? The chained skeleton of a man in the Sarrebourg mithraeum

blocks, we cannot even exclude the possibility that the unfortunate victim might even have been buried alive.

Whatever the precise circumstances of his death (excluding the slim chance that it was indeed the body of some prisoner who had died a natural death), we are almost certainly dealing with a brutal and sadistic crime. The conscious decision not to collect the money and other metal items whose value would have made it worth picking them up, as we have seen, and the systematic and thorough way in which the cult image was destroyed and parts of its remains used to build a stone cist are best explained as deep hate without any desire to plunder on the part of those responsible. It is hard to think of any motives for pagan invaders to demolish the image in such a time-consuming and systematic manner, and one wonders if they had slain the man what would have made them build a stone cist, rather than leaving him unburied. The coins prove that the temple continued to be used until at least AD 394. The general scarcity of artefacts datable to subsequent centuries north of the Alps does not allow us to exclude that we are dealing with a much later destruction. However, there are no positive indications so far that Mithraism survived anywhere into the sixth century, and the fact that no Mithraic sanctuaries north of the Alps were converted into churches equally points to an early end of this complex religion which would have been much harder to integrate into the medieval world or to excuse than nature worship. If the man had indeed some association with the cult, then we are probably dealing with events between the late AD 390s and the fifth century.

Are we thus witnessing here a case to prove that the Christianisation of the late Roman Empire did not only involve violence against monuments, but that missionaries did not even shrink from bloodshed? Famously, a Christian mob murdered in AD 415 the female philosopher Hypatia in Alexandria in a brutal manner. The well-known orator Libanius attests in a passionate appeal to the Christian Emperor Theodosius I that in Syria already by the AD 380s priests who resisted temple destruction were at mortal risk. Referring to gangs of black-robed monks he writes (speech 30,8):

> ... they assault the temple carrying wooden beams, stones and iron tools or even without these items with their hand and feet. Then they are an easy prey; even though they destroy the roofs, raze the walls to the ground, pull down the statues and tear down the altars, the priests have to keep silent or they have to die.

These unlawful acts occurred, according to the pagan author, even in towns, but were most frequently ventured in the countryside, and a single raid could lay waste to several temples. The emperor in power then, Theodosius I (AD 379-395), was a very pious man; he prohibited temple visits only five years after this speech had been delivered and imposed the death penalty on pagan animal sacrifices in AD 392. One would not have thought Libanius would have dared to accuse the monks of murder had there been no substance to these allegations. Yet, we are dealing both in the case of Hypatia and in the case of the Syrian monks with incidents of people transgressing the laws and accepted norms at the time. A wider survey of written sources confirms the impression that these are comparatively scarce excesses, which found no approval amongst Christian missionaries and authors. In Sarrebourg we may well have traced an incidence of mob-violence, probably by people who called themselves Christians; even so, it would be hard to find a parallel. Both literary sources and archaeology suggest that the Christianisation of the Empire in the fourth and fifth centuries involved violence against monuments on a massive scale, yet it was a revolution with little blood being spilled. And, to judge by the written evidence, the few who fell prey to lynch-law included both staunch pagans and Christian iconoclasts. It is true that the laws prescribed the death penalty for animal sacrifices; yet there is no evidence to suggest that these laws were stringently applied and led to a significant number of executions, with the sole exception of alleged cases of evil magic seen as a real danger to the emperor.

14

A PAST PHENOMENON OR FUTURE THREAT?

After the Christian victory

We have seen that cases of image destruction are often difficult to date by the means of archaeology. The written sources suggest that the phenomenon in north-western Europe and the Mediterranean reached its peak between the late fourth and the seventh century. It coincides with the gradual conversion of the population in this area from paganism to Christianity. Yet, it certainly was not a phenomenon exclusive to this period. Once much of the visible remnants of pagan religion had disappeared from view and most of the population had been won over to the new religion, anti-pagan iconoclasm lost its momentum – and except for the odd rock-carved image in a remote setting little survived to be destroyed. Pagan images and monuments, which had survived the onslaught in this turbulent period of change often escaped for good. Place names suggest that they played their part in local folklore. At Kindsbach (in modern Germany) in the foothills of a densely forested mountain range six pagan figures, three of them seated mother goddesses, had been carved out of a rock next to a sacred spring in the Roman period (**colour plate 23**). The image is now heavily weathered, but there is nothing to suggest that it ever suffered a single hit from the hands of an image-hater. Next to and in the immediate vicinity of the spring is another rock-cut relief depicting Mars beside another mother goddess and other deities (**colour plate 24**). This heavy rock, measuring no less than 3.10m by 1.75m, had been turned over at some stage. From then on, the side with the pagan images was lying face down, until the carvings were rediscovered by touch one century ago and the rock put back into its original position. Some damage to the faces can be observed and there is a hole in the rock where the head of one figure would have been. This may at least be partially due to weathering and accidental damage, and if the reliefs were subject to any attack at all, it was at most half-hearted iconoclasm. The turning over of the rock must have been a deliberate act to conceal the pagan figures. The discovery of several fragmented stone images from the same site provides further evidence for anti-pagan measures being implemented at the site from which the relief of the mother goddesses somehow escaped. The spring water contains boron and was still in the recent past used to cure eye diseases. Thus people probably never forgot about the site nor were they under any illusions about the origins of the figures as the toponym *Heidenfelsen* ('the pagans' rock') demonstrates. Nevertheless, no determined Christian iconoclast ever seems to have touched the easily destructible relief of the mother goddesses. We do not know why this relief escaped (especially since it was smaller than the other rock which had been turned over) and when the attack on the other images occurred. Whenever it was, the image must have been on display for centuries more and, almost certainly, in excess of a millennium without any longer being considered a threat to Christian dominance.

Isolated instances of iconoclasm still occurred here and there, such as at a monastery at Trier where a sixteenth-century inscription mocked the badly mutilated remains of an idol, the statue of the Roman goddess of love, Venus. Pilgrims used to hurl stones at the idol. While anti-pagan iconoclasm largely ebbed away once Christianity had won victory in Western Europe, it was, of course, a different matter in territories converted to Christianity after the seventh century, such as in northern Germany or, much later, in sixteenth-century America. The Renaissance had earlier revived the veneration of the images of Classical Antiquity, if no longer for their religious significance, but for their artistic merits. Today it is probably true to say that the destruction of pagan images, like the burning of 'witches', is, for the present at least, a closed chapter in the history of western Christianity.

Christians, as we have seen, often had an ambivalent and sometimes hostile attitude towards images, and this did not stop at pagan images. Did not God's commandments categorically rule out image veneration, and had Christianity transgressed divine rules when depicting Jesus and the saints in churches? Long periods of image production and veneration were in some countries interrupted by episodes of image destruction, notably in the eighth and ninth centuries in the Byzantine Empire and, much later, in the wake of the Hussite movement in Bohemia, during the Reformation in England etc.

Islam shared hostility towards images with Judaism and Christianity. In contrast to Christianity, image veneration never gained any significant place within Islam. The attitude towards paganism and pagan image worship, however, was similarly strict. By the time the forces of the new religion conquered Syria, Egypt, northern Africa and much of the Iberian peninsula in the seventh and early eighth centuries, much of the work in clearing pagan images from public view had been done. Nevertheless, there were still instances of image destruction. A striking case is the temple at Khirbet edh-Dharih in modern Jordan. The temple was abandoned as a result of an earthquake in AD 363. In the sixth century the temple *cella* was re-used as a church, but, interestingly, the pagan reliefs were not touched, despite the fact that the ancient village was less than 4km away from a late Roman military road station at a major traffic axis, the *Via Nova Traiana*. This is significant as it confirms that within the Christian clergy attitudes towards pagan images were not uniform. Not everybody necessarily shared the hard line zeal to reduce all pagan art to rubble, and in some regions there may have been some leeway for more tolerant procedures depending on the attitude of church authorities. The same, as we have seen, was probably true in Britain. In the seventh or eighth century the villagers converted to Islam. Feeding troughs in the church and former temple signal its conversion to an agricultural building. In the second half of the eighth century yet another earthquake occurred. Large parts of the temple and, notably, the upper sections of its façade collapsed. Some of the elaborate reliefs, which had decorated the façade, landed softly on a layer of dung; others fell on cattle. These animals, the new inhabitants of the once sacred building, paid with their lives for the survival of these works of art which bear no sign of deliberate damage. Strangely, it was precisely the earthquake which saved them. Soon after, in the late eighth or early ninth century, all images then still extant were systematically hammered off the stones, almost certainly by Muslims.

Also, when spreading to the East Islam did not refrain from using force against its opponents and their works of art. The modern visitor to the museum of Bodh Gaya, the birthplace of Buddhism in Bihar, India, is struck by a whole series of deliberately mutilated images (seen in January 2000). One of the reliefs, for example, depicts one large cross-legged Buddha flanked by two very small similar images. All three had their faces chopped off, rendering it unlikely that we are dealing with accidental damage. The right of the two small Buddhas appears to have been hit with a pointed tool. While attempts to gain information from the relevant authorities in India on these images and their circumstances of discovery have so far yielded no results, the beheading and smashing of statues has been observed at Bodh Gaya as well as at various Buddhist monasteries in the surroundings. It has been plausibly linked with the Muslim advance at the turn of the twelfth and thirteenth century. Secular revolutions, such as the French revolution, have equally used image destruction as a method to break off the people's link with the past.

Image destruction today

The destruction of anything which stands in the way of an intolerant religious doctrine – is this a phenomenon of the past, a closed chapter of history? Is the world now a better and more civilised place where people know to appreciate cultural heritage and art? Anybody who thought so will have had a rude awakening in March 2001 when Taliban and Al-Qaeda explosives blew apart the two colossal rock-cut Buddhas at Bamiyan, one 36, the other even 54m tall (**73-7** & **colour plate 25**). Already in 1999 the smaller of the two statues

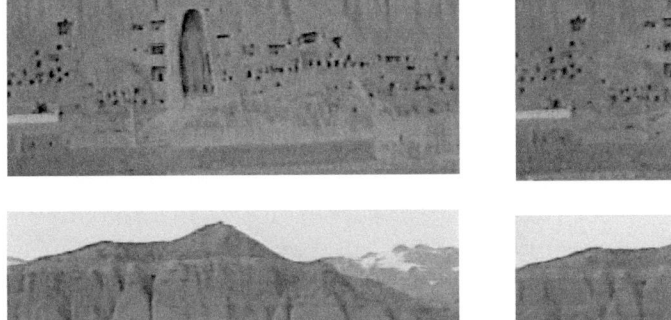

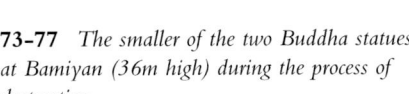

73-77 *The smaller of the two Buddha statues at Bamiyan (36m high) during the process of destruction*

had its head blown off, a loud warning signal to the world of what was to come. The images were between 1,300-1,800 years old, and Buddhism had been replaced by Islam in the area more than a millennium ago. Nobody in the region had venerated these images for centuries; yet, this did not save them. As war today is so much more destructive than it has ever been before in world history, so the prospect of a renewed wave of image destruction has become much more frightening than at any previous point in history. While iconoclasts in earlier periods of history depended on basic tools and manual labour which saved at least the colossal monuments partially or completely, such as Dendara or Bamiyan, modern explosives could turn whole countries into cultural deserts within days. The determination and fanaticism are the same and, where 'necessary', the iconoclast can still spend excessive amounts of manual labour and time to achieve their targets (e.g. in the case of smaller works of art in a building which itself is thought worth preserving, thus rendering the use of explosives unsuitable). The journal *Archaeology* (May/June 2002, 24) features a photograph of the devastation in the store-room of the Ministry of Information and 'Culture' at Kabul as a result of iconoclasm in 2001. Paul Bucherer-Dietschi, an insider of recent Afghan history and campaigner for the preservation and restoration of the little that remains of the once rich cultural heritage of this country comments (*ibid.* 22 & 24):

> Here's 18 cubic feet of primarily Gandharan and Bactrian artifacts from the Kabul Museum, in pieces no bigger than my little finger. The Taliban came in the morning, hammered until prayer time, paused, hammered again, paused for tea, then hammered for the rest of the day.

A daily routine which, chillingly, may not have differed very much from that adopted by the iconoclasts at Dendara (details aside) some one and a half millennia earlier; fortunately the latter did not have explosives.

Since monotheistic religions with a claim to absolute truth have come into being, iconoclasm has flared up again and again. However, it would not be fair to issue any blanket accusations against religions based on belief in just one God. The list of the Christians, Muslims and Jews who have made outstanding achievements in recovering, studying or preserving monuments and works of art of cultures and religions different to their own would exceed this present book in length. It is not monotheism as such which is to blame, but extremism – and not just religious extremism, but also secular ideologies. The Chinese Cultural Revolution, for example, has been no less devastating than religiously motivated waves of destruction. Frighteningly, iconoclasm is a phenomenon which can be latent for centuries only to erupt suddenly and to reduce the cultural heritage of whole regions to rubble. Where will it strike next?

15
CONCLUSIONS

The controversy about the end of paganism

Seven years ago, in 1996, I published an earlier monograph on the 'End of Paganism', which chose the cult of Mithras in the north-western provinces of the Empire as a case study. The book has attracted both support and criticism. Turcan (1997), whose belief in the collapse of Mithraism by and large without Christian intervention had been subject to criticism already in this book, responded by reiterating his views. While Clauss (1998), in sharp contrast to Turcan, concluded that the historical assessment was correct and judged the section on the coin evidence as knowledgeable and methodologically sound, Gordon (1999) came to diametrically opposed conclusions and felt entitled to reject the conclusions of my discussion of the coin evidence without providing a single counter-argument or even quoting the chapter on the value of coins. Griffith (1997), however, concluded that 'the strength of Sauer's investigation is his meticulous review of epigraphic and numismatic evidence.' Clauss, in contrast to his equally positive assessment of the numismatic section, was less impressed by the introduction and the chapter on inscriptions, but chose to keep to himself what he disliked about this section. It may not be without interest to note that I had argued in this very section that there was insufficient evidence to be sure about the area of origin of the Roman form of Mithraism in opposition to Clauss who had postulated that the mysteries were an Italian creation (on the basis of the origin of early dedicators of Mithraic inscriptions). Clauss's theory on the origins of the Mithras mysteries, incidentally, has now been put seriously into question by current research in the Doliche mithraea. At least the first of the two adjacent temples appears to have been in existence in the early first century at the very latest, well before any mithraeum so far discovered in Italy, the western and northern provinces of the Empire.

My hypothesis that the Mithras mysteries could have been substantially older than the earliest archaeological evidence and the earliest inscriptions of the late first century (as Christianity can only be traced by archaeology some one and a half centuries after its creation), by contrast, has been proven to be correct. Doliche was, interestingly, within the region stretching from Asia Minor to India where Mithras had been worshipped for centuries and, in places at least, for more than a millennium (albeit not in the framework of a mystery religion). It seems thus at least a strong possibility that the Roman form of the Mithras mysteries was created in the East. Italy was probably no more than a major springboard for the further spread of the cult. Be this as it may, it is worth noting that there is certainly no agreement whatsoever amongst fellow academics about the value of the archaeological evidence for the end of paganism and about its interpretation. The fact that the very same arguments have attracted both praise and criticism and that there is no common ground whatsoever between Gordon, Turcan, Clauss and Griffith, entitles us at least to the conclusion that doubters and supporters cannot both be right at the same time.

While well-founded criticism to progress our knowledge is always welcome, I felt that Gordon and Turcan rejected my unconventional arguments not because they had strong counter-arguments, but because they went against their preconceived opinions, especially against their implicit assumption that material evidence is always subordinate to written evidence and can be pushed in any direction to suit one's argument. If numerous late coins in temples contradict Turcan's assumption that most pagan sanctuaries ought to be abandoned at the time, he claims that they provide no evidence for continued worship, because profane installations, such as theatres, bath-houses, villas and pottery production centres have also yielded numerous coins. Yet it is precisely because there was intensive human activity within those installations that numerous coins were left behind. The same is true for late temples of Mithras with frequently exceptionally high concentrations of coins within a narrow space. Unless there are strong arguments for a collective re-use of all such temples for a different activity which would have involved the deposition of numerous coins, Turcan's objections are groundless; that normally within an area as small as the interior of a mithraeum in a theatre, bath-house, villa or pottery production centre only a minute fraction of the coins are found, the average mithraeum yields, is a fact Turcan (1997) wisely omits to mention.

The frequent occurrence of large numbers of late coins in mithraea excludes with certainty the assumption by Turcan or Nicholson (1995, 359) that they could have ended up there accidentally or even as a result of rubbish deposition. Similarly, if numerous late coins deliberately left behind in mithraea contradict Gordon's assumption that Christians played no major part in the wider decline of paganism, they are discounted as basically worthless small change which hostile 'vandals' might just as easily have left behind as Christians, even if there is clear evidence that their sheer metal value was quite substantial. One of the purposes of this book is to provide a response to such a vociferous refusal by these classical scholars to engage with any unconventional forms of evidence. It is deliberately a popular book. For once the end of paganism has shaped world history to the present day; these are issues which are of significance far beyond academic circles. Secondly, it was felt that archaeologists and those who work at the borderline of archaeology and history can make a major contribution by going beyond offering the one hundredth re-interpretation of well known textual and art-historical evidence. It is a plea to classicists not to reject 'ordinary' objects (like coins or pottery) only because it is unfamiliar territory. This is a deliberate attempt to widen the discussion beyond the narrow circle of, largely text and iconography-based, experts in religious history. For this reason many examples discussed in my earlier study have been used again beside much new material, since it is hoped that this book will attract a readership far beyond those who have read the first book. Thus there would be little point in presenting what I became aware of after 1996 in isolation of what I had been aware of before.

It is important to take a closer look at Gordon's review which attests to the author's rhetorical skill. Is Gordon (1999, 683) right in accusing me of strong preconceived opinion or is this a pre-emptive strike to avert attention from a certain bias in his own approach? Clauss (1998, 380 in translation) comes to diametrically opposed conclusions: 'Sauer is very careful, . . .' Gordon, undoubtedly, found it very tempting to produce a good piece of rhetoric. It is much easier to attack a one-sided approach – and if the original work is not one-sided, why portray it as such? In my previous book I had repeatedly pointed out that incidents of destruction perpetrated by invaders must have taken place, even though I felt that the evidence suggested that on the whole they were lower in number and intensity than those committed by Christians:

> . . . the reason why I have questioned in this paper many theories that Germanic invaders are to blame for the destruction of religious monuments is not because I want to rule out that they were indeed responsible for intentional damage in some cases, but because it is necessary to stress that mostly the published evidence is just insufficient to reveal the identity of the iconoclasts . . . The question which deserves further investigation is not whether Germanic invaders or early missionaries caused damage to religious monuments – both groups certainly did – the question is what differences there were in the extent of the deliberate damage, in the chosen targets, in the procedures and in the thoroughness of destruction and in the basic aims and motives.
>
> (Sauer 1996, 68)

Gordon (1999, 687) calls this 'the "Christians-did-it" thesis' and against this imaginary view he argues with much eloquence, yet without clear signs that he had taken much time to study the arguments under discussion or the evidence they are based upon. Indeed, a whole range of passages reveal that Gordon read the book rather cursorily before rejecting its conclusions. Coins are described as being of 'extremely low intrinsic value' allegedly not worth picking up (Gordon 1999, 687), while a chapter which assesses the value of coins from mithraea and states precisely the reverse (Sauer 1996, 32-36) is not mentioned with a single word, nor is a single counter-argument provided. He laments the fact that several pie charts refer to the same temple (Gordon 1999, 684) without realising that these charts compare coin numbers, weight and metal value, thus being essential to the same argument which had somehow eluded him. Gordon (1999, 685) states that the main cult relief from Mundelsheim had been 'carefully removed', while in fact it had probably been smashed into many small pieces, as both my book (Sauer 1996, 65) and the original report (Planck 1989, 181), both of which Gordon claims to have read, clearly state. The possibility that a three-aisled building in Leicester could be a temple of Mithras is discounted based, as Gordon (1999, 683 no. 8) in admirable frankness admits, at no more than a 'glance' at a single photograph; the evidence quoted in my book (Sauer 1996, 82 no. 5), especially the plan (Wacher 1995, 360 fig. 163) which would have revealed that its architecture is quite similar to that of the mithraeum at Ober-Florstadt in Germany, was not taken into consideration. Gordon (1999, 684) concedes that there are the remains of torchbearers in a building at Rockenhausen in Germany, but doubts that it is a mithraeum. Few buildings other than mithraea have yielded heads of torchbearers and that a building in the countryside has yielded the head of a torchbearer without being a mithraeum is unlikely to say the least. In my book episodes in biographies of saints, which clearly attest the destruction of pagan idols, are repeatedly mentioned, while Gordon in a seven-page-long review fails to mention a single passage except for the one well-known example that refers specifically to Mithraism. Is this because such post-classical texts are outside his field of interest or because an acknowledgement of the abundance of literary evidence for the destruction of images would have undermined his claim that it would be 'misguided to believe that direct violent intervention by Christians was the dominant or even critical factor in the wider process of the decline of paganism'?

Gordon (1999, 683-4) equally felt that the original study was geographically too narrow as it only dealt with Britain, Gaul and Germany. Yet, with a similar argument we could question the value of some 90 per cent of archaeological literature which deals with a geographic area as small or smaller than that. Is it really impossible to write a book on any aspect of history in a geographically limited area (e.g. the economy of Roman Britain or religion in Roman Gaul) only because hardly any region ever developed in isolation? Yet, not only the 'narrow' geographic focus but also the subject raises doubts. Gordon (1999, 682) claims that Mithraism was a badly chosen example for the wider decline of paganism, because 'the cult of Mithras has little claim to be considered typical in the context of Roman provincial paganism'. Of course he is right that the decline of paganism was not a uniform development. Spring and mountain veneration, for example, which outlasted Mithraism because of the very indestructibility of the places of worship, are quite different. Yet, one could argue, they are equally not an entirely typical example for the end of paganism. But is there any one typical example for the multi-faceted disappearance and transformation of the pagan heritage of Rome? If it is not allowed to take anything as an example, as everything is special in one way or another, does Gordon imply that the subject of the end of paganism should not be approached at all unless a multi-volume study of the subject in a global context is produced? I make no excuses for once again including many examples of destroyed images from the temples of Mithras while being fully aware of the fact that they constitute only a small proportion of all pagan sanctuaries. Mithraea are identifiable as such merely on the basis of their ground-plan, unlike temples dedicated to Minerva, Mars or Apollo, for example, and are often better preserved from later stone robbing and plough damage because of their frequent partial or complete subterranean location. This makes it very difficult to establish whether their cult inventory was more or less frequently removed by devotees fearing profanation and whether or not they were more frequently subject to savage attacks. The impression remains that there were strong local differences and that in some areas such as at Hadrian's Wall, Mithraism was indeed subject to earlier and more targeted attack than any of his fellow deities.

In most parts of the Empire the evidence is insufficient to tell one way or the other. Indestructible natural sanctuaries are by definition largely left out from a study on the material manifestations of religious hatred, but I hope to deal with some of them in a future study on 'Springs in Antiquity'. How can we explain Gordon's passion in denying that direct Christian intervention was a critical factor in the decline of paganism as a whole or of Mithraism specifically, notwithstanding the large numbers of temples with mutilated images? Gordon has established himself as a scholar by his criticism of Franz Cumont who laid the foundations to the subject of Mithraic studies in the late nineteenth century (Gordon 1975). He already stresses in the first paragraph of his review that Cumont had already argued that Mithraism had died a violent death (Gordon 1999, 682) and later (p.688) that such a theory on the end of Mithraism has 'a 19th-c. whiff about it' implying blanket contempt for scholarship of earlier generations and for Cumont in particular, without even acknowledging that an interpretation does not need to be wrong only because it found support in the nineteenth century.

Conclusions

While the wider approach adopted in this book is more likely to find mercy in the eyes of Richard Gordon, others might take the opposite standpoint. More has been written on Christianisation, paganism and the archaeology of religious monuments than could be read in a whole lifetime. When Frank Trombley (1993 & 1994) published his extensive study on 'Hellenic Religion and Christianization' in Late Antiquity academic referees were quick to point out important secondary works Trombley had failed to take into consideration. It is easy to criticise from the comparatively safe basis of expertise in a geographically or methodologically narrow field those who endeavour a wider synthesis and cannot have read as much about each aspect of their subject as the specialist. Trombley would probably have received kinder reviews had he limited himself to one smaller part of the Empire which might have enabled him to take all relevant works into consideration. The present popular book does not, in any way, try to compete with Trombley's detailed survey. Yet, its thematic scope is even wider. Trombley had been brave enough to deal with complex developments in much of the East of the Empire, while the present book uses examples from West and East alike. Trombley had confined himself largely to written evidence, while the present book seeks to look at the archaeological evidence against the background of the written evidence. Inevitably, it is full of gaps. It is not its aim to be comprehensive, but to point out how much further we might advance in future if we did not look only at written evidence in isolation. It is meant to be a first step, not the last word on the matter. Despite difficulties as a result of differential survival chances for different types of sacred sites, there is scope for the development of statistical models to compare and contrast the fate of different types of pagan sanctuaries and of different regions in the ancient world. To do this, we need a much larger database than it has been possible to assemble for this book. It will require a group of scholars spending several years on such a project. Furthermore, and this again is an observation which a thorough study of any one part of the ancient world could not have provided, even a random selection of examples of archaeological (as far as available) and literary evidence demonstrates quite convincingly that there is more uniformity than disparity in the way images were treated in various parts of the late Roman and early medieval world.

Images were destroyed by Christians. Few, if any, would disagree with such a conclusion. Yet, how widespread was the phenomenon? This is a much more difficult question. There is no doubt about the geographic scale. Image-haters were active in many and probably all of the provinces of the Empire and its early medieval Christian successor states. There is no way we will ever be able to give percentage figures as to what part of the visual heritage of the ancient world perished in the onslaught. Few works of art have survived undamaged and in the majority of cases that have survived with damage of one sort or another we cannot tell whether it was accidental or deliberate. Striking a statue with a blunt piece of wood can result in damage which is visually indistinguishable from that caused by a collapsing roof. The number of images, previously damaged or undamaged, that have perished over the past two millennia in lime kilns is anybody's guess. Only a small proportion of instances of iconoclasm have left such clear traces that we can identify them as such with ultimate certainty. We know no more than the tip of the iceberg. Even then questions often remain about the circumstances of destruction. A proportion of the 'easy' targets, especially in the frontier zone, were probably indeed attacked by hostile invaders though there is as yet no convincing evidence that they would ever have undertaken very labour-intensive forms of destruction, such as observed in Egypt.

Nicholson (1995) and Gordon (1999) have argued that in many instances votaries themselves brought cult images to safety, and I would agree. However, is this a viable counter-argument against the scale of violent Christian intervention, as Gordon believes? Was it not much rather a result of an atmosphere of fear and insecurity which brought devotees to hide what was holy to them? After all, they still cared enough to undertake the laborious task of concealing images, presumably because they had witnessed the ferocity of image destruction elsewhere. Had they lost their faith or had there been no threat, there would have been no incentive for doing so. It is irrelevant whether there were more cases of destruction or evacuation of cult inventory as the two phenomena are quite obviously interrelated. Late Roman legislation was ambivalent about temples as buildings; sometimes destruction was sanctioned and sometimes there was a desire to preserve the architecture as long as they no longer serve as places of pagan worship. Some temples which we find devoid of images today may have been emptied in an orderly fashion by state representatives, but this need not imply that such measures enjoyed the approval of the population. Undoubtedly, it is correct that only in a minority of cases can we prove iconoclasm in a temple. Yet, we equally cannot disprove in most instances that suppressive Christian intervention directly or indirectly led to the removal of images.

Whether images were hacked to pieces, thrown into water, buried outside sanctuaries or left in temples filled up with rubble, these actions all served the same purpose. Paganism in Roman tradition depended crucially on images. The population of Bregenz had nothing to replace their old and venerable bronze statues with once St Gallus had smashed them to pieces. Such acts were instrumental in making object-centred forms of pagan worship impossible. Quite irrespective of the precise percentage of images which perished in such a dramatic manner, image destruction was a crucial factor in ending central forms of pagan cult. Even Christian authors were not ashamed to admit that image destruction had significantly boosted the process of Christianisation. Let us hear the testimony of just two of them.

> Gaudentius and Jovius, commissioners of emperor Honorius, destroyed, as we know, on the 19th of March [AD 399] the temples of the false gods in the most famous and important city in Africa, Carthage, and smashed their idols. Who would not see how much the worship of the name of Christ has grown from then to our present time over nearly thirty years?
>
> (St Augustine, *The City of God* 18,54)

Sulpicius Severus similarly makes no attempt to deny that it was not persuasion alone which won over the population to Christianity, in this case in Gaul. He offers a detailed description of how St Martin destroyed a 'most ancient' temple and felled a nearby sacred pine tree. This was done against fierce resistance of the local population who were, we are told, eventually won over by a miracle. Following this account he concludes:

> And, in fact, before Martin fairly few, yes indeed, virtually none in these regions had adopted the Christian faith. Through his virtues and his example the faith has grown to such an extent that at the present time there is no place there which is no full of very large numbers of churches and monasteries. Since wherever he had destroyed pagan shrines, he instantly built either churches or monasteries.
>
> (*Life of St Martin* 13,9)

While we must not overlook the element or rhetorical exaggeration, e.g. in the number of churches and monasteries allegedly constructed, archaeology has proven that the sources are basically telling the truth, and archaeological evidence helps us to gain a visual idea of the events which unrolled themselves one-and-a-half millennia ago. Some modern scholars have set themselves the target of disproving such a dramatic end by pointing out that the number of pagan votive inscriptions, works of art and temple building projects declined prior to Christian victory in the AD 330s and continued to do so thereafter. Yet, they fail to notice that the same is true for most similar non-religious monuments, thus pointing to cultural, economic and psychological changes, sparked by the Third-Century Crisis, rather than being proof for people losing their pagan faith. Furthermore, once the avalanches of Christian image destruction had gathered momentum in the fourth century, it must have seemed increasingly pointless even for committed pagans to continue to erect stone monuments whose fate was predictable. Others believe they can disprove that violence against monuments played any major role in the total transformation of the religious landscape of the ancient world in the late Roman/early medieval transition by listing temples which have yielded no traces of violent damage. Of course, the phenomena of filling temples with debris, emptying them of the cult inventory, whether out of fear of profanation or for re-use and temple destruction, took place simultaneously. By arguing that one is in opposition to the other they are missing the point. There is undoubtedly a strong causal link between the disappearance of pagan monuments and the spread of Christianity, irrespective of how much disappeared as a result of direct destruction and how much as a result of indirect pressure.

As stressed above, Christianity had much to offer, such as a clear sense of purpose in life, the promise of a blissful afterlife etc. Indeed, it had been a successful and expanding minority religion within the Roman Empire even while it was still persecuted. Christianity, in particular the Nestorian denomination, had spread widely in the Persian Empire, India, central Asia and even China by the early Middle Ages. Undoubtedly it would have established itself as a world religion without the use of force and violence, yet one religion beside others (as it was in much of Asia). However, it is equally noticeable that, as far as I am aware, nowhere in Asia, Europe or Africa did it become the majority, let alone the sole, religion by the early Middle Ages with the exception of the western and eastern Roman Empire, many of its neighbours and successor states and their zones of influence. Image destruction has to be seen in the context of other oppressive measures, such as outlawing temple visits in the early AD 390s. Those who argue that paganism by and large collapsed in on itself as people had lost interest in it and waited for something more fulfilling, ought to explain why it is that Christianity became the sole religion precisely in those states which imposed it from above and normally outlawed pagan worship and tolerated or encouraged image destruction, while in the first millennium it failed to do so anywhere else.

BIBLIOGRAPHY

Preface
St Columbanus and St Gallus: MGHSRM 4, 1902, 259-60; 287-9; Fellmann 1988, 314-15; Frank 1975, 171-266; 307-28.
Kilcolman: Cuppage 1986, 331-4 no. 868; Macalister 1945, 186-8.
Ostia: Becatti 1954; Calza 1951, 129-31; 1966, 239-42; Meiggs 1973.
Mythological scenes in late Roman art: Killerich & Torp 1994.
Christianisation of sculpture: Delivorrias 1991.

1 The tip of the iceberg
Dieburg: Behn 1928; Gordon 1975, 233-42; Künzl 1989; Schallmayer 1989.
Image destruction in south-west Germany: Fischer 1991; Huld-Zetsche 1986, 46; Kuhnen 1992, 42-6; 91-4.
Güglingen: Joachim 1999.
Literature on other Mithras temples mentioned: Sauer 1996; 2003.
Re-dedication of temples to churches (not a subject investigated in any detail in this study): Deichmann 1939; 1954; Teichner 1996.
Hechingen-Stein: Schmidt-Lawrenz 1999.
Walheim: Planck 1991.
Carmona: Bendala Galán 1976a, 49-72; 1976b, pls. 10-16; 1986, 381-90; pls. 6.10-9.14; Hernandez Díaz et al. 1943, 108; Vermaseren 1986, 62-3 nos. 164-8.

2 Pagan 'vandalism' and iconoclasm in peacetime
Seeck 1908; Versnel 1981. Classical sources: Cassius Dio 40,47,3; 42,26,2; Josephus, *Jewish Antiquities* 18, 65-80; Suetonius, *Tiberius* 36; Tacitus, *Annals* 2,85; Valerius Maximus 1,3,4.
Melting down of metal votive gifts: Duncan-Jones 1994, 8-9; 15.
London riverside wall: Hill et al. 1980.
Mainz: Frenz 1986; 1992.
Mittelstrimmig: CIL XIII, 11975-6.
Palmyra: Gàssowska 1982; Collart and Vicari 1969, 76-7; 87; Drijvers 1976; Gawlikowski 1977; 1979a & b; 1983; 1995; Kowalski 1994; Krzyzanwska 1981; Starcky and Gawlikowski 1985, 71-2.

3 Destruction in war and peace
Mithras temple at Capua: Minto 1924; Vermaseren 1971.
Clermont-Ferrand: Fournier 1965; Provost & Mennessier-Jouannet 1994, 125; 143-51; Vieillard-Troiekouroff 1976, 103-4 no. 89.

Jupiter giant column at Ladenburg: Heukemes 1975; Wiegels 2000, 42-51 (kindly provided by Dr Heukemes); number of Jupiter giant columns from Ladenburg: letter of Dr Heukemes of 23 September 2002.
Fate of other Jupiter giant columns: Bauchhenß & Noelke 1981, 24-6; Klumbach 1973.
Bad Wimpfen: Filgis & Pietsch 1985; Pietsch 1986.
Walheim: Planck 1991, 46-53.
Entrains-sur-Nohain: Devauges 1988; Walters 1974, 95 no. 26-101 no. 34.
Well at Lower Slaughter: O'Neil & Toynbee 1958.
Britain: CSIR, Great Britain, vols I,1-8; Henig 1984.
Uley: Woodward & Leach 1993; see also Painter 1999.
Lydney: Wheeler 1932.
White Horse at Uffington: Lock & Gosden 1997; Miles & Palmer 1995.
Dura Europos: the impression that there was no iconoclasm is based on the illustrations and plates in various publications on the excavations at and finds from the town, too numerous to list here, notably the volumes of *The Excavations at Dura-Europos* series. On the Nemesis relief see Baur and Rostovtzeff 1929, 19, 62-8, pl. IV.1; Perkins 1973, 89, pl. 36.
Mithras temples in Syria: Hopfe 1990.
Mithras temple at Dura-Europos: Rostovtzeff *et al.* 1939, 62-134.
Mithras temple at Caesarea: Bull 1987, chapter 5; Hopfe 1975.
Mithras temple at Hawarte: Gawlikowski 1999; 2000a & b; 2001.
Mithras temples at Doliche: Bulgan *et al.* 2001; Schütte-Maischatz & Winter 2000; Winter 1999; 2000.

4 Image destruction seen through Christian eyes
Attitude to images in early Christianity: Kollwitz 1954; Snyder 1985.
Destruction of pagan images as a motif in art: Kemp 1970.
San Marco at Venice: Andaloro *et al.* 1991, 110, 112; Demus 1984, 219-25, 230, pls. 358, 361-2, 365, 373-4; 1988, 82-5; pls. 27-28b.
St Simon and St Jude: Acts of the Apostles (St Simon and St Jude) 6,22 (Fabricius 1703, 634 [in Latin]); 738-40; Lipsius 1884, 164-75.
Painting in Roman catacombs: De Rossi 1865; Gatti 1919, 44-5; Marucchi, 1918-19; 65; 1930s, 561-2; Seroux d'Agincourt 1823; Styger 1933, 240-1.

5 Hilltop sanctuaries
Christian asceticism: examples are too numerous to be listed here. See, for example, Theodoret of Cyrrhus, *A history of the monks of Syria* and O'Sullivan 2001.
La Ferté-sur-Chiers: Vieillard-Troiekouroff 1976, 120-2 nos. 110-11.
Tawern: Faust 1987; Faust *et al.* 1996, 82, 84-5 and 222-3.
Hochscheid: Weisgerber 1975; see also Dehn 1941; Haffner 1989.

6 Large Mithraic cult images
Strasbourg-Koenigshoffen: Forrer 1915; see also Hatt 1993, 25; Kern 1994.
Sarrebourg: Fisenne 1896.

7 Destruction at Dendara: a colossal task
Dendara: Bourbon 1996, 184-9; Cauville 1990; 1997; 1998-2001; 2000; Chassinat 1934a & b; 1935a & b; 1947; 1952; Chassinat & Daumas 1959; 1965; 1972; 1978; Daumas 1959; 1969; 1970; 1987; Dümichen 1877; Grossmann 2002, 171; 443-6; 528-36; Hölbl 2000, 72-87; Mariette-Pacha 1880; Shore 1979.

Opet temple at Karnak: De Wit 1962.
Other examples for image destruction and Christianisation of temples in Egypt: Frankfurter 1998, 265-84; Munier 1940; Watterson 1998; Winter 1976.

8 Destruction and re-use in Egypt and Palestine
Shenoute and his monastery: Bell 1983; Deichmann 1975; 54-60; figs. 22-5; El-Masry 2001; Monneret de Villard 1925 & 1926; Petrie 1908, 4-5; Wiseman 1931.
Gaza: Trombley 1993, 187-282 with further references.

9 The speed of Christianisation in Egypt
Speed of Christianisation of Egypt: Bagnall 1982; 1987; 1993, 261-289; 2001; De Lacy O'Leary 1938; Habachi 1972; Heinen 1998, 49-50; Krause 1998, 83-6; Parássoglou 1978, 207-8 no. 93; Rea and Sijpesteijn 1976; Snape 1996; Wipszycka 1986; 1988.
Luxor: El-Saghir 1991; El-Saghir *et al.* 1986.
Karnak: Traunecker & Golvin 1984, 32.
Karanis: Boak 1933, 15-16; 21.
Herakleopolis: Petrie 1905, 17.
Third-century demography at Alexandria: Parkin 1992, 63-4 with reference.
Qasr Ibrim: Adams 1991; Alexander 1999; Driskell *et al.* 1989; Edwards 2001; Horton 1991a & b; Kjølbye-Biddle 1994; Plumley 1975; Welsby 2002.
Pagan image worship and iconoclasm near Alexandria in the AD 480s: Trombley 1994, 1-15.

10 A world waiting for Christianity?
Views on the controversial subject of the speed of Christianisation and the degree of pagan resistance: Chuvin 1991; Grant 1968; Harnack 1924; Lane Fox 1986; MacMullen 1984; 1997; Martin 1989; Trombley 1993 and 1994; Turcan 1984; 1996; Vidman 1977; see also Frend 1984.
Late inscriptions: Mac Mullen 1982; Mrozek 1973.
Late inscription at Ongayo in northern Spain: Blázquez 1986, 248; Gómez 2000.
Comparison with Thirty Year's War: Sauer 1996, 71-2; 74-5 with further references.
Late coins and pottery from mithraea: Sauer 2003 with references.
Anatolia: Mitchell 1993; Trombley 1985; various excavation reports, too numerous to list here.
Temple foundations and use in Gaul, Germany and Britain: Fauduet 1993, 119-21; Gilles 1987; Horne 1981; Lewis 1966, 139-42; Rousselle 1990, 320-39.

11 Afterlife and oriental cults: serious competition for Christianity?
Turcan 1989.
The end of the Jupiter Dolichenus cult: Chini 2000; Hörig & Schwertheim 1987; Sarnowski *et al.* 1998; Speidel 1978, 72-5; Tóth 1973.
Late traces of Egyptian cults in Roman Germany: Grimm 1969, 89-90 (the archaeological evidence is rather limited).
St Prisca at Rome: Vermaseren & Van Essen 1965.
Debate on the origins of Mithraism (see also chapter on 'The controversy about the end of paganism'): Beck 1998; Gordon 1975.
Law against nightly ceremonies of AD 364: *Codex Theodosianus* 9,16,7.
Sarsina: Mansuelli 1967; see also: Leclant 1981, 867 no. 39; Malaise 1978, 634-5; Mancini 1940; Vermaseren 1978, 77-9 with nos. 187-94.

Selected examples for the felling of sacred trees: Callinicos, *Life of Hypatios* 30,1; Sulpicius
Severus, *Life of St Martin* 13,1-8; Merkelbach 1993; Wagner 1993, 53-4.

12 Money and Mithraism
Sauer 1996; 2003 with further references.
St Germanus from Auxerre: Constantius from Lyon, *Life of Germanus* 33.
Lux: Devauges 1971; 1976.
Crain: Devauges 1973; Meissonier 1973.

13 Christianisation and bloodshed
Anti-pagan laws: Noethlichs 1971 & 1986.
Sarrebourg: Fisenne 1896.

14 A past phenomenon or future threat?
So much information is available on the destruction of Christian images by Christians of different denomination and on iconoclasm within Christianity and on image destruction for political reasons throughout history that I do not attempt to include these subjects in this study or to provide a bibliography. For a wide-ranging survey of the phenomenon of image-destruction from Antiquity up to the Hussites in the fifteenth century see Bredekamp 1975.
Spring sanctuary at Kindsbach: Bernhard 1990; Fehr 1972, 99-103; pls. 111-13;
Geschwendt 1972, 86-8; Grünenwald 1906.
Trier: Binsfeld 1984; Florencourt 1848.
Khirbet edh-Dharih: Villeneuve 2000.
Bodh Gaya: Barua 1981, 41; 46-8; 233-4; 241-2; 244; Cunningham 1892, 56; 62; Jamuar
1985, 32; 90-1; 125; pl. 23; Kumar 1992, 51; Kumar 1999, 35-7; pl. X(B) and (C).
Bamiyan: Gilles 2000; http://www.photogrammetry.ethz.ch/research/bamiyan/destruction.html; Lewis 2001; Romey 2002; Vidale 2002.

15 Conclusions
Clauss 1998; Gordon 1999; Griffith 1997; Nicholson 1995; Sauer 1996; Turcan 1997.
Theory that Roman Mithraism was an Italian creation: Clauss 1990, 31-2 (= 2000, 21-2);
1992, 253. See chapter 3 on Doliche.
Reviews of Trombley 1993 & 1994: see list in *L'Année Philologique* 66, 1995, 805 nos.
10409-10.

General bibliography
Adams, W.Y., 1991 The United Kingdom of Makouria and Nobadia, a medieval Nubian anomaly, in Davies, W.V. (ed.), *Egypt and Africa, Nubia from Prehistory to Islam*, Dorchester, 257-63.
Alexander, J., 1999 A New Hilltop Cemetery and Temple of the Meroitic and Post-Meroitic Period at Qasr Ibrim. *Sudan & Nubia* 3, 47-59.
Andaloro, M., Da Villa Urbani, M., Florent-Goudouneix, I., Polacco, R. & Vio, E., 1991 *The Patriarchal Basilica in Venice, San Marco, The Mosaics, the Inscriptions, the Pala d'Oro* II, Milan.
Bagnall, R.S., 1982 Religious conversion and onomastic change in early Byzantine Egypt. *The Bulletin of the American Society of Papyrologists* 19, 105-24.
Bagnall, R.S., 1987 Conversion and Onomastics; A Reply. *Zeitschrift für Papyrologie und Epigraphik* 69, 243-50.
Bagnall, R.S., 1993 *Egypt in Late Antiquity*, Princeton.

Bagnall, R.S., 2001 Roman Occupation, in *The Oxford Encyclopedia of Ancient Egypt* III, Oxford, 148-56.
Barua, D.K., 1981 *Buddha Gaya Temple: its history*, Buddha Gaya.
Bauchhenß, G. & Noelke, P., 1981 *Die Iupitersäulen in den Germanischen Provinzen*, Cologne and Bonn.
Baur, P.V.C., & Rostovtzeff, M.I. (eds), 1929 *The Excavations at Dura-Europos. Preliminary Report of First Season of Work Spring 1928*, New Haven.
Becatti, G., 1954 *Scavi di Ostia II. I Mitrei*, Rome.
Beck, R., 1998 The Mysteries of Mithras: a new account of their genesis. *Journal of Roman Studies* 88, 115-28.
Behn, F., 1928 *Das Mithrasheiligtum zu Dieburg*, Berlin and Leipzig.
Bell, D.N., 1983 *Besa, The Life of Shenoute, introduction, translation and notes*, Chicago.
Bendala Galán, M., 1976a La necrópolis Romana de Carmona (Sevilla) I, Sevilla.
Bendala Galán, M., 1976b La necrópolis Romana de Carmona (Sevilla) II, Sevilla.
Bendala Galán, M., 1986 Die orientalischen Religionen Hispaniens in vorrömischer und römischer Zeit. *Aufstieg und Niedergang der Römischen Welt* II.18.1, Berlin & New York, 345-408.
Bernhard, H., 1990 Kindsbach, Quellheiligtum 'Heidenfels', in Cüppers, H. (ed.), *Die Römer in Rheinland-Pfalz*, Stuttgart, 412-14.
Binsfield, W., 1984 Venus von St Matthias, in *Trier. Kaiserresidenze und Bischofssitz. Die Stadt in spätantiker und frühchristlicher Zeit*, Mainz, 202-3.
Blázquez, J.M., 1986 Einheimische Religionen Hispaniens in der römischen Kaiserzeit. *Aufstieg und Niedergang der Römischen Welt* II, 18.1, Berlin & New York, 164-275.
Boak, A.E.R., 1933 *Karanis, the temples, coin hoards, botanical and zoölogical reports; seasons 1924-31*, Ann Arbor.
Bourbon, F., 1996 *Yesterday and today, Egypt: Lithographs and diaries by David Roberts, R.A.*, Vercelli.
Bredekamp, H., 1975 *Kunst als Medium sozialer Konflikte. Bilderkämpfe von der Spätantike bis zur Hussitenrevolution*, Frankfurt a. M.
Bulgan, F., Schütte-Maischatz, A. & Winter, E., 2001 Forschungen in Doliche. *Kazi Sonuçlari Toplantisi* 23.2, 163-74.
Bull, R.J., 1987 *The Joint Expedition to Caesarea Maritima, Preliminary Reports in Microfiche*, Madison.
Calza, G., 1951 Nuove testimonianze del Cristianesimo a Ostia. *Atti della Pontificia Accademia Romana di Archeologia Ser. III, Rendiconti* 25-26, 1949-1951, 123-38.
Calza, R., 1966 Le sculture e la probabile zona Cristiana di Ostia e di Porto. *Atti della Pontificia Accademia Romana di Archeologia Ser. III, Rendiconti* 37, 1964-1965, 155-257.
Cauville, S., 1990 *Le temple de Dendara*, Cairo & Paris.
Cauville, S., 1997 *Le temple de Dendara X.1-2. Les chapelles osiriennes*, Cairo.
Cauville, S., 1998-2001 *Dendara I-IV. Traduction*, Leuven.
Cauville, S., 2000 *Le temple de Dendara* XI.1-2, Cairo.
Chassinat, É., 1934a *Le temple de Dendara* I, Cairo.
Chassinat, É., 1934b *Le temple de Dendara* II, Cairo.
Chassinat, É., 1935a *Le temple de Dendara* III, Cairo.
Chassinat, É., 1935b *Le temple de Dendara* IV, Cairo.
Chassinat, É., 1947 *Le temple de Dendara* V.2, Cairo.
Chassinat, É., 1952 *Le temple de Dendara* V.1, Cairo.
Chassinat, É. & Daumas, F., 1965 *Le temple de Dendara* VI, Cairo.
Chassinat, É. & Daumas, F., 1972 *Le temple de Dendara* VII, Cairo.

Chassinat, É. & Daumas, F., 1978 *Le temple de Dendara* VIII, Cairo.

Chini, P., 2000 Il santuario di Giove Dolicheno, in Ensoli, S. & La Rocca, E. (eds.), *Aurea Roma. Dalla città pagana alla città cristiana*, Rome, 288-94.

Chuvin, P., 1991 *Chronique des derniers païens. La disparition du paganisme dans l'Empire romain du règne de Constantin à celui de Justinien*, 2nd ed., Paris.

CIL: *Corpus Inscriptionum Latinarum*.

Clauss, M., 1990 *Mithras, Kult und Mysterien*, Munich.

Clauss, M., 1992, *Cultores Mithrae* (Heidelberger Althistorische Beiträge und Epigraphische Studien 10), Stuttgart.

Clauss, M., 1998 Review [in German] of Sauer 1996. *Germania* 76.1, 379-80.

Clauss, M., 2000 *The Roman Cult of Mithras, the God and his mysteries*, Edinburgh.

Collart, P. & Vicari, J., 1969 *Le sanctuaire de Baalshamin à Palmyre* I, Neuchâtel.

CSIR: *Corpus Signorum Imperii Romani*.

Cumont, F., 1896 *Textes et monuments figurés relatifs aux mystères de Mithra* II, Brussels.

Cumont, F., 1923 *Die Mysterien des Mithra*, Darmstadt (reprinted 1975).

Cunningham, A., 1892 *Mahâbodhi or the great Buddhist Temple under the Bodhi tree at Buddha-Gaya*, London.

Cuppage, J., 1986 *Archaeological Survey of the Dingle Peninsula*, Ballyferriter.

Daumas, F., 1959 *Les mammisis de Dendara*, Cairo.

Daumas, F., 1969 *Dendara et le temple d'Hathor*, Cairo.

Daumas, F., 1970 *Le temple de Dandara*, Cairo.

Daumas, F. with Lenthéric, B., 1987 *Le temple de Dendara* IX, Cairo.

Dehn, W., 1941 Ein Quellheilitum des Apollo und der Sirona bei Hochscheid, Kr. Bernkastel. *Germania* 25, 104-11.

Deichmann, F.W., 1939 Frühchristliche Kirchen in antiken Heiligtümern. *Jahrbuch des Deutschen Archäologischen Instituts* 54, 105-36.

Deichmann, F.W. with Labriolle, P. de, 1954 Christianisierung II (der Monumente). *Reallexikon für Antike und Christentum* II, Stuttgat, 1228-41.

Deichmann, F.W., 1975 *Die Spolien in der spätantiken Architektur* (Sitzungsberichte der Bayerischen Akademie der Wissenschaften, philosophisch-historische Klasse 1975, 6), Munich.

De Lacy O'Leary 1938 The destruction of temples in Egypt. *Bulletin de la Société d'Archéologie Copte* 4, 51-7.

Delivorrias, A., 1991 Interpretatio Christiana. About the boundaries of the pagan and Christian worlds, in ΕΥΦΡΟΣΥΝΟΝ ΑΦΙΕΡΩΜΑ ΣΤΟΝ ΜΑΝΟΛΗ ΧΑΤΖΗΔΑΚΗ I, Athens, 123 (English summary); pls 53-60 [107-23 (Greek text)].

Demus, O., 1984 *The Mosaics of San Marco in Venice I. The Eleventh and Twelfth Century*, Washington, Chicago and London.

Demus, O., 1988 *The Mosaic Decoration of San Marco, Venice*, Chicago and London.

De Rossi, G.B., 1865 Un esplorazione sotteranea sulla via Salaria vecchia - Delle statue pagane in Roma sotto gli imperatori cristiani. *Bulletino di Archeologia Cristiana* 3.1, 1-8.

Devauges, J.-B. 1971 Découverte d'une stèle dédiée à Mercure près de Lux (Côte-d'Or). *Revue Archéologique de l'Est et du Centre-Est* 22, 155-9.

Devauges, J.-B., 1973 Le Fanum de Crain (Yonne). *Revue Archéologique de l'Est et du Centre-Est* 24, 169-213.

Devauges, J.-B., 1976 Circonscription de Bourgogne. Côte-d'Or, Lux. *Gallia* 34, 1976, 441-3.

Devauges, J.-B., 1988 *Entrains Gallo-Romain*, Entrains.

De Wit, C., 1962 *Les inscriptions du temple d'Opet à Karnak* II, Brussels.

Drijvers, H.J.W., 1976 Das Heiligtum der arabischen Göttin Allât im westlichen Stadtteil von Palmyra. *Antike Welt* 7.3, 28-38.

Driskell, B.N., Adams, N.K. & French, P. G., 1989 A newly discovered temple at Qasr Ibrim. Preliminary report. *Archéologie du Nil Moyen* 3, 11-54.

Dümichen, J., 1877 *Baugeschichte des Denderatempels und Beschreibung der einzelnen Teile des Bauwerks*, Straßburg.

Duncan-Jones, R., 1994 *Money and government in the Roman Empire*, Cambridge.

Edwards, D.N., 2001 The Christianisation of Nubia: some archaeological pointers. *Sudan & Nubia* 5, 89-96.

Effenberger, A. & Severin, H.-G., 1992 *Das Museum für spätantike und byzantinische Kunst, Staatliche Museen zu Berlin*, Berlin and Mainz.

El-Masry, Y., 2001 More recent excavations at Athribis in Upper Egypt. *Mitteilungen des Deutschen Archäologischen Instituts, Abteilung Kairo* 57, 205-18.

El-Saghir, M., 1991 *Das Statuenversteck im Luxortempel*, Mainz.

El-Saghir, M., Golvin, J.-C., Reddé, M., Hegazy, E.-S. & Wagner, G. with Migalla, R. & Gabolde, L., 1986 *Le Camp Romain de Louqsor* (Mémoires publiés par les membres de l'Institut Français d'archéologie orientale du Caire 73), Paris & Cairo.

Excavations at Dura-Europos, The.

Fabricius, J.A., 1703 *Codex Apocryphus Novi Testamenti* 2, Hamburg.

Fauduet, I., 1993 *Atlas des sanctuaires Romano-Celtiques de Gaule. Les fanums*, Paris.

Faust, S., 1987 Der gallo-römische Tempelbezirk von Tawern. *Kurtrierisches Jahrbuch. Funde und Ausgrabungen im Bezirk Trier* 27, 42-8.

Faust, S., Gilles, K.J., Goethert, K., Hupe, J., Klementa, S., Kuhnen, H.-P., Schwinden, L. & Unruh, F., 1996 *Religio Romana. Wege zu den Göttern im antiken Trier*, Trier.

Fehr, H., 1972 *Die vor- und frühgeschichtliche Besiedlung der Kreise Kaiserslautern und Rockenhausen*, Speyer.

Fellmann, R., 1988 Geschichte, Zivilisation, Kultur, Religion, in Drack, W. & Fellmann, R., 1988 *Die Römer in der Schweiz*, Stuttgart, 11-315.

Filgis, M.N. & Pietsch, M., 1985 Die römische Stadt von Bad Wimpfen im Tal, Kreis Heilbronn. *Archäologische Ausgrabungen in Baden-Württemberg* 1985, 139-46.

Fischer, F., 1991 Schicksale antiker Kultdenkmäler in Obergermanien und Raetien, in Weimert, H. (ed.), *4. Heidenheimer Archäologie-Colloquium 'Leben und Umwelt im Neolithikum'. 1. Verleihung des Kurt-Bittel-Preises der Stadt Heidenheim für Süddeutsche Altertumskunde, 8. September 1989*, Heidenheim, 29-45.

Fisenne, F. von, 1896 Das Mithräum zu Saarburg in Lothringen. *Jahr-Buch der Gesellschaft für lothringische Geschichte und Altertumskunde* 8.1, 119-75.

Florencourt, W.C. von, 1848 Der gesteinigte Venus-Torso zu St Matthias bei Trier. *Jahrbücher des Vereins von Alterthumsfreunden im Rheinlande* 13, 128-40.

Forrer, R., 1915 *Das Mithra-Heiligtum von Königshofen bei Strassburg*, Stuttgart.

Fournier, P.F., 1965 Le monument dit Vasso de Jaude à Clermont-Ferrand. *Gallia* 23, 103-50.

Frank, K.S., 1975 *Frühes Mönchtum im Abendland II. Lebensgeschichten*, Zürich and Munich.

Frankfurter, D., 1998 *Religion in Roman Egypt, Assimilation and Resistance*, Princeton.

Frend, W.H.C., 1984 *The Rise of Christianity*, London.

Frenz, H.G., 1986 Die Spolien der Mainzer Stadtmauer. *Jahrbuch des Römisch-Germanischen Zentralmuseums* 33, 331-68.

Frenz, H.G., 1992 *Denkmäler des römischen Götterkultes aus Mainz und Umgebung. CSIR, Deutschland* II,4, Mainz.

Gaidon-Bunuel, M.-A., 1991 Les mithraea de Septeuil et de Bordeaux. *Revue du Nord - Archéologie* 73, 49-58.

Gàssowska, B., 1982 Maternus Cynegius, Praefectus Praetorio Orientis and the destruction of the Allat temple in Palmyra. *Archeologia, Rocnik Instytutu Historii Kultury Materialnej Polskiej Akademii Nauk* 33, 107-23.

Gatti, E., 1919 Roma. Nuove scoperte di antichità nella città e nel suburbio. *Notizie degli Scavi di Antichità* 1919, 38-49.

Gawlikowski, M., 1977 Le temple d'Allat à Palmyre. *Revue Archéologique* 1977, 253-74.

Gawlikowski, M., 1979a Palmyre 1975. *Études et Travaux* 11, 267-70.

Gawlikowski, M., 1979b Palmyre 1976. *Études et Travaux* 11, 270-3.

Gawlikowski, M., 1983 Réflexions sur la chronologie du sanctuaire d'Allat à Palmyre. *Damaszener Mitteilungen* 1, 59-67.

Gawlikowski, M., 1995 Tempel, Gräber und Kasernen, Die polnischen Ausgrabungen im Diokletianslager, in Schmidt-Colinet, A. (ed.), *Palmyra, Kulturbegegnung im Grenzbereich* (Antike Welt Sonderheft), Mainz, 21-7.

Gawlikowski, M., 1999 Hawarti. Preliminary report. *Polish Archaeology in the Mediterranean* 10, 1998 (1999), 197-204.

Gawlikowski, M., 2000a Hawarte. Excavations, 1999. *Polish Archaeology in the Mediterranean* 11, 1999 (2000), 261-71.

Gawlikowski, M. (with comments by Turcan, R.), 2000b Un nouveau mithraeum récemment découvert à Huarté près d'Apamée. *Académie des Inscriptions & Belles-Lettres. Comptes rendus* 2000. 1, 161-71.

Gawlikowski, M., 2001 Hawarte. Third interim report on the work in the Mithraeum. *Polish Archaeology in the Mediterranean* 12, 2000 (2001), 309-14.

Geschwendt, F., 1972 *Der vor- und frühgeschichtliche Mensch und die Heilquellen*, Hildesheim.

Gilles, K.J., 1987 Römische Bergheiligtümer im Trierer Land - Zu den Auswirkungen der spätantiken Religionspolitik. *Trierer Zeitschrift* 50, 1987, 195-254.

Gilles, R., 2000 L'Afghanistan, cinquante ans d'archéologie, vingt ans de guerre. *Archéologia* 365, 16-31.

Gómez Fernández, F.J., 2000 Paganismo y cristianismo en la Hispania del siglo V. d. C. *Hispania Antiqua* 24, 261-76.

Gordon, R.L., 1975 Franz Cumont and the doctrines of Mithraism, in Hinnells, J.R. (ed.), *Mithraic Studies. Proceedings of the First International Congress of Mithraic Studies* I., Manchester, 215-48.

Gordon, R.L., 1999 The end of Mithraism in the northwest provinces. Review of Sauer 1996. *Journal of Roman Archaeology* 12, 682-8.

Grant, M., 1968 *The Climax of Rome*, London.

Griffith, A.B., 1997 Review of Sauer 1996. *American Journal of Archaeology* 101, 429.

Grimm, G., 1969 *Die Zeugnisse Ägyptischer Religion und Kunstelemente im römischen Deutschland*. (Études préliminaires aux religions Orientales dans l'Empire Romain 12), Leiden.

Grossmann, P., 2002 *Christliche Architektur in Ägypten* (Handbook of Oriental Studies 1,62), Leiden, Boston & Cologne.

Grünenwald, L., 1906 Matronensteine in der Pfalz. *Westdeutsche Zeitschrift für Geschichte und Kunst* 25, 239-58; pl. 5.

Habachi, L., 1972 The destruction of temples in Egypy, in Hanna, S.A. (ed.), *Medieval and Middle Eastern Studies in honor of Aziz Suryal Atiya*, Leiden, 191-8.

Haffner, A., 1989 *Gräber – Spiegel des Lebens, zum Totenbrauchtum der Kelten und Römer am Beispiel des Treverer – Gräberfeldes Wederath-Belginum*, Mainz.

Harnack, A. von, 1924 *Die Mission und Ausbreitung des Christentums in den ersten drei Jahrhunderten* vols. 1 & 2, 4th ed., Leipzig.

Hatt, J.J., 1993 *Argentorate, Strasbourg*, Lyon.
Haussig, H.W., 1983 *Die Geschichte Zentralasiens und der Seidenstraße in vorislamischer Zeit*, Darmstadt.
Heinen, H., 1998 Das spätantike Ägypten (284-646 n.Chr.), in Krause, M. (ed.), *Ägypten in spätantik-christlicher Zeit. Einführung in die koptische Kultur*, Wiesbaden, 35-56.
Henig, M., 1984 *Religion in Roman Britain*, London.
Hernandez Díaz, J., Sancho Corbacho, A. & Collantes de Teran, F., 1943 *Catalogo Arqueologico y Artistico de la Provincia de Sevilla*, Sevilla.
Heukemes, B., 1975 Die Jupitergigantensäule von Ladenburg in antiker Zeit und heute, dreimal zerstört und zweimal wiederhergestellt. *Denkmalpflege in Baden-Württemberg* 4.2, 38-43.
Hill, C., Millett, M. & Blagg, T., 1980 *The Roman Riverside Wall and Monumental Arch in London*, London.
Hölbl, G., 2000 *Altägypten im Römischen Reich. Der römische Pharao und seine Tempel*, Mainz.
Hopfe, L.M. & Lease, G., 1975 The Caesarea Mithraeum: A Preliminary Announcement. *The Biblical Archaeologist* 38.1, 2-10.
Hopfe, L.M., 1990 Mithraism in Syria. *Aufstieg und Niedergang der römischen Welt* II.18.4, Berlin & New York, 2214-35.
Hörig, M. & Schwertheim, E., 1987 *Corpus Cultus Iovis Dolicheni (CCID)*. Études préliminaires aux religions Orientales dans l'Empire Romain 106, Leiden, New York, Copenhagen and Cologne.
Horne, P., 1981 Romano-Celtic temples in the third century, in King, A. & Henig, M. (eds), 1981 *The Roman West in the Third Century* i, Oxford: British Archaeological Reports, International Series 109(i), Oxford, 21-6.
Horton, M., 1991a Africa in Egypt: new evidence from Qasr Ibrim, in Davies, W.V. (ed.), *Egypt and Africa, Nubia from Prehistory to Islam*, Dorchester, 264-77.
Horton, M., 1991b First Christians at Qasr Ibrim. *Egyptian Archaeology* 1, 9-12.
Huld-Zetsche, I., 1986 *Mithras in Nida – Heddernheim*, Frankfurt a. M.
Jamuar, B.K., 1985 *The Ancient Temples of Bihar*, New Delhi.
Joachim, W., 1999 Ein römisches Mithräum mit römischen und alamannischen Siedlungsresten in Güglingen, Kreis Heilbronn. *Archäologische Ausgrabungen in Baden-Württemberg* 1999, 139-43.
Kemp, W., 1970 Götzenbild. *Lexikon der christlichen Ikonographie* 2, Rome, Freiburg, Basel and Vienna, 179-82.
Kern, E., 1994 Strasbourg-Koenigshoffen, in Petit, J.-P. & Mangin, M. (eds), *Atlas des agglomérations secondaires de la Gaule Belgique et des Germanies*, Paris, 157-9.
Killerich, B. & Torp, H., 1994 Mythological sculpture in the fourth century A.D.: the Esquiline group and the Silahtaraǧa statues. *Istanbuler Mitteilungen* 44, 1994, 307-16.
Kjølbye-Biddle, B., 1994 The Small Early Church in Nubia with reference to the Church on the Point at Qasr Ibrim, in Painter, K. (ed.), *Churches Built in Ancient Times*, London, 17-47.
Klumbach, H., 1973 *Der römische Skulpturenfund von Hausen an der Zaber (Kreis Heilbronn)* (Forschungen und Berichte zur Vor- und Frühgeschichte in Baden-Württemberg 5), Stuttgart.
Kollwitz, J., 1954 Bild III (christlich). *Reallexikon für Antike und Christentum* II, Stuttgart, 318-41.
Kowalski, S.P., 1994 The Praetorium of the Camp of Diocletian in Palmyra. *Studia Palmyreńskie* 9, Warsaw, 39-70.
Krause, M. 1998 Heidentum, Gnosis und Manichäismus, ägyptische Survivals in Ägypten, in Krause, M. (ed.), *Ägypten in spätantik-christlicher Zeit. Einführung in die koptische Kultur*, Wiesbaden, 81-116.

Krzyzanwska, A., 1981 A hoard dating the destruction of a temple at Palmyra, in Casson, L. & Price, M. (eds), *Coins, Culture and History in the Ancient World. Numismatic and other Studies in honor of Bluma L. Trell*, Detroit, 39-41.

Kuhnen, H.-P. (ed.), 1992 *Gestürmt – geräumt – vergessen? Der Limesfall und das Ende der Römerherrschaft in Südwestdeutschland*, Stuttgart.

Kumar, A., 1992 *Art and Architecture of the Gaya and Bodh Gaya*, New Delhi.

Kumar, N., 1999 *Archaeological excavations in Bihar since independence*, Patna and New Delhi.

Künzl, E., 1989 Religion und Kunst, in Baatz, D. & Herrmann, F.-R. (eds), *Die Römer in Hessen*, 2nd ed., Stuttgart, 157-209.

Lane Fox, R., 1986 *Pagans and Christians*, London.

Leclant, J., 1981 Anubis. *Lexicon Iconographicum Mythologiae Classicae* I,1, Zürich & Munich, 862-73.

Lewis, J., 2001 Il sacrificio dei giganti. *Archeo* 191/17.1, 52-61 (see also p.5).

Lewis, M.J.T., 1966 *Temples in Roman Britain*, Cambridge.

Lipsius, R.A., 1884 *Die apokryphen Apostelgeschichten* 2.2, Braunschweig.

Lock, G. & Gosden, C., 1997 Hillforts of the Ridgeway Project: excavations on White Horse Hill 1995. *South Midlands Archaeology* 27, 64-9.

Macalister, R.A.S., 1945 *Corpus Inscriptionum Insularum Celticarum* I, Dublin.

MacMullen, R., 1982 The Epigraphic Habit in the Roman Empire. *American Journal of Philology* 103, 233-46.

MacMullen, R., 1984 *Christianizing the Roman Empire*, New Haven and London.

MacMullen, R., 1997 *Christianity & Paganism in the Fourth to Eighth Centuries*, New Haven and London.

Malaise, M., 1978 Documents nouveaux et points de vue récents sur les cultes Isiaques en Italie, in De Boer, M.B. & Edridge, T.A. (eds), *Hommages à Maarten J. Vermaseren* II. (Études préliminaires aux religions Orientales dans l'Empire Romain 68), Leiden, 627-717.

Mancini, G., 1940 Il culto di Cibele e di Attis in Sarsina. *Studi Etruschi* 14, 147-53; pls. 19-21.

Mansuelli, G.A., 1967 Monumenti dei culti Orientali scoperti a Sarsina. *Mitteilungen des Deutschen Archäologischen Instituts, Römische Abteilung* 73-74, 1966-1967, 147-89; pls. 51-61.

Mariette-Pacha, A., 1880 *Dendérah, description générale du grand temple de cette ville*, Paris.

Martin, L.H., 1989 Roman Mithraism and Christianity. *Numen* 36, 2-15.

Marucchi, O., 1918-19 Resconto delle adunanze tenuta dalla Società per la conferenze d'archeologia cristiana. *Nuovo Bulletino di Archeologia Cristiana* 24-25, 1918-1919, 51-72.

Marucchi, O., 1930s *Le Catacombe Romane*, Rome.

Meiggs, R., 1973 *Roman Ostia*, Oxford.

Meissonnier, J., 1973 Le Fanum de Crain (Yonne). Supplément no. 1. Les monnaies. *Revue Archéologique de l'Est et du Centre-Est* 24, 215-48.

Merkelbach, R., 1993 Ein heiliger Baum der Heiden wird abgehackt. *Zeitschrift für Papyrologie und Epigraphik* 96, 58.

MGHSRM: *Monumenta Germaniae Historica Scriptorum Rerum Merovingicarum*.

Miles, D. & Palmer, S., 1995 White Horse Hill. *Current Archaeology* 142, 372-8.

Minto, A., 1924 S. Maria di Capua Vetere – Scoperta di una cripta mitriaca. *Notizie degli scavi di Antichità* 1924, 353-75.

Mitchell, S., 1993 *Anatolia. Land, Men and Gods in Asia Minor* 2, Oxford.

Monneret de Villard, U., 1925 *Les couvents près de Sohâg* I, Milan.

Monneret de Villard, U., 1926 *Les couvents près de Sohâg* II, Milan.

Mrozek, S., 1973 A propos de la répartition chronologique des inscriptions Latines dans le Haut-Empire. *Epigraphica* 35, 113-18.

Munier, H., 1940 Les monuments coptes d'après les explorations du Père Michel Jullien. *Bulletin de la Société d'Archéologie Copte* 6, 141-68.

Nicholson, O., 1995 The end of Mithraism. *Antiquity* 69, 358-62.

Noethlichs, K.L., 1971 *Die gesetzgeberischen Maßnahmen der christlichen Kaiser des vierten Jahrhunderts gegen Häretiker, Heiden und Juden*, Cologne.

Noethlichs, K.L., 1986 Heidenverfolgung. *Reallexikon für Antike und Christentum* 13, Suttgart, 1149-90.

O'Neil, H. & Toynbee, J.M.C., 1958 Sculptures from a Romano-British well in Gloucestershire. *Journal of Roman Studies* 48, 1958, 49-55; pls. VIII-IX.

O'Sullivan, D., 2001 Space, Silence and Shortage on Lindisfarne, The Archaeology of Asceticism, in Hamerow, H. & MacGregor, A. (eds), *Image and Power in the Archaeology of Early Medieval Britain, Essays in honour of Rosemary Cramp*, Oxford, 33-52.

Painter, K., 1999 Natives, Romans and Christians at Uley? Questions of continuity of use of sacred sites. *Journal of Roman Archaeology* 12.2, 694-702.

Parássoglou. G.M., 1978 *The Archive of Aurelius Sakaon. Papers of an Egyptian farmer in the last century of Theadelphia* (Papyrologische Texte und Abhandlungen 23), Bonn.

Parkin, T.G., 1992 *Demography and Roman Society*, Baltimore and London.

Patsch, C., 1899 Archäologisch-epigraphische Untersuchungen zur Geschichte der römischen Provinz Dalmatien III. II. Das Mithräum von Konjica. *Wissenschaftliche Mittheilungen aus Bosnien und der Hercegovina* 6, 186-211.

Perkins, A., 1973 *The Art of Dura-Europos*, Oxford.

Petrie, W.M.F., 1905 *Ehnasya 1904* (The Egypt Exploration Fund 26), London.

Petrie, W.M.F., 1908 *Athribis* (British School of Archaeology in Egypt and Egyptian Research Account 14), London.

Pietsch, M., 1986 Bad Wimpfen im Tal. Die neuen Ausgrabungen: Töpferwerkstatt und Kultbezirk, in Filtzinger, P., Planck, D. & Cämmerer, B. (eds), 1986 *Die Römer in Baden-Württemberg*, 3rd ed., Stuttgart and Aalen, 221-5.

Planck, D., 1989 Ein römisches Mithräum bei Mundelsheim, Kreis Ludwigsburg. *Archäologische Ausgrabungen in Baden-Württemberg* 1989, 177-83.

Planck, D., 1991 *Das römische Walheim* (Archäologische Informationen aus Baden-Württemberg 18), Stuttgart.

Planson, E., Lagrange, A., Minot, A. & Herard, L., 1973 Le mithraeum des Bolards à Nuits-Saint-Georges. *Archéologia* 54, 54-63.

Plumley, M., 1975 Qasr Ibrîm, 1974. *The Journal of Egyptian Archaeology* 61, 5-27.

Pross, Gabrielli, G., 1975 Il tempietto ipogeo del dio Mitra al Timavo. *Archeografo Triestino* Ser. 1, 35, 5-34.

Provost, M. & Mennessier-Jouannet, C., 1994 *Carte Archéologique de la Gaule 63/1, Clermont-Ferrand*, Paris.

Rea, J.R. & Sijpesteijn, P.J. (eds), 1976 *Corpus Papyrorum Raineri V, Griechische Texte II, Textband*, Vienna.

Romey, K.M., 2002 The Race to Save Afghan Culture. *Archaeology* May/June 2002, 18-25.

Rostovtzeff, M.I., Brown, F.E. & Welles, C.B. (eds), 1939 *The Excavations at Dura-Europos. Preliminary Report of the Seventh and Eighth Seasons of Work 1933-1934 and 1934-1935*, New Haven.

Rousselle, A., 1990 *Croire et guérir. La foi en Gaule dans l'Antiquité tardive*, Mesnil-sur-l'Estrée.

Sarnowski, T., Zubar, V.M. & Savelja, O.J., 1998 Zum religiösen Leben der Niedermoesischen Vexillationen auf der Südkrim. *Historia* 47.3, 321-41.

Sauer, E., 1996 *The End of Paganism in the North-Western Provinces of the Roman Empire. The example of the Mithras cult.* British Archaeological Reports, International Series 634, Oxford.

Sauer, E., forthcoming 2003 Not just small change – coins in Mithraea, in Martens, M. & De Boe, G. (eds), *Proceeding of the International Conference on Roman Mithraism: the evidence of the small finds, 7-8 November 2001, Tienen, Belgium.*

Schallmayer, E., 1989 Dieburg, in Baatz, D. & Herrmann, F.-R. (eds), *Die Römer in Hessen*, 2nd ed., Stuttgart, 250-5.

Schmidt-Lawrenz, S., 1999 *Die römische Gutsanlage von Hechingen-Stein* (Führer zu archäologischen Denkmälern in Baden-Württemberg 21), Stuttgart.

Schütte-Maischatz, A. and Winter, E., 2000 Kultstätte der Mithrasmysterien in Doliche, in: Wagner, J. (ed.), *Gottkönige am Euphrat. Neue Ausgrabungen und Forschungen in der Kommagene*, Mainz, 92-9.

Seeck, O., 1908 Zur Geschichte des Isiskultus in Rom. *Hermes* 43, 642-3.

Seroux d'Agincourt, J.B.L.G., 1823 *Histoire de l'art par les monuments depuis la décadence au IVe siècle jusqu'à son renouvellement au XVIe siècle* volumes II, III and V, Paris.

Shore, A.F., 1979 Votive Objects from Dendera of the Graeco-Roman Period, in Ruffle, J., Gaballa, G.A. & Kitchen, K.A. (eds), *Orbis Aegyptiorum Speculum, Glimpses of Ancient Egypt, Studies in Honour of H.W. Fairman*, Warminster, 138-60.

Snape, S., 1996 *Egyptian temples* (Shire Egyptology 24), Princes Risborough.

Snyder, G.F., 1985 *Ante Pacem: Archaeological Evidence of Church Life before Constantine*, Mercer.

Speidel, M.P., 1978 *The Religion of Iuppiter Dolichenus in the Roman Army.* (Études préliminaires aux religions Orientales dans l'Empire Romain 63), Leiden.

Starcky, J. & Gawlikowski, M., 1985 *Palmyre*, 2nd ed., Paris.

Styger, P., 1933 *Die Römischen Katakomben*, Berlin.

Teichner, F., 1996 Signa Venerandae Christianae Religionis: On the Conversion of Pagan Sanctuaries in the Dioceses of Africa and Aegyptus. *Libyan Studies* 27, 1996, 53-66.

Tóth, I., 1973 Destruction of the sanctuaries of Iuppiter Dolichenus at the Rhine and in the Danube Region (235-238). *Acta Archaeologica Academiae Scientiarum Hungaricae* 25, 109-16.

Traunecker, C. & Golvin, J.-C., 1984 *Karnak. Résurrection d'un site*, Fribourg.

Trombley, F.R., 1985 Paganism in the Greek World at the end of Antiquity: the case of rural Anatolia and Greece. *Harvard Theological Review* 78, 327-52.

Trombley, F.R., 1993 *Hellenic Religion and Christianization c. 370-529* vol. I. Religions in the Graeco-Roman World (ÉPRO) 115/1, Leiden, New York and Cologne.

Trombley, F.R., 1994 *Hellenic Religion and Christianization c. 370-529* vol. II. Religions in the Graeco-Roman World (ÉPRO) 115/2, Leiden, New York and Cologne.

Turcan, R., 1984 Les motivations de l'intolerance chrétienne et la fin du mithriacisme au IVe siècle ap. J.-C., in Harmatta, J. (ed.), *Proceedings of the VIIth Congress of the International Federation of the Societies of Classical Studies* II, Budapest, 209-26.

Turcan, R., 1989 *Les cultes Orientaux dans le monde Romain*, Paris [quoted only where there is a significant discrepancy between the English translation (Turcan 1996) and the French original].

Turcan, R., 1996 *The Cults of the Roman Empire*, Oxford [translation of Turcan 1989].

Turcan, R., 1997 Review [in French] of Sauer 1996. *Revue Archéologique* 1997, 436-7.

Vermaseren, M.J., 1956 *Corpus Inscriptionum et Monumentorum Religionis Mithriacae* vol. I, The Hague.

Vermaseren, M.J., 1960 *Corpus Inscriptionum et Monumentorum Religionis Mithriacae* vol. II, The Hague.

Vermaseren, M.J., 1971 *Mithriaca I, The Mithraeum at S. Maria Capua Vetere*, Leiden.
Vermaseren, M.J., 1978 *Corpus Cultus Cybelae Attidisque* 4 (Études préliminaires aux religions Orientales dans l'Empire Romain 50), Leiden.
Vermaseren, M.J., 1986 *Corpus Cultus Cybelae Attidisque* 5 (Études préliminaires aux religions Orientales dans l'Empire Romain 50), Leiden.
Vermaseren, M.J. & Van Essen, C.C., 1965 *The Excavations in the Mithraeum of the Church of Santa Prisca in Rome*, Leiden.
Versnel, H.S., 1981 Römische Religion und religiöser Umbruch, in Vermaseren, M.J. (ed.), *Die Orientalischen Religionen im Römerreich* (Études préliminaires aux religions Orientales dans l'Empire Romain 93), Leiden, 41-72.
Vidale, M., 2002 Afghanistan, tesori nel vento. *Archeo* 206/18.4, 42-79.
Vidman, L., 1977 Isis, Mithras und das Christentum, in Irmscher, J. & Treu, K. (eds), *Das Korpus der griechischen christlichen Schriftsteller*, Berlin, 237-42.
Vieillard-Troiekouroff, M., 1976 *Les monuments religieux de la Gaule d'après les œuvres de Grégoire de Tours*, Paris.
Villeneuve, F. with Al-Muheisen, Z., 2000 Nouvelles recherches à Khirbet edh-Dharih (Jordanie du Sud, 1996-1999). *Académie des Inscriptions & Belles-Lettres Comptes Rendus.* 2000.4, 1525-71.
Wacher, J., 1995 *The Towns of Roman Britain*, 2nd ed., London.
Wagner, G., 1993 Trois inscriptions grecques chrétiennes d'Egypte. *Zeitschrift für Papyrologie und Epigraphik* 96, 53-7.
Walters, V.J., 1974 *The Cult of Mithras in the Roman Provinces of Gaul* (Études préliminaires aux religions Orientales dans l'Empire Romain 41), Leiden.
Watterson, B., 1998 *The House of Horus at Edfu. Ritual in an Ancient Egyptian Temple*, Stroud.
Weisgerber, G., 1975 *Das Pilgerheiligtum des Apollo und der Sirona von Hochscheid im Hunsrück*, Bonn.
Welsby, D.A., 2002 *The Medieval Kingdoms of Nubia. Pagans, Christians and Muslims along the Middle Nile*, London.
Wheeler, R.E.M. & Wheeler, T.V., 1932 *Report on the Prehistoric, Roman, and Post-Roman Site in Lydney Park, Gloucestershire*. Reports of the Research Committee of the Society of Antiquaries of London 9, Oxford.
Wiegels, R., 2000 *Lopodunum II, Inschriften und Kultdenkmäler aus dem römischen Ladenburg am Neckar* (Forschungen und Berichte zur Vor- und Frühgeschichte in Baden-Württemberg 59), Stuttgart.
Winter, E., 1976 Die Tempel von Philae und das Problem ihrer Rettung. *Antike Welt* 7.3, 2-15.
Winter, E., 1999 Ein historisch-topographischer Survey in Kommagene 1997. *Araştirma Sonuçlari Toplantisi, 25-29 Mayis 1998, Tarsus* 16.1, 365-79.
Winter, E., 2000 Mithraism and Christianity in Late Antiquity, in Mitchell, S. & Greatrex, G. (eds), *Ethnicity and culture in Late Antiquity*, London & Swansea, 173-82.
Wipszycka, E., 1986 La valeur de l'onomastique pour l'histoire de la christianisation de l'Egypt. A propos d'une étude de R. S. Bagnall. *Zeitschrift für Papyrologie und Epigraphik* 62, 1986, 173-81.
Wipszycka, E., 1988 La christianisation de l'Égypte aux IVe-VIe siècles. Aspects sociaux et ethniques. *Aegyptus* 68, 117-65.
Wiseman, H., 1931 *Sinuthi Archimandritae Vita et opera omnia* III, Paris.
Woodward, A. & Leach, P., 1993 *The Uley Shrines. Excavations of a ritual complex on West Hill, Uley, Gloucestershire: 1977-9* (English Heritage Archaeological Report 17), London.

PICTURE CREDITS

(All reasonable efforts were taken to contact the copyright holders for permission to reproduce illustrations. The names of those who kindly provided pictures, permission to reproduce them or other help with the illustrations are listed separately in the Acknowledgements.)

Cover: see (**2**)
1: E.S.; **2:** Soprintendenza per i Beni Archeologici di Ostia, Becatti 1954 pl. 4.2; **3:** Soprintendenza per i Beni Archeologici di Ostia, Becatti 1954 pl. 4.3; **4:** Soprintendenza per i Beni Archeologici di Ostia, Calza 1966, 241 figs. 50 & 50a; **5:** E.S.; **6:** Behn 1928, pl. 1; **7:** *ibid*. pl. 2; **8:** *ibid*. 3 fig. 1; **9:** *ibid*. 29 fig. 27; **10:** *ibid*. 29 fig. 28; **11:** E.S. with kind permission of Mrs Porzenheim; **12:** Behn 1928, 30 fig. 30; **13:** *ibid*. 31 fig. 32; **14-15:** E.S. with kind permission of Mrs Porzenheim; **16:** Behn 1928, 34 fig. 34; **17:** Cumont 1896, pl. 7; **18:** *ibid*. pl. 8; **19-20:** Museum Hanau, Schloß Philippsruhe, Hanauer Geschichtsverein; **21:** Bendala Galán 1986, 382 fig. 5a; **22:** *ibid*. pl. 9.14; **23:** *ibid*. pl. 7.11; **24:** Bendala Galán 1976b, pl. 56.3; **25:** Hill *et al*. 1980 frontispiece, drawn by Peter Warner, reproduced with kind permission of the Museum of London; **26:** Drijvers 1976, 38 fig. 12; **27-30:** kindly provided by Professor Gawlikowski and Dr Zuchowska, originally published by Gàssowska 1982, 117 fig. 12; 116 figs. 10c & 10a; 117 fig. 11; **31:** Wiegels 2000, 50 fig. 10r (= Heukemes 1975, 43 fig. 7); **32:** Musée des Antiquités nationales, Saint-Germain-en-Laye (inv. 70063); **33:** O'Neil and Toynbee 1958, 50 fig. 5; **34:** *ibid*. pl. 9 bottom left; **35:** *ibid*. pl. 9 bottom right; **36:** De Rossi 1865, 4; **37:** Effenberger and Severin 1992, 147 no. 60; **38:** Weisgerber 1975, 9 fig. 1; **39:** *ibid*. pl. 50; **40:** *ibid*. pl. 51; **41:** *ibid*. pl. 74.1; **42:** Vermaseren 1956, fig. 236; **43:** Musée Archéologique de Strasbourg; **44:** source: Forrer 1915, pl. 1; **45:** *ibid*. pl. 14.1; **46:** *ibid*. pl. 15; **47:** Chassinat 1934a, pl. 34; **48:** Chassinat 1934b, pl. 90; **49:** *ibid*., 95; **50:** *ibid*., pl. 112; **51:** Chassinat 1935a, pl. 182; **52:** Chassinat 1935b, pl. 281; **53:** Chassinat 1934b, pl. 145; **54:** *ibid*., pl. 148; **55:** Oriental Institute of the University of Chicago, Epigraphic Survey Chic. Or. Inst. photo 8596/ Oriental Institute Photograph P. 38278, De Wit 1962, pl. 27; **56:** Monneret de Villard 1925, pl. 7; **57:** Monneret de Villard 1926, pl. 146; **58:** MacMullen 1982, 235; **59:** *ibid*., 243 fig. 5 (original in Mrozek 1973, 114); **60:** E.S. based on Fauduet 1993, 119-20; **61:** Horne 1981, 24 fig. 3.3; **62:** Horne 1981, 22 fig. 3.1; **63:** Vermaseren and Van Essen 1965, pls. 55-8, Brill Academic Publishers, Leiden; **64:** Patsch 1899, pl. 12; **65-7:** Museo Archeologico Nazionale di Sarsina; **68:** Gaidon-Bunuel 1991, 55 fig. 7; **69:** Pross Gabrielli 1975, 20 (drawing by Dr G. Pross Gabrielli); **70:** Service régional de l'archéologie de Bourgogne, photo by J.-B. Devauges, 1971; **71:** Devauges 1973, 180 fig. 10; **72:** Cumont 1923, pl. 2.2; **73-7:** http://www.photogrammetry.ethz.ch/research/bamiyan/ destruction.html, kindly provided by Fabio Remondino.

Colour plate 1: Stiftsbibliothek St Gallen, Cod. Sang. 602, p. 33; **2:** E.S.; **3:** Deborah Miles-Williams; **4-5:** E.S.; **6:** Minto 1924, pl. 17; **7-8:** E.S.; **9:** Schütte-Maischatz and Winter 2000, 98 fig. 143 (photo by Dr Jörg Wagner); **10:** Andaloro 1991, 112 figs. 1 & 2; **11:** *ibid*. 110 fig. 3; **12:** British Museum (photo by Dr Sebastian Rahtz, cf. Woodward and Leach 1993, 75 fig. 68); **13:** E.S.; **14:** Deborah Miles-Williams; **15:** Hölbl 2000, 80 fig. 90 (photo by Professor Günther Hölbl); **16:** *ibid*., 81 fig. 91 (photo by Professor Günther Hölbl); **17:** *ibid*., 74 fig. 81 (photo by Professor Günther Hölbl); **18:** *ibid*., 77 fig. 86 (photo by Professor Günther Hölbl); **19:** E.S. (see Sauer 2003 for a B&W version of this map with much more detailed comments and a bibliography); **20:** E.S.; **21-2:** Dijon, Musée Archéologique (photos by F. Perrodin); see also Planson *et al*. 1973, 57 and 63; **23-4:** E.S.; **25:** kindly provided by Dr Volker Thewalt (see http://www.thewalt.de/afghanistan/ haibak_bamiyan/pages/74r05-04.htm).

INDEX

Bold page numbers refer to illustrations in the text (with or without additional references in the text on the same page). Note that some references refer to the subject rather than to the precise word.

Abraham, 45, **66**, 68
Acheron (river in the underworld), 134
Acts (New Testament), 114, 118
Adriatic, **20**, 132
Aemilius Lepidus Paullus, Lucius (consul of 50 BC), 47
Africa (Roman province), **20**, 46, 115, 161, 172
Afterlife, 41, 85, 118, 131, 134-5, 137-8, 173, 176, *see also* Elysian Fields, Hades, Heaven, Hell, Paradise, Rebirth, Resurrection, Salvation, Underworld
Agathangelos (author), 154
Akhenaten (pharaoh, 1372-1355 BC), 46
Alamanni, 10, **11**, 26, 30, 39, 53-4, 56, 147, *see also* Germans
Alexandria (in Egypt), **21**, 88, 109, 113, 158, 176
Allat (Arab goddess of war), 49, **50-2**, **colour plate 5**
Alps, **20**, 22, 73, 89, 132, 151, 153, 158
Al-Qaeda, *see* Taliban
Altars, 12, 14, 18, **26**, 27, 34, 48, 52, 55, **56**, 59, 73, **83**, 84, 86, 88, 122, 147, 149-50, 159, **colour plate 24**
America, 161
Amida, **21**, 117
Anatolia, 9, 41, 117, 126, 176, *see also* Asia Minor, Turkey *and* individual sites
Anti-pagan laws and policy, 8-9, 53, 74, 100, 105, 116, 129, 138, 147, 152, 159, 171, 173, 176-7
Anubis (Egyptian god), 47
Apennines, 10, **20**, 139
Apollo, **75-6**, 77-9, 169

Apollonius of Tyana, 45
Apuleius, 133-4
Arabian peninsula, 9
Arbon, **11**, 12
Ardennes, **20**, 71
Armenia, **21**, 154
Arson, *see* Fire
Artemis, 73, 114
Asceticism (Christian), 70, **71**, 143, 175
Asia (as a Roman province), **21**, 114, 118
Asia Minor, 115, 117, 126-7, 166, *see also* Anatolia, Turkey *and* individual sites
Astrology, 135
Aten (Egyptian god), 46
Athena, 50, **colour plate 4**
Athribis, **21**, 102
Attis (eastern god), **40**, 41, 83, 120, 139
Aurelian (emperor, AD 270-75), 49-52
Auxerre, **20**, 143
Axes (used in image destruction), 47, **134-5**, 142

Baalshamen (Syrian god), 51
Babylon, **21**, 68
Bad Wimpfen, **20-1**, 57, 175
Bamiyan, 162, **163**, 177, **colour plate 25**
Baptism, 85, 111
Bastet (Egyptian goddess), **94**
Bel (Syrian god), 51
Belginum, **20**, **74**, 75
Betyl (a holy stone), 41
Bible, 13, 64, 68-9, 131, 139, *see also* individual books *and* the Old Testament
Biesheim, **20**, 152, **colour plate 19**
Bithynia and Pontus, **21**, 117
Bloodshed (and Christianisation), 83, 157, **158**, 159, 177

Bóbbio, 10, **20**
Bodh Gaya, 162, 177
Bolards, *see* Nuits-Saint-Georges
Bregenz, **11**, 12-13, 171
Britain, 9, 48, 59-61, 122, 129, **130**, 151-2, 162, 168, 175-6, **colour plate 12**, *see also* individual sites
Bronze images, 12-13, 23, 171
Buddha and Buddhism, 162, **163**, 164, **colour plate 25**
Bull (as cult image), *see* Mithraism
Byzantium, *see* Constantinople *and* icons

Caernarfon, **20**, 152, **colour plate 19**
Caesarea (in Palestine), **21**, 62, 175
Callinicos (biographer of Hypatios), 117
Capua, **20**, 53, 174, **colour plate 6**
Caria, **21**, 118
Carmona, **20**, 39, **40**, 41, **42-3**, 174
Carrawburgh, **20**, 152, **colour plate 19**
Carthage, **20**, 115, 172
Catacombs, **66**, 67, 69, 175
Chinese Cultural Revolution, 164
Chi-rho symbols, 18, **19**
Chisels (used in image destruction), 23, **24**, 27, 33, 63, **colour plate 3**
Christ, 9, 12, 45, 47, 71, 117, 172, *see also* Jesus
Christian cross, 14, 63, 70, **colour plates 2** & **9**
Christian names (spread of), 110-11, 114
Chrocus (Alamannic king, third century), 54-5

188

INDEX

Churches or monasteries (on the site of former temples), 12, 18, **19**, 38-9, 51, 61, 63, 70, 99, 101-2, 105-6, 112, 118, 135, 151, 158, 161-2, 172, 174, **colour plates 4, 9 & 17**

Cissonius (native god in E. Gaul and Germany), 84

Cleopatra (Egyptian queen, 52/1-30 BC), 89

Clermont-Ferrand, **20**, 54, 174

Closing and sealing off of temples, 53, 100, 105, *see also* 62, 171 *and* Filling of religious monuments with debris

Coins, 18-19, 38, 42, 51, 53, 61, 63, 65, 73, 86, 88, 112, 123-7, 129, 132-3, 138, 143-58, 165-8, 176-7, **colour plate 19**

Colman, **colour plate 2**

Commagene, **21**, 138

Communion (Christian), 35, 85, 136

Constantine (emperor, AD 306-37 and his sons, AD 337-61), 31, 106, 111, 115, 129

Constantine (city in Africa), **20**, 132, 152

Constantinople, 9, **21**, 117

Contamination (with pagan objects), 144, 148

Coptos, **21**, 101

Cornelius (bishop of Rome, AD 251-53), 119

Crain, **20**, **154-5**, 156, 177

Crusades, 65

Cybele (eastern goddess), 41, 120, 139, **142**

Dacia, **21**, 152

Damnation (of political figures), 46

Daniel (Old Testament), 68

Danube, **20-1**, 26, 116, 121, 133, 152

Danube lands, 122, 125

Decius (emperor, AD 249-51), 119

Demetrios (silversmith from Ephesus), 114

Demons, 11, 14, 65, 67, 69, 93, 103, 105, 107, **colour plate 10**

Dendara, **21**, 38, 89, **90**, 91, **92-8**, 99-103, 107, 150, 163-4, 175, **colour plates 14-18**

Deuteronomy (Old Testament), 14, 145

Devil, 72, *see also* 138

Diana, 71-3

Dieburg, **20-1**, **24-6**, **28-9**, 30-1, **32**, 33-5, 37-9, 41, 43, 53, 57, 62, 174, **colour plates 3 & 19**

Diyarbakyr, *see* Amida

Doliche, **21**, 63, 133, 138, 165-6, 175, 177, **colour plate 9**

Dragon, 67, **colour plate 11**

Druidism, 47

Dülük, *see* Doliche

Dura-Europos, **21**, 61-2, 175, **colour plate 8**

Eagle (as an image), 46

Egypt, 9, 31, 49, 64, 88-107, **108**, 109-15, 128, 142, 161, 171, 176

Elephant (as a cult image), 41, **43**

Elysian Fields, 134, *see also* Afterlife, Heaven, Paradise, Rebirth, Resurrection, Salvation

Entrains-sur-Nohain, **20**, 57, **58**, 175

Ephesus, **21**, 73, 114-15, 117-18

Epidemics, 109, 123-4, *see also* Population decline

Erudinus (Hispanic deity), 122

Ethiopians, 67

Eusebius (church historian), 119

Exodus (Old Testament), 14, 64

Falcon (Egyptian gods in the guise of), **94**, **97-8**, 112

Fayum oasis, **21**, 109

Felling of sacred trees and groves, 14, 117, 142, 145, 172, 177

Ferté sur-Chiers, La, **20**, 71, 73, 175

Filling of religious monuments with debris, 42, 53-4, 63, 102, 135-6, 171-2, **colour plate 6**, *see also* Closing and sealing off of temples

Fire or arson (associated with destruction), 8, 11, 14, 23, 33, 54-5, 57, 87-8, 101, 105, 112-13, 117, 139, 144, 153, 155

Frankfurt-am Main-H eddernheim, **20-1**, 30, **34-5**, 36, 53, 136, **colour plate 19**

Franks and Frankish kingdoms, 10, 54, 71, 147

French revolution, 162

Gallo-Roman temples, **127-8**, **130**, **154**, **colour plate 13**

Gaudentius, 172

Gaul, 9, **20**, 54, 57-8, 60, 73, 86, 88, 122-3, 125, **127-8**, 129, 132, 142, 145, 153-4, 168, 172, 176, *see also* individual sites

Gaza, **21**, 48, 104-6, 143, 146, 154, 176

Genii (Roman deities), **26**, 27, **29**

Germanicus, 54

Germans (or Germanic invaders), 26, 30-4, 36-7, 39, 54-8, 61, 75, 77, 145, 152, 158, 167, *see also* Alamanni

Germany (ancient and modern), **11**, **20-1**, 24, 26, 33-4, 36, 39, 48, 53-5, 59-60, 86, 122, 124, 132, 136, 150, 153, 160-1, 168, 174, 176, *see also* individual sites

Giants, 55, *see also* Jupiter giant columns

Globe, 68

Granada, **20**, 30

Greece, 17, **21**, 122

Gregory of Tours, 54-5, 71-3

Griffons, 62, **75**

Groß-Gerau, **20-1**, 35-6

Güglingen, **20-1**, 33, 174, **colour plate 19**

Hades, 131-2, *see also* Underworld

Hadrian's Wall, **20**, 84, 138, 152, 169

Hagenbach, **20-1**, 145, 148

Halos, **134-5**, 136, **colour plate 1**

Hammers (used in image destruction), 23, 27, 71, **colour plate 3**

Harpocrates (Horus as a child), 139

Harsomatus (Egyptian god), **92**, 97, **98**

Hathor (Egyptian goddess), 89, **90**, **93-5**, 96-7, 99, **colour plate 15**

Hawarte, **21**, 63, 132, 151, 175
Heaven, 25, 64, 143, *see also* Afterlife, Elysian Fields, Paradise, Rebirth, Resurrection, Salvation
Hechingen-Stein, **20-1**, 39, 174
Heddernheim, *see* Frankfurt-a.M.-Heddernheim
Heidelberg-Neuenheim, **20-1**, 36, **colour plate 19**
Hell, 14
Herakleopolis, **21**, 109, 176
Hercules, **26**, 27; **28-9**
Herod, 46
Hieroglyphs, 89, **90**, **92-8**, **100**, 102-3
Hilltop and mountain sanctuaries, 70-8, 118, 120, 129, 139, 169, 175, **colour plate 13**
Historia Augusta, 45
Hochscheid, **20**, **74-6**, 77-9, 175
Honorius (emperor, AD 393/5-423), 172
Horus (Egyptian god), **94**, 97, 112
Housesteads, **20**, 152, **colour plate 19**
Human head (cult of), 61
Human sacrifices, 47, 68
Hussite movement, 161, 177
Hypatia (pagan philosopher), 158-9
Hypatios (abbot in Bithynia), 117

Iberian peninsula, 9, 42, 161, *see also* Spain
Icons (Byzantine), 64, *see also* 161
Ihy (Egyptian god), **93**, **colour plate 15**
India, 162, 166, 173
Inscriptions (chronology of), 121, **122**, 123-5, 129-30, 172
Ireland, **20**, **colour plate 2**
Iron tools, *see* metal tools
Isaac, **66**, 68
Isis (Egyptian goddess), 47, 73, **92**, 113, 120, 132-5, 138-9
Islam, 9, 45-6, 64, 99, 142, 161-4, *see also* Muslims
Israelites, 68, 145
Italy, 10, 45, 122, 132, 139-43, 150-1, 165-6, *see also* individual sites
Jerusalem, **21**, 46

Jesus, 12, 14, 64, **66**, 68, 115, 136, 143, 161, *see also* Christ
Jews, 46, 68, 144, 164, *see also* Israelites, Judaism
John from Diyarbakyr, 117-18
Jonah, **66**, 68
Jovius, 172
Judaism, 45-7, 64, 161, *see also* Jews, Old Testament
Julian (emperor, AD 360/61-63), 31, 151
Juno, 27, **29**
Jupiter, 55-7, **66**, 68-9
Jupiter Dolichenus, 132-3, 176
Jupiter giant columns, 55, **56**, 57, 175, **colour plate 7**
Justinus (Christian author), 136, 138

Kabul, 164
Karanis, **21**, 109, 176
Karnak, **21**, **100**, 109, 176
Khirbet edh-Dharih, **21**, 161-2, 177
Kilcolman, **20**, 174, **colour plate 2**
Kindsbach, **20**, 160, 177, **colour plates 23 & 24**
Koenigshoffen, *see* Strasbourg-Koenigshoffen
Konjic, **20**, 136, **137**, 151, **colour plate 19**

Ladenburg, **20-1**, 36, 55, **56**, 57, 136, 175, **colour plate 7**
La Ferté sur-Chiers, *see* Ferté sur-Chiers
Lake Constance, **11**, 12-13, 23, **colour plate 1**
Lakes (as depositories for pagan objects), 11-12, 23, 57
Lake Zürich, **11**, 23
Lares (Roman house gods), 45
Lavinium, **20**, 132
Lazarus, **66**, 68
Leicester, **20**, 168, **colour plate 19**
Les Bolards, *see* Nuits-Saint-Georges
Libanius (pagan author), 159
Linz, **20**, 150, **colour plate 19**
Lion (as cult image), 35, 49-50, **83**, 149, **colour plates 5 & 21**, *see also* Bastet
London, **20**, 48, **49**, 174, **colour plate 19**
Lotus, *see* Water lily

Lower Slaughter, **20**, **59-60**, 175
Lucius (fictional hero in Apuleius's *Metamorphoses*), 133
Luna, *see* Moon goddess
Lux, **20**, 153-4, 177
Luxeuil, 10, **20**
Luxor, **21**, 89, 108, 176
Lydia, **21**, 118
Lydney, **20**, 61, 175

Mackwiller, **20**, 147, 152, **colour plate 19**
Magic, 138, 159
Mainz, **20**, 48, 174, **colour plate 19**
Mandelieu, **20**, 125, 148, **colour plate 19**
Mani (founder of Manichaeism), 47
Manichaeism (religion), 45, 47
Mark (biographer of Porphyrios), 104-5, 144
Marnas (chief god at Gaza), 105
Mars, 65, 67, 145, 155, 160, 169, **colour plates 11 & 24**
Marsi, **20**, 54
Martigny, **20**, 150-1, **colour plate 19**
Matthew (New Testament), 143
Maximinus Thrax (emperor, AD 235-38), 133
Meal (Mithraic), 25, **35**, 136, **137**, 138
Meal (pagan), 39, 41
Melting down of metal votives, 23, 48, 146, 174
Mercury, **26**, 27, **29**, 31, **32**, 35, 43-4, 55, 61, 73, 79, 153, **colour plate 12**
Merovingian period (fifth to eighth century in Gaul and Germany), 87
Mesopotamia, **21**, 117
Metal/iron tools (used in image destruction), **24**, 26-7, 31, **51**, 57, **58**, 60-3, 72-3, 82, 91, **92-8**, **134-5**, 139, **149**, 159, 162, **colour plates 3, 9 & 14-16**, *see also* Axes, Chisels, Hammers, Picks
Minerva, 27, 32, 57, 155, 169

Minorca, **20**, 144
Mithras (oriental god), Mithraism and Mithraea, **16-17**, 18-19, **24-6**, 27, **28-9**, 30-3, **34-7**, 41, 53, 57, **58**, 60-3, 79, **80-1**, 82, **83-5**, 86-8, 120, 124-5, 129, 132-3, **134-5**, 136, **137**, 138-9, 143, 146-8, **149-50**, 151-4, 156-7, **158**, 165-6, 168-9, 174-7, **colour plates 3, 6, 9 & 19-22**
Mittelstrimmig, **20**, 48, 174
Mohammed, 9
Moon goddess, 65, 67, 84, **85**, **colour plate 10**
Moorish incursions, 43
Morocco, 122
Mosaics with pagan subjects, 61
Mosel, **20**, 48
Moses, **66**, 68
Mother goddesses, **26**, 160-1, **colour plates 23-4**, *see also* Cybele
Mühlthal, **20**, 146-9, **colour plate 19**
Mundelsheim, **20-1**, 30, 168, **colour plate 19**
Muslims, 42, 46, 121, 162, 164, *see also* Islam
Mythological scenes in art, 14, 24-5, 55, 174

Nakedness, 27, 31-2, 38, 43, 65, 67, 75, 78, 139
Naples, **20**, 132
Natural sanctuaries and nature worship, 38, 116, 120-1, 132, 139, 142, 158, 169, *see also* Felling of sacred trees and groves, Hilltop and mountain sanctuaries, Spring cult
Nebuchadnezzar (Babylonian king, 605-562 BC), 68
Neckar, **20-1**, 30, 57
Nectanebo I (Egyptian pharaoh, 379/378-361/360 BC), 100
Nekhbet (Egyptian goddess), **95**
Nemesis (goddess of revenge), 62, 175
Neoplatonism, 116
Nero (emperor, AD 54-68), 89, 99, **colour plate 15**
Nestorian denomination, 173
Neumagen, **20**, 48
Neupotz, **20-1**, 145, 148-9
Nile, **21**, 89, 100, 101, 114
Nubia, **21**, 112-13

Nudity, *see* Nakedness
Nuits-Saint-Georges, Les Bolards, **20**, 149, **colour plates 19 & 21-2**

Ober-Florstadt, **20-1**, 168, **colour plate 19**
Offertory box, **154-5**, 156
Ogham, **colour plate 2**
Oil lamps, 51
Ointments, 112
Old Testament, 46, 64, 68, 107, *see also* Bible, Daniel, Deuteronomy, Exodus
Ongayo, **20**, 122, 176
Opet (Egyptian festival), **100**, 176
Orpheus (mythical musician), 45
Osiris (Egyptian god), 134
Ostia **16-17**, 18, **19-20**, 174
Ostraca (pottery sherds with texts), **108**

Pacifist movement, 15
Palestine, 48, 62, 102, 104, 106, 176
Palmyra, **21**, 49, **50-2**, 174, **colour plate 5**
Palmyrene gods, **50**
Panopolis, **21**, 101
Papyri, **108**, 110
Paradise, 15, 131, 134, *see also* Afterlife, Elysian Fields, Heaven, Rebirth, Resurrection, Salvation
Patera (bowl for wine offerings), 68
Persecutions (of the Christians), 9, 14-15, 30, 47-8, 68-70, 115, 117-19, 173
Persians and Persian Empire, 9-10, **21**, 47, 61-3, 123, 133, 173, **colour plate 8**
Personifications of cities or virtues, 65
Phaeton (mythical son of the sun god), **25**
Philae, **21**, 98, 100, 113
Philosophers and philosophy, 14, 116, 131-2, 135, 158
Phrygia, **21**, 118
Phrygian cap, 69
Picks (used in image destruction), 91, 97, **colour plate 14**
Pliny (the younger), 117-19, 126, 132

Pontifex maximus, 131
Population decline (in the third century), 55, 109, 123-4, 129
Porphyrios (bishop of Gaza), 104-6, 143
Pottery, 18-19, 55, 87, 109, 112-13, 123-5, 127, 155-6, 166-7, 176
Ptolemy XII (Egyptian king, 80-51 BC), 89, 102
Ptuj, **20**, 151, **colour plate 19**
Publicola (north-African Christian), 42, 144

Qal'at Sim'Çn, **21**, 70, **71**
Qasr Ibrim, **21**, 112-13, 176

Rebirth, 97, *see also* Afterlife, Elysian Fields, Heaven, Paradise, Resurrection, Salvation
Reformation (in England), 161
Reichenau, **11**, 13
Renaissance, 14, 161
Resurrection, 12, 68, 134, 137, *see also* Afterlife, Elysian Fields, Heaven, Paradise, Rebirth, Salvation
Re-use of stone monuments and quarrying of temples, 31, 38, 44, 48, **49-50**, 59-61, 86, 102-3, **104**, 105, 108-9, 112, 153, 173, 176, **colour plate 5**
Revolving cult images (in Mithraism), 23, **24-6**, **34-7**, **colour plate 3**
Rhine, 10, **11**, **20**, 26, 30, 58, 86, 116, 120-1, 133, 145, 149, 151-2
Rivers (as depositories for pagan objects), 47, 57, **58**, 101, 145
Rockenhausen, **20**, 150, 168, **colour plate 19**
Romans (New Testament), 13
Rome (the city), 18, **20**, 41, 47, 65, **66**, 67, 119, 132-3, **134-5**, 175-6
Ropes (used to pull down statues), **66**, 67-8, 71, **colour plate 11**
Rouphinianai, **21**, 117
Rückingen, **20-1**, **34-5**, **36-7**
Rudchester, **20**, 152, **colour plate 19**

Sacrifices (of animals), 11-12, 14, 65, 88, 113, 117, 119, 138-9, 159, *see also* Mithraism

191

Sacrificial tools, 27
St Augustine, 42, 139, 144-5, 154, 172
St Aurelia, 12
St Columbanus, 10, **11**, 12-13, 37, 143, 174, **colour plates 1-2**
St Gallen, **11**, 13
St Gallus, 10, **11**, 12-13, 23, 37, 171, 174, **colour plates 1-2**
St Germanus from Auxerre, 143, 177
St Gregory, the 'illuminator', 154
St Jude, 65, 175, **colour plate 10**
St Martin, 72, 88, 172
St Paul, 73, 114-15, 117, 126
St Philip, 67, **colour plate 11**
St Simon, 65, 175, **colour plate 10**
St Symeon, 70, **71**
Salvation, 12, 25, 68, 115, 120, 132, 136-8, *see also* Afterlife, Elysian Fields, Heaven, Paradise, Rebirth, Resurrection
Sarrebourg, **20-1**, 31, 79, **80**, 82-3, 86, 88, 147, 149, 157, **158**, 159, 175, 177, **colour plate 19**
Sarsina, **20**, 139, **140-2**, 176
Sea of Marmara, **21**, 117
Septeuil, **20**, 125, **149**, 152, **colour plates 19-20**
Septimius Severus (emperor, AD 193-211), 86, 122
Serapis (Graeco-Egyptian god), 73, 88, 139, **140-1**
Serpent, 97, **98**
Severan period (AD 193-235), 121-3
Severus (bishop of Minorca), 144
Severus Alexander (emperor, AD 222-35), 45, 86
Sevilla, **20**, 39
Shapur I (Persian king, AD 240/42-72), 63
Shenoute (Egyptian abbot), 101-7, 110, 176
Shenoute's monastery, **21**, 101-2, **103-4**, 105, 176
Sicily, **colour plate 4**
Sidon, **21**, 62, 132
Silvestrius Perpetus, Silvinus and Aurelius from Dieburg, 24-5
Sirona (native goddess in E. Gaul and Germany), 75, **76**, 77

Sofia, **21**, 132
Sol, *see* Sun god
Spain, 30, 39, 42-3, 122, 176, *see also* Iberian peninsula
Sparing of unrecognised pagan art, 38, 97, **98**, 149-50, **colour plates 21-2**
Spoils, *see* Re-use of stones
Spring cult, 75, 77, 120, 129, 132, 139, 142, 149, 160-1, 169, 177, **colour plates 20 & 24**
St = Saint, *see* above
Stones (hurled at deities), **66**, 68, 161
Strasbourg-Koenigshoffen, **20-1**, 31, 33, 79, **81**, 82, **83-5**, 86-9, 138, 175, **colour plate 19**
Styx (river in the underworld), 134
Sulpicius Severus (biographer of St Martin), 88, 172
Sun god, 18, **24-5**, 57, **58**, 62, 65, 67, 79, **80**, **134-5**, 136, 139, **colour plate 10**, *see also* Aten
Synagogues, 144
Syracuse, **20**, **colour plate 4**
Syria, 9, 49, 62, 70, **71**, 132, 151, 159, 161, 175, **colour plate 8**

Taliban, 75, 162-4, **colour plate 25**
Tamm, **20-1**, 124
Tanfana (Germanic goddess), 54
Tawern, **20-1**, 73-4, 79, 175, **colour plate 13**
Tertullian, 14, 115, 118-19, 137-8
Tetrarchy (rule of four emperors, AD 293-311), 116
Theadelpheia, **21**, 109
Theodoret (church historian), 88
Theodosius I (emperor, AD 379-95), 116, 159
Third-Century Crisis (AD 235-84/85), 48, 120-4, 172
Thirty Years' War (AD 1618-48), 124, 176
Three men in the burning fiery furnace, 68-9
Tiber, **20**, 47
Tiberius (emperor, AD 14-37), 47, 54, 89

Timavo, **20**, **150**, 151, **colour plate 19**
Tomb of the Elephant, 39, **40**, 41, **42-3**
Torch-bearers, *see* Mithraism
Trajan (emperor, AD 98-117), 99, 117
Tralles, **21**, 118
Trees, 120, *see also* Felling of sacred trees and groves
Trier, **20-1**, 73, 129, 150, 161, 177, **colour plate 19**
Tuggen, **11**, 12-13, 23
Turkey, 9, 49, 62, 114, 117, 122, 126, 133, 138, *see also* Anatolia, Asia Minor *and* individual sites
Tyana, **21**, 45

Uley, **20**, 60, 175, **colour plate 12**
Underworld, 134, *see also* Hades

Valens (emperor, AD 364-78), 31, 138, 151
Valentinianus I (emperor, AD 364-75), 31, 138, 151
Vandals (Germanic tribe), 43
Venice, **20**, 65, 175, **colour plates 10-11**
Venus, 161
Victoria (Roman goddess of victory), 65
Visigothic period (fifth to eighth century in Spain), 42
Vosges, 10, **20-1**
Vulfilaicus (deacon in sixth-century Gaul), 71-4, 77, 79, 82, 88

Walahfridus (biographer of St Gallus), 10-11, 13
Walheim, **20-1**, 39, 57-8, 174-5
Water lily, 97, **98**
Weapons (as offerings), 126
Wells (as depositories for pagan objects), **26**, 27, **29**, 31, 39, 41-2, 43, 55, **56**, 57-8, **59-60**, 73, 175, **colour plates 7 & 13**
Wetti (biographer of St Gallus), 10, 13
White Horse at Uffington, **20**, 61, 175
White Monastery, *see* Shenoute's monastery

Zenobia (queen and empress, AD 267-72), 50
Zeus, 50